STRATEGIC PLANNING
THE CHIEF EXECUTIVE AND THE BOARD

Forthcoming Titles in the *Best of Long Range Planning* Series:

Entrepreneurship: Creating and Managing New Ventures (Number 2)
Edited by Bruce Lloyd

Making Strategic Planning Work in Practice (Number 3)
Edited by Basil Denning

Planning for Information as a Corporate Resource (Number 4)
Edited by Alfred Collins

The titles in this series can be obtained on annual subscription at an advantageous rate. Further details can be obtained from Brian Cox, Journal Sales Director, Pergamon Press plc, Headington Hill Hall, Oxford, OX3 0BW, UK.

STRATEGIC PLANNING
THE CHIEF EXECUTIVE AND THE BOARD

Edited by

BERNARD TAYLOR

Henley - The Management College

PERGAMON PRESS

OXFORD · NEW YORK · BEIJING · FRANKFURT
SÃO PAULO · SYDNEY · TOKYO · TORONTO

U.K.	Pergamon Press plc, Headington Hill Hall, Oxford OX3 0BW, England
U.S.A.	Pergamon Press, Inc., Maxwell House, Fairview Park, Elmsford, New York 10523, U.S.A.
PEOPLE'S REPUBLIC OF CHINA	Pergamon Press, Room 4037, Qianmen Hotel, Beijing, People's Republic of China
FEDERAL REPUBLIC OF GERMANY	Pergamon Press, Hammerweg 6, D-6242 Kronberg, Federal Republic of Germany
BRAZIL	Pergamon Editora, Rua Eça de Queiros, 346, CEP 04011, Paraiso, São Paulo, Brazil
AUSTRALIA	Pergamon Press Australia Pty Ltd., P.O. Box 544, Potts Point, N.S.W. 2011, Australia
JAPAN	Pergamon Press, 5th Floor, Matsuoka Central Building, 1-7-1 Nishishinjuku, Shinjuku-ku, Tokyo 160, Japan
CANADA	Pergamon Press Canada Ltd., Suite No. 271, 253 College Street, Toronto, Ontario, Canada M5T 1R5

First edition 1988

Reprinted 1989

Library of Congress Cataloging-in-Publication Data

Strategic planning: The Chief Executive and the Board / edited by Bernard Taylor.—1st ed.
p. cm.—(The Best of Long Range Planning, ISSN 0889 3136: no. 1)
1. Strategic planning. I. Taylor, Bernard. 1931–
II. Series.
HD30.28.S735 1988 658.4′012—dc19 88-19506

British Library Cataloguing in Publication Data

Strategic Planning: The Chief Executive and the Board
1. Business firms. Management. Long-range planning
I. Taylor, Bernard, 1931– III. Series 658.4′012

ISBN 0 08 036566 3

Printed in Great Britain by Aberdeen University Press

Contents

Strategic Planning: The Chief Executive and The Board

Bernard Taylor, Editor, Long Range Planning

Introduction to the Series

Our aim in *The Best of Long Range Planning* is to bring together in each volume the best articles on a particular topic previously published in *Long Range Planning* so that readers wishing to study a specific aspect of planning can find an authoritative and comprehensive view of the subject, conveniently in one volume.

Whereas each issue of *Long Range Planning* normally contains a 'horizontal slice' of *Long Range Planning* at a particular point in time, in different fields and in various kinds of organizations across the world, each volume in the new series will take a 'vertical slice' through more than a hundred issues, pulling out the outstanding articles on a given subject.

The first group will cover four areas of vital interest,

(1) Strategic Planning: The Chief Executive and the Board.

(2) Entrepreneurship: Creating and Managing New Ventures.

(3) Making Strategic Planning work in Practice.

(4) Planning for Information as a Corporate Resource.

Later volumes will deal with other topical themes, such as:

☆ Strategic Management in Major Multinational Companies.

☆ Developing Strategies for Competitive Advantage.

☆ Strategic Planning for Human Resources, and

☆ Implementing Corporate Strategy: Turning Strategy into Action.

We also plan to publish a number of volumes on planning for functional areas which will appeal to specialists in finance, marketing, research and development, personnel, production and operations.

Each volume will contain 10–12 articles, and about 100 pages. They may be bought individually or on subscription. In due course they will provide a comprehensive and authoritative reference library, covering all important aspects of Strategic Planning.

This first volume of *The Best of Long Range Planning* is about the place of strategic planning or strategic management in the leadership and direction of major businesses. The authors are dealing with three issues:

(1) What should be the role of the chief executive and the board in making and implementing strategy?

(2) How do most chief executives and directors work in practice? and

(3) What happens when major companies adopt strategic management as a management style?

The Board's Responsibility for Planning

Strategic planning is one of the two key tasks of top management. Their other job, of course, is making sure that the business is running smoothly. There are five main reasons for the Board to get involved in planning:

(1) to improve the performance of the business, for the benefit of the shareholders, the managers, the employees and other stakeholders;

(2) to provide a philosophy and a set of principles which will guide the actions of the people involved in the enterprise;

(3) to set the strategy and direction of the business —usually for growth in products and markets, divestments and acquisitions;

(4) to monitor and control the company's operations, not just in the form of immediate financial results, but also in building for the future through improved productivity, quality, customer service, new products, the recruitment and training of staff, and

(5) to provide a set of policies which can be presented publicly in discussions with governments and other external bodies.

Current Boardroom Practice

The first six chapters report the present situation in the boardroom and the chief executive's office. The results are remarkably consistent, whether the research was carried out in Western Europe, North America or elsewhere.

(1) The chief executive has a dilemma: he is worried about the future of his business, but he spends most of his time dealing with the day to day operations. To solve this problem he must find a way to delegate to his subordinates some of his operational responsibilities.

(2) Boards have a different problem. Usually, they simply rubber stamp the decisions of the executive team. To operate effectively they need to be more independent. They should be in a position to control and, where necessary, remove the chief executive. In the U.S.A. and in Britain, the problem has not been solved. The Board is often still the creature of the chief executive.

(3) In recent years the task of the chief executive and the board has been further complicated because of the widespread intervention of governments, the growing power of employees and unions, pressure groups and the media. At one time it seemed as if business was losing the war on all fronts. In his article, 'The New C.E.O.', George Steiner describes how America's largest businesses organized themselves to mount a major political offensive to stem the tide of regulation.

This then is a typical situation in a large company: the chief executive is overburdened with operational problems, the board is unable to take an independent line and top management are often spending a good deal of their time dealing with governments, pressure groups and employee representatives.

Strategic Management

In spite of these pressures, and in many cases as a result of the crises of the early 1980s, a substantial number of leading companies are using strategy to steer their businesses.

In the 1980s a new generation of chief executives has appeared: Jan Carlzon of SAS, Lee Iacocca of Chrysler, John Harvey-Jones of ICI, Wisse Dekker of Philips, Carlo de Benedetti of Olivetti, and others. Strong individual leaders with some common characteristics: they emerged in a crisis: they achieved dramatic improvements in performance: they re-structured their companies, and often changed whole industries by creating new market segments, forming new alliances and mergers, and making new deals with trade unions and governments.

The second half of this volume provides eight company case studies which demonstrate how some remarkable top managers have used a strategic management approach to change the structures and the corporate cultures of their organizations.

It is evident from these cases that strategic management has a number of distinctive features:

(1) *The Executive Team are the planners.* They delegate operational control to the level below the board; they develop objectives and strategies for the corporation as a whole; and they require the chief executives of each business unit to present their strategies to the board for approval.

(2) *The organizations are decentralized.* Their organizations are divided into autonomous units which are treated as separate businesses.

(3) *The Chief Executive is a visible leader.* The top managers make a public commitment to a philosophy, a set of objectives, and a broad strategy and this is publicized inside and outside the organization.

(4) *Project teams accountable to top management.* Task forces and Project Teams are formed which cross functional and divisional boundaries and report directly to the chief executive.

(5) *Internal marketing.* The company philosophy, objectives and strategies are communicated throughout the organization via meetings and conferences, and by using modern marketing techniques.

(6) *Problem-solving teams.* Teams are formed at section and departmental level to review their own performance continuously, and to make recommendations which will improve the company's productivity, quality, cost levels and customer service. This usually involves large investments in training.

(7) *Profit-sharing and performance-related pay.* The top management encourage greater employee involvement in company affairs by promoting share ownership and incentive payments related to results.

Twelve Key Articles

The articles in this volume reflect the wide spread of contributors who write for the journal. They include senior academics, researchers, chief executives and line managers from major companies, and consultants who live in the U.S.A., Britain, France, Israel, South Africa, Sweden and Holland.

Part I consists of six research reports which cover three areas:

(1) the job of the chief executive,

(2) the role and responsibilities of the board of directors, and

(3) the need for the board to exercise strategic control.

Part II includes six company cases which describe the approach to strategic planning and strategic management in Texas Instruments, ICI, Philips, Scandinavian Airlines, 3M and the National Freight Consortium.

They cover a range of themes: Corporate Self Renewal, Planning by the Executive Team, Competing through Quality and Customer Service, Developing Strategies for a Global Business and Setting up an Employee Buy-out.

The significance of each article and its contribution to our theme Strategic Planning: The Chief Executive and the Board, is set out below so that readers can appreciate how the subject is developed, and they can turn immediately to the articles which they find interesting.

* * *

Strategic Leadership and the Chief Executive

André and Sandra van der Merwe's fascinating and well-documented study of Chairmen and Managing Directors in South Africa's major companies spells out the top manager's dilemma in relation to strategy and planning.

Planning—including formulating corporate objectives and growth plans, organization structure, high level manpower, and other future requirements of the company' is universally recognized as one of their primary responsibilities, and an activity which cannot be delegated. To quote the van der Merwes:

> By far the largest proportion—two-thirds—rank planning as their most important activity. Of course planning, in the sense used here, is all encompassing. Among chief executives who do not give this broad category of activity highest ranking, relatively few rate it less than third in importance. No other activity matches planning, or more appropriately concern with the future.

On the other hand,

> The allocation of the individual chief executive's time does not always square with the relative importance he assigns to the specific activity. Collectively speaking, less than half of the chief executives profess to be able to devote most of their time to the item they consider most important. And only 18 per cent say they are able to allocate their time in accordance with all their relative priorities. Comparing the chief executives' top priorities in terms of importance with their time priorities, 66 per cent rank planning as their most important activity, yet only 34 per cent devote most of their time to it.

What is it that takes most of their time? Two main areas:

> Inspection and Control—checking and appraising individual and company performance through on-the-spot visits, inspection and written reports,

and

> People—dealing with internal personalities and personal problems, inter-personal conflicts, stimulating individual and group performance.

And when asked 'What aspect of the business has consistently given you the most perplexing problems' 48 per cent again quote 'People problems—development and training for succession and growth, and motivation'.

The chief executives who make space for strategy and planning do so by adopting a decentralized or divisionalized organization structure: appointing capable and properly trained subordinates; and delegating to them routine, day-to-day decisions. As one chief executive put it: 'In theory I delegate everything possible in order to make sure I don't get bogged down with detail. In practice, I retain control of a number of key functions . . .'—and top of the list of decisions which cannot be delegated for 60 per cent of the executives is Corporate Planning and Strategy in the major areas.

The New Class of Chief Executive Officer

In this classic article, published in 1980, George Steiner documents the rise of the Public Affairs function, and the sea-change which occurred in the role of the chief executives in America's largest companies in response to the growth of single interest groups, and the tidal wave of legislation, regulation and litigation which occurred in the 1970s.

In the 1970s, private enterprise became unfashionable. Multinational corporations in particular were seen as robber barons who exploited the societies which sustained them. One stakeholder group after another sought to call them to account. Ethnic minorities claimed their civil rights. Women's emancipation groups fought for equal opportunity. Ralph Nader spoke up for consumer protection, claiming that many products were a danger to health and to life itself. Environmentalists called for a reduction in air and water pollution. Trade union leaders and socialist parties lobbied for new laws to protect jobs and to improve the quality of working life. Profits were cut as social costs increased. Plants were closed, new projects were stopped and chief executives were called upon to put their case publicly in the media.

George Steiner interviewed the top managers of 47 leading U.S. corporations and he describes their response in detail.

(1) The chief executives are spending around 25–50 per cent of their time dealing with governmental and public affairs.

(2) Their corporations have abandoned their traditional low-profile approach and are involved in a dialogue with government agencies and special interest groups.

(3) The top managers recognize that they should respond positively to the legitimate demands of their stakeholders—principally, their employees, customers, shareholders and the communities in which they operate.

(4) Their new role in public affairs means that the 'new class of chief executive' must become a public figure. In addition to being a business leader, he must be capable of acting as spokesman for the company, a good communicator and a practiced politician.

(5) To enable the CEO to take on these extra duties, the companies have reorganized their Corporate Office:

 (a) Boards of Directors, include more outside directors, and they have special committees which regularly review social and political issues.

 (b) To enable them to take on these extra duties dealing with external affairs, many of them delegate most of the day-to-day operations to a President or Chief Operating Officer, whilst still retaining overall control of the business.

(6) Certain corporate activities are controlled centrally, e.g. compliance with legislation relating to environmental protection, product liability and conditions at work.

(7) At the same time line managers are being trained to make them more capable of dealing with pressure groups at the local level.

(8) Public Affairs, a new and powerful corporate staff function, has appeared which manages relations with government bodies, shareholders and investment analysts, consumer associations, environmentalists and other special interest groups, and the media.

(9) The public affairs activity involves monitoring social and political trends, identifying four or five public issues which are reviewed by the Board's Social Policy Committee, and the development and implementation of political lobbying and communications programs to employees, shareholders, suppliers, customers and local communities.

George Steiner describes how in the 1970s, particularly between 1975 and 1980, a sizeable Public Affairs 'industry' emerged in the U.S.A. By 1980, 500 corporations had established offices in Washington to lobby the federal government. Nine hundred and twenty Political Action Committees had been formed to support the election of business-oriented legislators. Over a half of the major companies had communications programs aimed at influencing public opinion on specific social issues. The success of President Reagan and the reversal of the trend towards 'socialism' was no doubt helped by these professionally-managed campaigns.

But it is not possible to turn the clock back. The special interest groups and the anti-business lobbies are still operating. The legislation remains on the statute book and the regulatory agencies are active and well-organized. Today's chief executive still has to be a public advocate for the business. This article is a reminder of what can happen to businesses which adopt a low profile, and it describes the arrangements which are needed to protect the corporation from social and political attacks.

* * *

What is the Board of Directors Good For?

Dan Bavly is chief executive—or more precisely Executive Partner—for a large firm of accountants in Tel-Aviv. His article, written after the recession of the early 1980s, asks the question 'How did U.S. Boards of Directors safeguard the shareholders' interests during the recent crisis?' His answer is: 'They failed to do so'. They did not develop new strategies ahead of time. They did not remove the chief executives when it was clear that they were incompetent. In fact, to quote Peter Drucker: 'In every major business catastrophe (since the Great Depression) down to recent debacles, the board members were apparently the last people to be told anything was awry'.

Dan Bavly then goes on to quote surveys of chief executive officers, the opinions of leading businessmen, and academics. He concludes that the U.S. Board of Directors provides advice and counsel, serves as a sounding board and often acts in crisis situations. However, it is not usually a critical contributor to a company's success. The Board does not establish basic objectives, corporate strategies or the broad policies of the company.

The Board is the creature of the chief executive officer. In practice it is the CEO who determines who should serve on the Board; he sets the Board agenda, often in consultation with the Chairman of the Board; and he, or one of his executives, prepares the material to be studied and discussed. Audit Committees, made obligatory by the New York Stock Exchange in 1978, seem to have had little effect. To quote Miles Mace of Harvard Business School: 'There have been some cosmetic approaches by many companies to create the impression that directors have a lot more to do on the Board . . . But there has been no real improvement in what directors do or don't do. Directors do not perceive themselves as representing the shareholders except at the annual meeting.'

There is clearly a wide gap between what the Board is expected to do, legally and by the general public, and what they do in practice; and there is a strong case for reform—in particular by making the Board more independent of the chief executives.

* * *

The British Boardroom: Time for a Revolution?

David Norburn is currently Director of the Management School at Imperial College, London.

He contrasts the theory and practice of directors in British boardrooms. Academics and businessmen are agreed that the board should 'determine the longer term strategy and see that the management is running the business properly'. However, research in Britain suggests that 'the entire picture of objective-setting is one of confusion, and is in marked contrast to the recommendations of the academic and consultancy world'. The information provided to directors is usually inadequate and often irrelevant. Also, in Britain and Commonwealth countries the majority of board members are usually executives. A recent survey puts the percentage of non-executive directors at 30 per cent.

A key issue for British business is how to make the board independent of the executive, particularly as 'the board has only one supreme executive act to perform: to hire and fire the chief executive'. In practice, there is little evidence to suggest that boards perform this task. The chief executive is rarely fired and he usually chooses his own successor.

From his survey of the literature, David Norburn concludes that the Board of Directors should meet four important requirements. It should: endorse the company strategy: be adequately informed to evaluate strategy: be independent of the executive, and hire and fire the chief executive. In a survey of 418 executive directors from the Times 1000 companies he found them wanting in each area. They tend to focus on short term results. They have worked in only two or three companies and have had a narrow functional training, usually in finance and accounting or a technical and professional area: only a minority have experience of sales and marketing, or production and manufacturing, and very few have worked overseas. Being executives themselves, they are clearly not independent of the executive management, and are unlikely to hire and fire the chief executive.

* * *

Strategic Control

Professor Jacques Horovitz of ESSEC, a leading French business school, reports on a study of top management planning and control systems in industrial firms in France, Britain and West Germany. He concludes that a good deal of progress has been made in shifting the emphasis of planning systems from short-term to long-term and from operations to strategy. However, management control systems still focus on the short term. Therefore new techniques and new procedures are needed so that the chief executive can monitor the company's performance in relation to its long-term objectives and strategies.

Corporate Planning was more developed in Britain and Germany where about 75 per cent of firms had a long-range plan, compared with 31 per cent in France. However, in Great Britain most plans contained some sort of strategic analysis, whereas in most French and German companies the plans were simply extended budgets. In Germany and France planning was part of the financial control function and most of the planning information was provided by the accounting or control departments.

In the area of control, chief executives in all three countries were solely concerned with short-term results—biased by culture. In Britain, where many chief executives were accountants the controls were primarily financial, whereas in France and Germany, where more chief executives were engineers, there was more concern with production.

Surprisingly, in all three countries the researchers found that chief executives did not generally monitor their company's performance in relation to key factors for success such as competitive performance in relation to product quality, price and customer service. They seemed not to be checking directly to ensure that their company strategies were being implemented. There were some exceptions: e.g. a British electronics firm which ensured that no equipment sold to a customer was out of order for more than 12 hours.

The author concludes that top management should set up a strategic control system to monitor:

(1) changes in the key assumptions about trends in the business environment and the competitive situation in each industry segment;

(2) company performance in relation to major competitors in key areas such as marketing, production, personnel, and research and development; and

(3) the extent to which specific strategic projects and programmes are being achieved.

As Jacques Horovitz comments: 'a plan is worthless without control'.

* * *

The Directors' Role in Planning

John Aram and Scott Cowen of Case Western Reserve University in Cleveland, Ohio report on the roles of directors in three companies with a reputation for adding shareholder value. On the basis of this research, they describe the procedures which are necessary for effective board involvement in planning. The work of the board is analysed in terms of the structures and systems used for setting corporate goals and strategies, monitoring and controlling management performance and motivating executives through appropriate pay and incentives.

Each board sets management goals in terms of increasing shareholder value, comparing the results of the firm with competitors and with leading shares on the stock market, making due allowance for risk. In addition, divisional targets are set in finance, in various functional areas, e.g. marketing, technical development, manufacturing and materials management, and in acquisitions and divestments.

The boards become involved in strategy by receiving and reviewing business unit presentations, and by reviewing key strategic issues, either as a full board or through board committees.

Each board reviews the company's performance each quarter, against the objectives it has set, back-up information is provided for major items and there is a break-down for each division.

Executives receive a cash bonus based on the achievement of goals set for each senior manager and targets usually include personnel development, progress in research and new product development. It is also usual for the top management to receive stock options, based on the achievement of return-on-equity targets. Each board has a compensation committee which reviews executive rewards and makes recommendations to the full board.

The study also emphasizes the importance of allocating adequate time to enable directors to brief themselves on key strategic issues. This may mean holding board meetings away from the company headquarters. Board agendas should be structured to encourage the discussion of important issues, and directors should be supplied with relevant and timely information. The authors provide detailed checklists and formats for the board information system.

* * *

Corporate Self Renewal

'Corporate Self Renewal', the article by Patrick Haggerty, is a classic statement of the business philosophy which he used to build Texas Instruments into a world leader in electronics. To quote the author:

> We are convinced that corporate self renewal begins with innovation . . . that both useful products and services and long-term profitability are the result of innovation, and that as a matter of fact profitability at a level above the bare fee for the use of the assets results only from the innovation advantage and disappears as soon as the innovation has become routine.

However, innovation must not be interpreted too narrowly.

> Too often in this technological age we associate innovation automatically with research and development based on the physical sciences, but the fact is that critical innovation—regardless of the field—may occur in the make and market functions as well as in the creative function. Further, effective innovation is the integral part (that is, the sum total) of the innovation in all three of the categories: create, make and market.

To Patrick Haggerty, then, the success of the business depends on planned innovation:

> Self renewal at TI begins with deliberate planned innovation in each of the basic areas of industrial life—creating, making and marketing in all product and service areas—and with our long-range planning system, we attempt to manage this innovation so as to provide a continuing stimulus to the company's growth in usefulness to society and as a business institution.

In other words, 'at Texas Instruments our long-range planning system is fundamentally a system for managing innovation'.

Patrick Haggerty then goes on to explain how the system breaks down into various elements: OST (objectives-strategies-tactics) and TAPS (tactical action programs).

Finally, he considers the role of the Board and, not surprisingly, he concludes 'Our deliberations have convinced us that our prime responsibility as a board of directors is to ensure our corporate self renewal'. This means evolving mechanisms which will drive continual renewal in three areas:

(1) the up-dating of corporate structures, policies and practices;
(2) the development of products and services; and
(3) the recruitment and training of professional managers, scientists and other specialists.

In addition, the Board itself must be renewed—for example, by bringing in senior executives with experience in government and in international business.

* * *

Strategic Leadership through Corporate Planning at ICI

'The Executive Team are the planners' writes Alan Pink, ICI's General Manager, Planning, 'but the role of the Executive Directors in strategic planning has not always been as it is today'. In his article, he explains how the style of the direction and management was changed in a 6-year period, and how this helped to transform the performance of the company. The new management took ICI from losses, and cuts in dividends in 1980, to record profits in 1986. In the period 1982–1986 the return on sales doubled and the return on assets, and earnings per share both increased three-fold.

Alan Pink describes how the Executive Directors changed their role. They delegated profit and operating responsibility to the next level of management and this left a smaller team of Executive Directors (reduced from 14 to 8) free to concentrate on Group financial performance and corporate direction, without being personally accountable for profits in the individual parts of the company. The Executive Team then developed and carried through a new strategy which shifted the portfolio of products from commodities towards speciality chemicals, and moved the balance territorially away chemicals, and moved the balance territorially away from the U.K. towards the U.S.A., Japan and selected Less Developed Countries.

With regard to strategy, the Executive Team became responsible for:

(1) formulating the strategy for the Group as a whole;

(2) agreeing and reviewing the strategies of the major businesses with their Chief Executives;

(3) launching at the centre strategic initiatives, such as acquisitions, divestments, new organization structures and new ventures.

The implications of the strategies are also followed through by:

(1) the agreement of 3-year budgets, 'a contract between the Executive Team and the Chief Executive of the unit';

(2) the approval of capital investment projects; and

(3) monitoring strategic milestones which indicate 'whether the unit is proceeding along its agreed

strategic path, and whether the milestones are being passed'.

The role of the ICI Planning Department has also changed dramatically. In 1980 there was a large planning staff engaged in budgeting and forecasting and often 'second-guessing' management in the divisions. By 1986, the planning group was half the size, but more influential, serving an Executive Team which had adopted a strategic planning role, and also working as consultants to the chief executives of the Business Units.

* * *

Global Strategic Planning at 3M

The 3M Company of St Paul, Minnesota has a reputation second to none for product innovation. One of its corporate objectives is that a quarter of its annual sales must come from products invented or improved upon in the last 5 years. As the company has had this rule since it was founded in 1901, and it now has global sales of $8·6bn, it is not surprising to find that they now sell nearly 50,000 products, including sandpaper, scotch tape, kitchen scourers, video cassettes, reflective road signs, and surgical masks. More than 100 products are introduced every year—one of the most recent being the fabulously successful Post-it Notes.

On the other hand, the company has had no reputation for Strategic Planning. You might say the culture was hostile to it. 3M was one of the last bastions of entrepreneurship. Until 1982 that is, when the Chairman and CEO, Lewis Lehr, decided that something must be done to improve the company's performance, and Strategic Planning might do the trick.

Typically, decisions were taken at the product level of the company in around 200 units operating in 49 countries. In the words of the Corporate Planner, 'cross-functional teams were doing a pretty good job but they were not steering the company'. The problem for top management was how to set priorities for corporate investment and disinvestment for the main business and for different territories without imposing the dead hand of bureaucracy and damaging the entrepreneurial spirit which is the life-blood of the organization.

Lewis Lehr decided to reorganize 3M along two dimensions.

(1) Operations were re-structured into four main sectors along technological lines—graphics, life sciences, electronics and information, and consumer and industrial (industrial abrasives, adhesives, coatings, sealants, etc.). Within these sectors it was expected that product champions in adjacent divisions would plan their technologies together.

(2) In addition, a new structure was established for strategy. This consisted of 20 Strategic Business Centers. This was not a large staff function—simply a requirement that the managers of each operating unit should formulate strategies for the global businesses they were involved in. The global strategies are discussed and agreed in the first 6 months of the year from January to June, and the priorities which emerge provide guidelines for the operating plans and budgets which are produced between July and December.

The SBC's are 'essentially data gathering and "thought centres"' designed to assist the corporate managers in setting priorities between the company's major businesses. The system has enabled top management to take a global view of the company and to take key decisions: disinvesting from photocopiers and investing in video cassettes, pulling out of several African states and investing in the Pacific Basin. The Strategy Centers have also served to coordinate and promote strategy development throughout the company. In the first year of the system 700 key managers were taught the elements of strategic thinking in a series of intensive seminars. This was just the first step in a significant change of management style towards strategic management.

* * *

The Quest for Quality at Philips

Philips is one of the few western companies which still competes with the Japanese in consumer electronics. The company can only survive by matching Japanese standards in quality and reliability. This article, written by Kees van Ham, Senior Director of Organization and Efficiency at Philips International, and Roger Williams of Erasmus University, Rotterdam, describes how Wisse Dekker, the President of Philips, led a company-wide Quality Improvement Programme to enable the company to compete on quality. He made it clear that the programme was 'of the utmost importance to the continuity of our company' and the Board of Management announced that they would give 'vigorous direction to a company-wide approach'.

These statements were followed up. The President outlined a new quality policy. He then invited all the senior executives to a series of seminars and asked them to start the change process personally within agreed guidelines. Then, 'the whole company entered an era of intensive learning by experimentation' with a central unit providing consultancy and information. The campaign was strongly marketed inside the company, through video tapes, newsletters, booklets, case presentations and a wide range of meetings and seminars. They also launched a Philips Quality Award Scheme.

Progress was reviewed annually by the Board of Management. In the first $2\frac{1}{2}$ years the company arranged 250 quality improvement seminars, for over 15,000 managers. Programmes were established in more than 150 organizational units employing over 60,000 people, including not just production workers but staff in sales, administration and various support groups. In addition to the usual quality standards, a variety of other measures were used: quicker product development, an increase in the number of approved suppliers, reduced inventories, fewer errors in invoicing, decreased sales costs, etc.

* * *

Competing through Service at SAS

The story of how Jan Carlzon turned around Scandinavian Airlines is a modern legend. In his article, Olle Stiwenius, an organization consultant with SAS, describes how Jan Carlzon initiated the move from a bureaucracy to a 'service culture' which triggered off a revolution in SAS, later led to the adoption of similar approaches in other airlines like British Airways and KLM, and also had an impact on other service businesses around the world.

Jan Carlzon's comprehensive programme for changing SAS had seven key elements:

(1) *a new philosophy* focused on the customer as the company's 'most important asset';

(2) *a new strategy* offering the 'frequent business traveller' the type of product he required;

(3) *a new organization structure* which broke the company into smaller 'result-oriented' units;

(4) *a new corporate culture* with greater delegation of responsibility, open access to information, more supportive management and clear goals and strategies;

(5) *new programmes for staff development*—these included $20m invested in 150 projects to improve customer service: a management development programme for 2000 managers and a 2-day course for 10,000 front line staff in Personal Service through Personal Development: and discussions on Market Value Analysis to cut out 'services nobody was prepared to pay for';

(6) *a new image*—The idea of SAS as the Businessman's Airline was promoted inside and outside the organization. This involved refurbishing the aircraft, office interiors and passenger lounges, new uniforms, and new corporate advertising;

(7) *new leadership*—Jan Carlzon is a real leader with charisma as well as ideas. He gave his organization a clear vision, specific goals and good information: then he encouraged them to take initiatives in line with his broad programme for change.

The result was astonishing. In less than 3 months SAS was the most punctual airline in Europe. The next year European businessmen voted SAS their favourite airline, the company increased its market share and went back into profit.

* * *

The NFC Buy-out—A New Form of Industrial Enterprise

Leveraged buy-outs are a phenomenon of the 1980s—a device which boards and chief executives have discovered can transform company results in traditional businesses, which appear to have little potential for development. In his article, Sir Peter Thompson, Chairman of the National Freight Corporation, reveals how he and his board injected new life into an aged haulage business and increased the value of the shares from £1 to £16 in just a few years. By the autumn of 1987, before the stock market crash, the shares were valued at £54! This turnaround was achieved not through a management buy-out but by an *employee* buy-out. NFC was Britain's largest employee buy-out which included over 10,000 employees and pensioners as shareholders. Now it seems likely to be followed by employee buy-outs in other transport organizations and many of the nation's bus companies.

The NFC buy-out was arranged in 1982. Sir Peter describes how the board negotiated with the government, the banks and the trade unions, then marketed the idea of share ownership to 25,000 employees and their families, 18,000 pensioners and 2500 managers. They used videos, brochures and face-to-face meetings, and in due course the issue was hugely over-subscribed.

The Board then faced the daunting task of communicating its strategies and plans and the company's results, to thousands of employee shareholders. They decided to hold quarterly meetings, chaired by directors in eight regions of the U.K., and they produced surveys of shareholders' views on business development, shareholder communication and other issues. At the Annual Meeting, the Chairman usually addresses over 2000 well-informed employee shareholders.

The top management have found that the key to successful communication is to sell their strategy to the employees, keep them well informed about company performance, consult them on key issues, and constantly expand share ownership among the work force. The next step will be to float the company on the Stock Exchange to expand the market for NFC shares.

Acknowledgements

I would like to express my personal thanks to the authors for submitting their articles to *Long Range Planning*, and for kindly agreeing to have them reprinted in this first volume of *The Best of Long Range Planning*. I hope readers will find this summary of the best thinking and practice in Strategic Planning stimulating and useful.

PART ONE

The Job of the Chief Executive

Strategic Leadership and the Chief Executive

Andre van der Merwe, Professor of Business Administration and Sandra van der Merwe, Professor of Marketing, University of Witwatersrand

This article is based on research undertaken among South African chief executives occupying the most senior operational positions in public-quoted companies. In looking at distinctive characteristics in these individuals the research attempts to bring together the activities that shape the chief executive's job and explore possible trends in their background; career route and behaviour patterns, and from the compositie picture to provide guidelines for executive development.

The enigma of the chief executive will never disappear until a sufficiently well researched data bank is built up on who he is and what he does. Are there, for instance, managerial skills and activity grounds common to these achievers? What is the main substance of their role and day-to-day functions and satisfactions? Are they made or born . . .?

Research up to now has tended to concentrate on work content and the intrinsic ingredients of the job.[1] Few studies, globally speaking, have actually looked at the issue in depth or produced a representative model or profile which could be used for planning or educational purposes.

The project is not intended as an all-purpose guide for the chief executive. Its focus is to provide a significant body of views and experience that any chief executive can draw on in evaluating his own approach to the job of heading a corporation. It is also not intended to be prescriptive. Rather it tests some of the commonly accepted notions and assesses the practical working value of classic concepts propounded over the years.

At the time of writing this article the authors were, respectively, Professor of Business Administration and Professor of Marketing at the Graduate School of Business Administration, University of the Witwatersrand, 2 St. David's Place, Parktown, Johannesburg, South Africa.

The composite drawn from the responses finally provides guidelines for more meaningful executive development and succession efforts and a role model for aspirant achievers with sights set on the top rung in their organizations.

The Survey Method—An Attempt to Characterize the Group

Clearly there is no average chief executive. On reading the report some may find themselves agreeding or disagreeing with parts of the picture that emerges. But from the participating chief executives it is possible to draw a profile, not of the average chief executive but of the group as a body.

To ensure a representative profile, random data had to be captured and a random sample of 50 chief executives by name was drawn from Johannesburg Stock Exchange list of quoted industrial companies. Respondents defined as the persons 'having overall responsibility for a more or less self-contained business unit'[2] were addressed personally by a letter with a pretested questionnaire.

Six refusals were replaced. Contributors to the research cover a broad spectrum of industries, encompassing a full range of corporations in the industrial sector with a normal distribution representation of employee numbers and annual turnover levels. The sets of answers received were combined with information gathered at personal interviews with about half the sample. The data assembled was analysed and forms the basis of the report which follows.

A Look at Demographic Profile and Career Route

Table 1 outlines the demographic profile of South African chief executives and also highlights career

Table 1. Profile of the chief executive background and career route

Titles	No.	%
Group MD & CE	1	2
MD	17	34
Deputy Chairman & CE	5	10
Deputy Chairman & MD	3	6
Deputy Chairman & Joint MD	1	2
Deputy Chairman	1	2
Chairman	1	2
Chairman & MD	12	24
Executive Chairman	3	6
Joint Chairman & MD	2	4
Group Director	1	2
GM & Director	1	2
Chief Executive	1	2
Vice Chairman & MD	1	2

Age	
Over 30 up to 40	20%
Over 40 up to 50	40%
Over 50 up to 60	30%
Over 60 up to 70	10%

Years as chief executive	
5 years or less	48%
Over 5 up to 10	28%
Over 10 up to 15	14%
Over 15	10%

Directorships		
0	48%	(of which 2/3 CEO's less than 5 years)
1	12%	
2	14%	
3	6%	
4	10%	
5 and more	10%	

Number of other companies worked for		Cumulative
0	14%	
1	32%	46%
2	16%	62%
3	18%	80%
More than 3	20%	100%

Years with company	
5 years or less	36%
Over 5 up to 10	18%
Over 10 up to 15	16%
Over 15	30%

mobility patterns from a collective point of view. In Table 2 their educational and functional experience is set out together with views on what additions they feel would have benefited them in their period of office.

Titles and Directorships
Looking at titles first, a wide array of terms is used to describe these high-ranking individuals. 'Chief executive' itself is seldom used and confirms a worldwide finding that it is an American term still largely confined to companies in the United States.

'Managing director' is the title which occurs most frequently among the sample. Thirty-four per cent of the participants carry it. The other dominant title is 'Chairman and Managing Director' which 24 per cent use. All of the other titles mentioned are less characteristic.

Typically, chief executives assume some responsibility for Chairman or deputy chairman duties. By far the majority, some 78 per cent, are not in a family-controlled environment and just over half serve on boards of other companies. Only 10 per cent serve on five boards or more—a far larger proportion, 26 per cent, restrict themselves to one or two of these outside commitments.

Age
On the whole there is a fairly 'normal' age distribution among South African chief executives. If anything they tend to be slightly older than the group which have emerged in research done in other countries with the highest concentration in the age group 40–50 years (some 40 per cent) followed by 30 per cent between 50 and 60 years, 20 per cent under 40 years and 10 per cent in the more-than-60 category.

Years as Chief Executive
A large proportion of individuals at present occupying chief executive positions in South African companies are relative newcomers to the field. About three-quarters of the group have been chief executives for 10 years or less and just under

Table 2. Profile of the chief executive education and functional experience

Functional background	
General administration	68%
Operations	42%
Sales/marketing	64%
Finance/accounting	64%
Personnel	26%
Engineering/production	32%
Research & development	20%
Legal	14%
Other	6%

Educational background[1]	
Finance/accounting	40%
Engineering/physical sciences	36%
Business/commerce	30%
Legal	18%
Humanities	6%
Social sciences	4%

Years of formal education	
8–12	12%
13–16	50%
17–18	26%
19 or more	12%

Functional experience for better preparation[1]	% of total sample	% of positive answers
None	72%	NA
Marketing	18%	64%
Finance/accounting	8%	29%
Personnel	4%	14%
CEO of another company	2%	7%

Educational background for better preparation[1]	% of total sample	% of positive answers
None	28%	NA
Business administration	46%	64%
Finance/accounting	40%	56%
Humanities/social sciences	24%	33%
Engineering/physical sciences	16%	22%
Law	8%	11%

[1] Multiple responses add up to more than 100%.

half have occupied their posts for less than half that time. This new generation of top achievers is reasonably young. In fact, a third who have been in office for 5 years or less are in the under-40-year-old bracket, while 87 per cent are below the 50 year mark.

Entry Ages

It seems that 50 is the cut-off age for aspirant chief executives in the Republic. Looking at the sample's present ages relative to their years in office shows that nearly half had become chief executives before their fortieth birthday; another 48 per cent of the incumbents got the top spot before reaching 50.

The data reveals an undoubted emphasis on younger men. About 80 per cent of the group became chief executives before they were 45. Only 6 per cent did so after their fiftieth birthday.

Years With Their Company

Quite a large number of incumbent chief executives are relative newcomers to their organizations. More than a third, 36 per cent in all, have been employees for 5 years or less and more than half for 10 years or less. Forty-six per cent can count more than 10 years of service, 16 per cent of these have been with their company for 10–15 years, 30 per cent for more than 15 years.

For three out of five, the chief executive position represented a promotion from within. However, looking in more detail at the data there is a bias toward promotion from outside for the recent comers to their organizations. Of the under-5-year-service category 75 per cent were brought in from the outside, whereas only a quarter progressed on an in-house route. Of those who have been at their jobs for longer than 5 years, 88 per cent came from inside their companies and 12 per cent from other organizations.

The implication of this is that recently wider experience tends to have had the upper hand and that possible weakness in managerial development and succession planning in many companies has led to a situation where the chances are 3:1 against an internal promotion to the top job. This has been quite a dramatic reversal from the case prior to 5 years ago were nine out of ten of these appointments were made from the inside.

Just about half the individuals promoted from within are in family-controlled situations or founded the company themselves. Thirty-five per cent of these executives have family interests while 16 per cent are founders of the firms they now head. All family-controlled institutions appoint chief executives from the inside.

Only one out of every seven of the respondents has spent his total working life with the company he now leads. Just less than half have worked with one or two other companies; the others have moved among three companies or more.

Prior Positions

With the exception of two people, all in the sample held some general executive position immediately prior to assuming their posts as chief executives. The exceptions were both in the accounting function.

The route to the top seems to be mainly through three prime titles, viz., general manager, managing director and working director. Twenty-six per cent moved to the chief executive spot from general manager rank, 26 per cent from managing director and 22 per cent from working director. Numbers are divided equally in each of these categories between those promoted from inside and those brought in from outside, except in the case of working director where a greater portion were promoted from within than without.

Functional Experience

Regardless of the position occupied immediately prior to becoming chief executive, 70 per cent of the responding chief executives had extensive experience in general administration. The other two prominent functional avenues to the top are marketing/sales to which 68 per cent of the sample professed a strong exposure, and finance/accounting in which 68 per cent of the sample claimed wide experience.

Other functional areas which featured in responses by the sample are operations (42 per cent), production (32 per cent), personnel (26 per cent), research and development (20 per cent) and law (14 per cent).

Educational Background

Indications of years of 'formal' education can never cover the full equivalent of years of learning or knowledge. However, most chief executives in the country do have sufficient years of formal education to have gained a 3-year degree or equivalent qualification. Thirty-eight per cent claim more than 17 years—enough to qualify for a post-graduate or other higher degree. On the lower end of the spectrum, 12 per cent acknowledge 12 years of less formal schooling. They tend to be in the older age category.

Most of the chief executive officers enumerate one field only of major formal study. This is contrary to their overseas counterparts who tend to have wider educational backgrounds. The disciplines that stand out as the major fields of study of the group are finance/accounting (40 per cent), engineering and physical sciences (36 per cent), and commerce and business administration (30 per cent). Law, too, has been followed by a number (18 per cent) of top-post South African achievers, unlike the liberal arts (humanities and social sciences) which have not figured prominently in their earlier careers. This is contrary to the situation overseas where they are well supported as a formal study base and are second to engineering and physical science and followed by finance, business and law.

Their Background in Retrospect

In retrospect, how adequate do the chief executives feel their prior experience to have been? More to the point, what, if any, additional functional experience might have provided better preparation for their present jobs?

Three-quarters of the chief executives feel that they needed no supplementary functional exposures that would have helped them cope with their current responsibilities. However, two out of every three who say that some additional experience would have been beneficial single out marketing, and one out of every three, finance, as something they would miss.

Retrospectively, what additional fields of study do these chief executives now wish they had? On this question, the chief executives are more responsive than on additional functional exposures. Three out of ten say 'none', but seven out of ten are willing to volunteer multiple additional fields that could have been helpful.

Business Administration got an answer from 64 per cent of these, primarily respondents whose formal schooling was in engineering and physical sciences, finance/accounting and law. Finance/accounting is cited next highest by 56 per cent of the sample and this comes mostly from engineering/physical sciences and law individuals. Thirty-three per cent of the respondents, mainly from finance/

accounting, would add humanities and social sciences to their formal education.

Handling the Job of Chief Executive

Ultimate responsibility stands out as a major element of the chief executive's job. To many that is what being a chief executive is all about—to produce the results.

By virtue of his singular position, though, the chief executive must reserve certain activities, duties and decisions. Others he can delegate. This section examines his judgment of success, mode of managing, reserved priorities, activities and responsibilities and his process of accountability. The data for this analysis are in Tables 3, 4 and 5.

Accountability

Looking at accountability first: accountability to whom? Almost half (46 per cent) of the responding chief executives say they report to the chairman, another 46 per cent to the board. The largest group (34 per cent), mention only the board as the body to whom they are accountable. A minority, but a sizeable minority of 26 per cent, report that they feel accountable to the chairman and 12 per cent to shareholders and the board. A handful of respondents insist they are accountable to themselves only.

Appraisers and Appraisals

A significant part of accountability is highlighted when the chief executive answers a related question, 'Who appraises your performance and what measures are used?' Just as few chief executives say they are accountable to no one, a few say that no one appraises their performance (11 per cent). As for standards, 13 per cent report no set standards and 8 per cent, unknown criteria. One respondent states that his own conscience is his standard. Most of these company heads work on a management-by-exception basis and the kind of comment they make is '. . . if they're not satisfied they let me know quick enough . . .'

The larger body of chief executives, however, say the board as a whole appraises their performance (46 per cent), while 43 per cent see their chairman as the appraiser. Some believe they are evaluated by some general standards which most of the responding chief executives characterized as 'performance targets agreed on' (13 per cent), or 'overall corporate achievements' (29 per cent). Some volunteered such more specific measures as profit (47 per cent), cash flow (18 per cent), return on equity (16 per cent), increase in net worth

Table 3. Profile of the chief executive reporting line and accountability

Report to	
Chairman	46%
Board	46%
Group MD	2%
GM Holding Company	2%
Nobody	4%

Accountable to	
Board—only	34%
—& shareholders	12%
—shareholders & myself	2%
—& chairman	10%
—chairman & shareholders	4%
Chairman—only	26%
—& shareholders	4%
Myself—only	4%
Auditors—only	2%
Holding Company representative on board	2%

Who appraises CEO's performance[1]	
Board	46%
Chairman	43%
Shareholders	11%
Stock Exchange	7%
Financial Press	4%
Myself	4%
Nobody	11%
(Total respondents 46 out of 50)	

What standards are used[1]	
Results of performance	
'Targets agreed on'	13%
'Overall achievements'	29%
Specific performance standards	
Profit	47%
Cash flow	18%
Return on equity	16%
Increase in net worth	13%
Development of subordinates	3%
Product strength	3%
No formal standards	13%
Unknown criteria	8%
My own conscience	3%
(Total respondents 38 out of 50)	

[1]Multiple answers.

Table 4. Delegation pattern of chief executive

Number that report to chief executive	
2	0%
3	4%
4	14%
5	30%
6	20%
7	16%
8 or more	16%

Evaluation of number who report to you	
Do too many executives report to you	20%
Do not enough executives report to you	6%
Do just enough executives report to you	74%

Evaluation of amount delegated	
Too much	2%
Too little	20%
About enough	78%

(13 per cent). Development of subordinates was only raised by one respondent, market share was also mentioned once only and referred to as 'product strength'.

A few of the responding participants include in their orbit of accountability a group larger than just the board or chairman. Shareholders were mentioned by 11 per cent of the group, the Stock Exchange by 7 per cent and the Financial Press by 4 per cent. In a broader sense many expressed their obligation to the expectations of community interests they and their companies serve. Whether these are formally spelled out or not, they feel that producing results in accord with them is a substantial part of their ultimate accountability.

His Own Measure of Success

There is evidently a self-judging quality as well which is the source of what the chief executive himself makes of his performance. In short, there is a large measure of consensus as to how heads of South African companies measure their own success.

All the chief executives participating in this survey were asked: 'When you leave the job of chief executive, how will you judge whether you have been successful?' The following were the major multiple responses:

Company's financial growth and prosperity	76%
Depth and continuity of management	40%
Continued performance of successor and company	38%

Table 5. Priority ranking of importance of and time spent in major activities[1]

Activity		Ranking 1st	2nd	3rd	4th	5th	6th
Planning	Importance	66%	18%	10%	6%	—	—
	Time spent	34%	28%	24%	8%	6%	—
Inspection & control	Importance	28%	26%	24%	20%	2%	—
	Time spent	36%	30%	14%	16%	4%	—
Meetings	Importance	10%	8%	14%	16%	20%	20%
	Time spent	2%	16%	16%	14%	14%	—
People	Importance	10%	36%	36%	10%	4%	4%
	Time spent	18%	18%	34%	12%	6%	6%
External relations	Importance	6%	12%	6%	18%	24%	14%
	Time spent	6%	10%	14%	20%	20%	23%
Personal development	Importance	—	2%	6%	12%	20%	26%
	Time spent	—	—	12%	8%	24%	20%
Other (those mentioned most often)							
Top level customer contact	Importance	—	4%	6%	4%	6%	4%
	Time spent	—	2%	10%	8%	4%	4%
Mergers & take-overs	Importance	—	2%	6%	10%	18%	26%
	Time spent	—	4%	6%	12%	6%	6%
Rest, such as developing dealer network, expanding export business, etc.							
	Importance	—	14%	18%	14%	24%	6%
	Time spent	5%	4%	9%	18%	30%	21%

[1]Multiple answers result in % totally over 100.

Company's market position, reputation and image	30%
Employee morale, loyalty and reaction to my leaving	16%
Smoothness of transition	14%

From the various executives came replies focusing on the end result similar to that of one respondent who said: 'By keeping together and building a competent team of executives to continue with objectives and aims of the company', and from another: 'That the company has an image of solidarity and strength'. Other executives looked to future events to judge whether they had succeeded or not. One respondent commented: 'If the company continues to grow for at least 3 years after I leave, I'll know I've done a good job'. Another said: 'If the company does better after I leave'. One executive offered: 'If the board attempts to retain my services'.

Core Responsibilities

There is a reasonable degree of concurrence among chief executives as to certain essential responsibilities. Differences in responses of 'newcomers' and those who have been in the top seats for longer periods are too small to attach any significance to their varying perception.

Of course there are variations, not only in the responsibilities mentioned but in the relative emphasis on them. Even so there is evidently a body of duties that chief executives recognize as reserved to their office. This is manifest in their replies to the questions 'What do you consider to be your primary responsibilities?' 'What are the factors or bases that determine what you delegate?' and 'What aspects of your job, if any, do you believe cannot be delegated and must be reserved to you as chief executive?

What follows is a composite drawn from the voluntary statements in answer to the first question.

(1) Determine Overall Objectives and Plans

This is stated in a variety of ways but is emphasized by a good proportion of the sample. Some examples are:

'Do forward planning and strategy'	32%
'Ensure adequate corporate growth'	28%
'Maintain rewards for shareholders'	14%
'Guide company into future'	12%
'Ensure adequate marketing planning'	12%
'Attend to meaningful acquisitions'	6%

One chief executive provides a statement which summarizes this strategic task: 'My primary responsibility as chief executive is to submit to the board and gain their acceptance of the group's current and long-term objectives. Then I need to see that these goals are adhered to'.

Only 16 per cent mentioned the word policy which probably means that to many of the chief executives responding, there is no substantiative difference between policy formulation and establishing objectives. The comment: 'Ensuring that necessary policies exist for effective cooperation' was made by 16 per cent, and another 'Ensuring that the company meets its social responsibilities' was spelled out by 16 per cent of the respondents.

Planning, of course, goes a long way toward establishing priorities. But in addition to the plans themselves, part of the executive's job is regarded as the allocation of resources, principally financial, that back up the plans. Forty per cent of the executives felt that ensuring adequate liquidity was a priority. Quite a few, 20 per cent, mentioned 'ensuring that the company adapts to technological and market changes' as of prime concern. The establishment of overall corporate budgets and targets was mentioned by 10 per cent of the sample.

(2) Organization and Key Executive Selection and Development

The job of organizing and selecting key executives is given as much emphasis by the chief executives as establishing objectives and policies. From the relative weight given to the morale and development of top management teams within organizations, it is evidently a major area of concern to chief executives and a key factor in determining how the existing organization can be structured and what responsibilities and authority can be delegated. Phrases like 'to ensure well-motivated staff' were mentioned 40 per cent of the time, 'appointing and leading a strong, effective top management team' 32 per cent, and 'having a sound organization structure' 14 per cent. No one mentioned the development and designation of a successor.

(3) Key External Relationships

For a reasonable number of responding individuals, external relationships of various types are a significant part of the job. This was mainly expressed as the 'establishing and maintaining of external contacts' (24 per cent). Few, 10 per cent, mentioned their relationship with the board as a body or with board members.

(4) Control

A fundamental part of the chief executive's task is control. This is evidenced by remarks like 'my major task is to ensure the effective operation of the whole company including subsidiaries'. This sentiment was expressed by 32 per cent of the group in one way or another. Eighteen per cent talked more of operating control, . . . 'that operating policies are adhered to'.

It is obvious that the financial health of the organization gets first place in terms of their responsibilities as perceived by South African executives. As one executive put it: 'the chief executive must at all times ensure that the company's profits increase'. Liquidity was also emphasized strongly and by several of the respondents in the group.

Delegation Pattern

The size and the scope of the chief executive's job responsibility rests, to a large extent, on delegation ability. His patterns of delegation can be looked at in at least two ways. First, it may be viewed through a number of people to *whom* he delegates (his span of control measured in terms of the number of people who report directly to him). The second equally significant aspect is looking at the factors that determine *what* he delegates.

Looking at the *to whom or how many*: among these chief executives only 4 per cent have more than three people reporting to them, 14 per cent have four, 30 per cent have five, 20 per cent have six, 16 per cent have seven and 16 per cent have eight or more.

Most, 75 per cent, say the number reporting to them is about right. Relatively few (6 per cent) say that 'not enough' people report to them. A larger group (one fifth) say 'too many'. Most of the chief executives who find their spans too broad have more than eight people reporting to them. Seventy-eight per cent reckon they delegate 'about enough'. Twenty per cent feel they delegate 'too little'. One respondent said 'too much'.

The next significant issue is the factors determining *what* chief executives delegate. 'Routine' and 'operational' matters are the ways most of the chief executives characterize what they delegate. 'All decisions which are not major corporate policy ones' say 42 per cent of the respondents. 'When it does not include financial policy decisions' was expressly itemized by 14 per cent.

As one executive put it 'Overall assessment of projects and action must not be clouded by too much involvement in routine or attention to detail'. Quite a large number (40 per cent) point out specifically that 'all matters which fall under a functional manager or a subsidiary' should be left to that individual. As one comment sums it up 'If a member of a top management team is delegated authority over areas for which he has responsibility he must be trusted to make day-to-day decisions or be replaced . . .' Another company head comments: 'A properly trained and motivated executive reporting to a managing director should be able to take 85 per cent of the decisions himself. The other 15 per cent will affect other divisions or company policy and therefore the managing director will have to participate . . .'

Implicit in these statements of delegation boundaries is the chief executive's subjective judgment of his subordinates' capabilities. In fact, 'confidence in the ability of the subordinate' got the highest number of responses (44 per cent) from the executives and was mentioned in a variety of ways.

It is quite clear from comments and descriptions that there is more to delegation patterns than just having confidence or faith in the demonstrated competence of subordinates. The question of morale was raised by 20 per cent of the executives who are prepared to delegate to 'develop and encourage' subordinates and, in one executive's phrasing, 'to make sure ultimately that there is commitment so that I can perform'.

Another 14 per cent use delegation 'to encourage decentralization'. This, say a number of executives, must be actively worked at. Especially, one points out, 'in a multi-company conglomerate where effective control makes delegation easy'.

Time-pressure is singled out by 14 per cent of the sample as governing when and how they delegate. This is invariably seen in relation to what priorities the chief executive gives to the various managerial elements of his job and obviously, too, against the impact of decisions on the company's future. Clearly though these factors are subjective and depend on the disposition and managing style of the chief executive. One respondent frankly admits '. . . in theory I delegate everything possible in order to make sure that I don't get bogged down with detail. In practice I retain control of a number of key functions . . .'

The 'novelty' factor is a determinant of only 6 per cent. Although this is not often expressly mentioned, there is a wariness evident among the chief executives questioned about delegating in areas where the company has had insufficient experience and where estimation of outcomes of any actions or decisions is perceived as high risk and in cases where the corporate head is afraid to be landed with consequences he cannot handle. A few executives also admit that they delegate on the basis of their own particular interests or familiarities—says one respondent: 'I delegate all matters that bore me . . .'

In talking about decisions that cannot be delegated there were half-a-dozen areas which stood out as reserved for the company head. The most significant of these are:

Corporate planning and strategy in major discipline areas (finance and marketing in particular)	60%
Appointment, remuneration and motivation and control of senior staff	54%
Top level negotiations and contracts with Government, key suppliers and key customers	30%

Reporting and liaising with chairman and board	20%
Acquisition and merger planning and negotiations	14%
Co-ordination of activities within group	14%
Public speeches and important press statements	14%

Apart from these specific areas where there seems to be reasonable consensus about what a chief executive can or cannot delegate, there is a more emotional element which governs these decisions. This comes from executives who associate 'gut feel' with aspects of their jobs and as one respondent candidly makes the point 'I can delegate almost anything except gut feel'. Says another on the same score 'I just cannot delegate in matters for which I feel I have a flair'.

On the issue of support and advice rather than outright delegation, the respondents offer the following list in answer to the question 'What sources do you turn to for advice?'

Executives, functional and operational	72%
Chairman and board members	70%
Consultants	30%
Merchant Bankers	6%
Wife	4%
Colleagues in similar overseas positions	2%

Activities and Priorities

Establishing over-all priorities is an important reserved responsibility of any chief executive. Not only is it significant in terms of his company's direction but of special relevance for himself and his own work as well. Notwithstanding the maximum amount of delegation, the chief executive has to establish some of his own priorities in allocating his effort and time.

Almost all of the co-operating chief executives have a fairly clear idea of priorities in terms of the relative importance of various parts of the job. Table 5 shows the results when they were asked to rank the following set of activities that correspond very closely to the reserved responsibilities already identified:

A: Planning—including formulating corporate objectives and growth plans, organization structure, high level manpower, and other future requirements of the company.

B: Inspection and Control—checking and appraising individual and company performance through on-the-spot visits, inspection and written reports.

C: Meetings—with staff and other contacts and with the company board of directors.

D: People—dealing with internal personalities and personal, interpersonal conflicts, stimulating individual and group performance.

E: External Relations—with the community, other companies and government or educational institutions.

F: Personal Development—reading, attending meetings, seminars, courses primarily for personal development (relative to their work).

G: Other—any other activity that takes a major segment of time, e.g. actually selling to major customers, working on an acquisition or merger . . .

By far the largest proportion—two-thirds—rank planning as their most important activity. Of course, planning, in the sense used here, is all-encompassing. Among the chief executives who do not give this broad category of activity highest ranking, relatively few rate it less than third in importance. No other activity matches planning, or, more appropriately, concern with the future.

Second in importance is 'inspection and control'. Two out of seven chief executives rate this their most important activity. But more than three-quarters rate it among the top three activities.

'Meetings' with the board, staff, and those with outside involvements, and 'People' are next in line in terms of the relative importance associated with activities by the respondents and are the only other two factors cited to any real degree of significance. In both cases they were ranked number one by 10 per cent of the group. However, 'People' comes out as a greater priority—72 per cent of the sample put it in the top three whereas only 32 per cent put 'meetings' in the top three.

When 'what is most important to the chief executive' is looked at in relation to 'how the executive spends his time', 'Inspection and Control' followed by 'Planning' is where the time goes. Thirty-six per cent of them rank 'Inspection and Control' as the activity taking the most time. 'Planning' according to 34 per cent of the chief executives is the Number One time consumer. For 18 per cent time spent on people problems is tops. While 'meetings' were only rated as taking the most time by 2 per cent, 16 per cent ranked it number two and another 16 per cent number three. 'External relations' was also rated highest by only a handful of respondents (6 per cent): it was ranked second by 10 per cent and third by 14 per cent.

The allocation of the individual chief executive's time does not always square with the relative importance he assigns the specific activity. Collectively speaking, less than half the chief executives profess to be able to devote most of their time to the item they consider most important. And only 18 per cent say they are able to allocate their time in accordance with all their relative priorities. Comparing the chief executive's top priorities in terms of importance with their time priorities in Table 5, 66 per cent rank planning as their most important activity, yet only 34 per cent devote most of their time to it.

Hours of Work and Vacation

Even with a maximum of delegation and best efforts to budget his time, the chief executive works a long day and a very long week. For some chief executives any quantitative figures on hours of work would be an understatement. Several comments were made to this effect, like: 'Your job is your life', 'office hours are for clerks', 'your job never ends', 'you've got to work until the work is done'.

To the extent that they can quantify their work time, 68 per cent of the responding chief executives estimate that they work more than 50 hours a week on business activities. Eighteen per cent claim the hours are more than 60. The distribution of responses is:

up to 40 hours	6%
more than 40 hours up to 50	26%
more than 50 hours up to 60	50%
more than 60 hours up to 70	16%
over 70 hours	2%

To the majority of South African chief executives, the many hours required by the job are not a formidable complaint. Seventy-eight per cent are satisfied that the hours they work are about right. Here is how the respondents rate their work time:

Too great	22%
Too little	—
About right	78%

Three- and 4-week periods are those most often taken off by chief executives for vacations. Roughly a third take a month a year and another 30 per cent allow themselves a 3-week break. Of the remaining third of the group, 16 per cent take off 2 weeks, 4 per cent only 1 week and 2 per cent less than a week annually. There is one isolated case of 6 weeks or more.

Is this enough time off? The respondents are about evenly split: just over half (52 per cent) say yes, 48 per cent say no. Those saying no are in the less-than-a-month-off category.

Problems, Expectations and the Future

The job of chief executive is not without its problems although most individuals in this position make it abundantly clear that the satisfactions outweigh the minor complaints or major frustrations.

Problems and Frustrations

The chief executives in most instances are very cryptic in describing problem aspects of the business. When asked 'What aspect of business has consistently given you the most perplexing problem?', one word or phrase was usually given. The majority of the responses can be grouped into the following categories:

People problems—development and training for succession and growth and motivation	48%
Marketing problems—moving into sophisticated products, maintaining market leadership, fighting multinationals	30%
Finance problems—raising finance, funding new products, expenditure control, getting rid of unsuitable investments, forward planning and budgeting in a fluctuating market	16%
Production problems—technical problems with products, high technology industries, productivity and product development	12%
Organizational structure—setting up a structure, changing a structure	8%

In answer to 'what part of your job do you find least satisfying?' several frustrations, large and small, were brought out. Complaints centred on half a dozen or so areas but the one that was singled out over and over again was 'staff'. It seems, therefore, that not only are 'people' of particular concern to these chief executives and the largest continuing problem, but they are also at the root of what many cite as the least satisfying aspect in the job situation.

Looking at the people side of things, by far the most perplexing problem is getting the 'right' people and by 'right' some executives mean 'motivated' while others refer to their training and ability. The dimensions of the problem are expressed often and, by at least half of the respondents, in many ways. Some phrases referred to . . . 'the lack of drive and job interest of younger employees'. Others talk of middle management and the weakness there seems to be in getting suitably trained people. Some refer to the constant 'interpersonal conflicts and having to sort out personality clashes and internal politics'. Then, say others, there is the frustration of 'having others do assignments that I could do better'. Another comment which cropped up regularly was 'the continuous need for staff reprimanding' and of course the anguish of 'staff dismissals'.

All of this points to a possible weakness in executive development and training systems in South African corporations, a point that has been brought out previously in this report. Identifying individuals worthy of becoming, and developing them into top calibre executives need to be incorporated into more formal and long-term career development programmes if top executives are to be spared at least the day-to-day hazards and frustrations related to the human element in business.

Next in turn in the volume of complaints is paperwork and routine matters that need to get done. Some executives talk of the 'daily grind'. Others speak of meetings, reporting time to overseas parents and time wasted at board level during meetings and on reports.

Another body of dissatisfaction revolves around dealing with governments and government policies and what is referred to as the uncontrollable effects of government legislation. Here, applying influx control, and restraints placed on business with regard to Black labour, are singled out. Fluctuations in foreign currency was also mentioned and what was termed 'continual weaknesses in our economy because of the political isolation'.

Other miscellaneous remarks included 'dealing with dissatisfied customers', 'air travel', 'big group bureaucracy' and the odious task of 'mixing business with private lives'.

Chief Satisfactions
When it comes to satisfaction, money isn't it. Only half-a-dozen respondents mentioned it and as some pointed out, high taxation can make the financial rewards secondary and in fact a source of dissatisfaction. A few executives make the point that it is necessary to have an income sufficient to free the executive to focus on important issues. But words like 'fulfilment' and 'stimulation' came much closer to describing their sentiments. As one person put it . . . 'the hunt, the chase and the victory'.

Nor are status or prestige the chief satisfiers, although these are mentioned quite a few times. The main satisfaction springs, it seems, from the opportunity to build something worthwhile and the sense of achievement and recognition that goes with it.

The accomplishments that appear to give the chief executives their greatest satisfaction are, in a large measure, of general types.

(1) The satisfaction of knowing he has proved himself capable of leading an organization and being successful in exercising power, initiative and creativity. One chief executive writes . . . 'the opportunity to develop and use one's own ideas constructively and with purpose . . .' The power to make their own decisions also stands out as a dominant feature. From several executives come comments like these: 'the opportunity to build and act on my own without reporting on a regular and detailed basis', . . . 'the right to do things my way'.

(2) The satisfaction of having allowed or encouraged the personal growth of other individuals. Many respondents mentioned the exhilaration of building people and the business concurrently. And a good few executives expressed their enjoyment in 'working as a team with my people' and the kick they get out of 'seeing a company grow in strength and stature plus developing strong people around me'.

(3) The satisfaction of having built something worthwhile and in a wider sense, having made a constructive impact on the economy and society as a whole. The companies whose operations are international in character talk of the wider implications of their efforts. Says one executive: 'the opportunity to build a truly South African enterprise that can compete in world markets with the multinationals'.

Why They Accepted the Job
The character of the satisfactions the chief executives identify as making the job worthwhile goes a long way, in many instances, toward explaining why they took the job in the first place. Only 14 per cent mention money as the reason they accepted the job. And just as a sense of achievement is what they found most satisfying, challenge and the desire to accomplish are the strongest reasons for accepting the job.

Here are their main reasons for taking on the top spot:

Challenge	70%
Job satisfaction	26%
Had no option	20%
Succeeding father or started company	18%
Fulfilment of life-time ambition	18%
Income	14%
Power	10%

How Long as Chief Executive
All responding chief executives agree that the fire they bring to the job has a limited life. Quite a substantial number, 42 per cent, refuse to set a specific time-span. According to them, it depends on the individual. To quote one such response, . . . 'you can stay as long as you are up to it'. The rest are willing to quantify the optimum period. Five years is optimum, say 4 per cent. Twenty-four per cent opt for 10 years and 28 per cent put the point at about 15 years. Typical of comments that go with these responses is 'you need at least 5 years to familiarize yourself with the job in all its aspects and to gain confidence—thereafter one has to worry about succession which takes at least as long a time . . .'. One proviso they make . . . 'this is fine as long as you can recognize change and can accommodate it'.

Among chief executives in South African companies, about 70 per cent are subject to compulsory retirement, most often at 65. Eighty-four per cent of these give this age, while 16 per cent give 70 as a cut-off point. Should their experience and know-how continue to be available to the company? Or is there more to be gained by a complete break with no continued association? On this point, there is some disagreement among the responding chief executives.

A large majority (66 per cent) say the ex-chief executive should continue his association with the company in some or other capacity, primarily as a member of the board and then for a limited period. The 'Yeses' are qualified by remarks to the effect that there is no general rule that can be applied—it depends on the individual, his financial status, acceptability and health.

Expectations and the Future

Long before the executive contemplates retirement, he thinks of succession. And as already indicated, the quality of his successor is one of the criteria he often uses to measure his own success in the job.

As a group, most responding chief executives have apparently fulfilled the responsibility of having a replacement ready. Seven out of ten state that there is someone within the company who could replace them tomorrow were they to step down as chief executive. They make the point though that finding a successor is not easy. On qualities that the chief executive looks for in developing and selecting a successor, most agree that apart from personal qualities such as integrity, the will to win, decision-making ability, flexibility and so on, know-how has an edge.

In looking back over the years, does the job match up to expectations? Are the responsibilities about what they expected?

Two-thirds say the actual responsibility of the job match quite accurately what they expected. Twenty-odd per cent say the task is a greater one than they anticipated and a few describe it as a heavier load. The gulf is mainly described in terms of the amount of commitment necessary to undertake the job well . . . 'I never knew one had to be so dedicated', retorts one respondent while another observes . . . 'one can only accept the minimum outside interest'. One respondent points out: 'I hadn't realized how important a wife was in the scheme of things', and says another: 'In retrospect, I would have liked to be more careful about seeing to it that my family life wouldn't suffer'. Another executive says pointedly 'I didn't allow sufficiently for how much understanding and affection for people is needed', and yet another interesting thought: 'It's a lonelier job than I ever imagined'.

Another view of the situation comes from executives whose comments revolve around the amount of knowledge that is needed and the fact that there are 'very few rules of the game—you're basically on your own'. (Only 20 per cent of South African chief executives purported to having job descriptions.)

As it turns out though, given the opportunity, nine out of ten would do it all again. Ultimately, they say, the job of the chief executive is made up of many parts and if the total is desired, the individual elements have to be accepted. It is an occupation out of the ordinary and unique . . . 'the chief executive has to be a renaissance man. He must have a wide knowledge and the constant thirst for more. He must achieve through his staff, coerce without appearing to do so. He must innovate without making people feel it's his idea. He must lead without seeming to run in front of everyone else. He must have ethics that set the tone for the whole company . . .'

Notes

The authors gratefully acknowledge: A grant from the Human Sciences Research Council which contributed to the costs of this research project. The co-operation and effort of the chief executives who took part in the study. Permission by Dr Harold Stieglitz and the Conference Board to use their *Personnel Policy Study* No. 214 entitled *The Chief Executive and his Job* as a foundation for developing the questionnaire used in this research project and as a comparative data resource. Unless otherwise stated reference to overseas research data and trends comes from this report. Sample = 50. Due to questions unanswered or multiple response figures do not always total 100.

References

(1) (i) For examples see Henry Mintzberg, The manager's job: folklore and fact, *Harvard Business Review*, p. 53, July–August (1975).
(ii) Jack Schofield, The effectiveness of senior executives, *Journal of Management Studies*, **5**, 219–234, May (1968).
(iii) Sidney Lecker, Personality could be the key to business success, *International Management*, pp. 23–24, May (1981).
(iv) Henry Mintzberg, *The Nature of Managerial Work*, Harper & Row, New York (1973).
(v) Rosemary Stewart, *Managers and Their jobs*, Macmillan, London (1967).
(vi) Leonard R. Sayles, *Managerial Behaviour*, McGraw-Hill, New York (1964).
(vii) Harry Levinson, Criteria for choosing chief executives, *Harvard Business Review*, pp. 113–120, July/August (1980).
(viii) Donald H. Thain, The ideal general manager, *Business Quarterly*, **43**, 75–81, Summer (1978).
(ix) D. H. Thain, The functions of the general manager, *Business Quarterly*, **43**, 53–61, Autumn (1978).
(x) T. Mitchell Ford, Changing rules for the CEO, *S.A.M. Advanced Management Journal*, **44**, 39–43, Autumn (1979).
(xi) George A. Welmer, Finance favoured as key to executive boardroom, *Iron Age*, pp. 35–38, 16 April (1979).

(2) Jack Schofield, op. cit., p. 220.

(3) Louis E. Boone and James C. Johnson, Profiles of the 801 men and one woman at the top, *Business Horizons*, pp. 47–52, February (1980).

The New Class of Chief Executive Officer*

George A. Steiner, Harry and Elsa Kunin, Professor of Business and Society, and Professor of Management

This article summarizes the results of research into the ways in which environmental forces are changing the management task of chief executive officers of large corporations. The article comments on the changing business environment; on the time spent by managers on environmental forces; changes in the basic strategies of managers concerned with major social and political environmental forces, the characteristics which chief executive officers believe their successors must have to be effective managers; major ways in which the impact of environment on the CEO is changing the infra-structure and decision-making process; and, finally, a brief look at the future.

Everyone knows that the business environment is changing. Not everyone fully appreciates, however, the extent to which it is affecting business. Today's environmental forces that impact importantly on business—externally as well as internally—are powerful, fundamental, numerous and generally threatening. My research study concluded that Chief Executive Officers of the larger corporations are spending an increasing amount of their time on environmental factors, that they have changed their basic strategies which deal with social and political forces in the environment, and that they believe the requirements needed by a person in order to be an effective CEO (today and in the future) are far broader than in the past. Indeed, so different are these qualities from the past that it is not any exaggeration to speak of a new class of CEO. This new class of CEO is clearly represented in the sample of CEOs upon which basis the full study has been prepared.†

Early in the study it became clear that the changes being made in the managerial task of the CEO were also altering the internal organization structure: the relationships of the CEO with the board of directors, line managers and staff; and the functions of different groups in the organization. The study dealt with major recent developments in these areas and these will of course, be touched upon here.

The sample of CEOs and other executives upon which basis the study was prepared is admittedly highly selective. Forty-seven executives were interviewed, most of whom were CEOs of very large corporations. Beyond that, speeches and other written materials of a great many more were read. It certainly cannot be said that CEOs in much smaller corporations face either the problems of the CEOs of the larger corporations or have responded in the same way to environmental forces as their peers in the largest companies. However, the example of how environment is influencing the larger corporations in the study, is more likely than not to be felt by an increasing number of companies in the future. Thus, the example of the sample for this study, while admittedly small and select, is one which is likely to spread.

The Changing Business Environment

The concept of environment in the study is the total environment, externally and internally. It includes, externally, such forces as government regulations, economic conditions, law, attitudes of people which directly and indirectly affect business, the proliferation of single-issue and intransigent pressure groups, new demands made by people on corporations, criticisms of corporations, and unsettling conditions in other parts of the world. Internally, in addition to the traditional economic and technical forces, there are changes in attitudes, expectations, and demands of managers, staff, and hourly employees that top managers of corporations must deal with.

---

*Presented at the AACSB Annual Meeting, Chicago, 11–13 June 1980.

†The full study has been completed and is now in process of publication by the Macmillan Publishing Company.
The author is Harry and Elsa Kunin, Professor of Business and Society and Professor of Management at the Graduate School of Management, University of California, Los Angeles, CA 90024, U.S.A.

Space does not permit any examination of these and other forces, but no one can consider them without a sense that there has been a basic change in our society which in turn significantly affects business. We may well be in the midst of what cultural historians describe as an 'axial age', or one of monumental transition. At least, so far as business is concerned there is little doubt that the rules of the game have changed dramatically from even a decade ago. The scope of environmental concerns has enormously expanded for the CEO of the large company and his priorities of attention have altered significantly within the past few years. The impact of these phenomena on the managerial task of the CEO of the large company has indeed been powerful as will now be described.

CEO Time Allocated to Environmental Forces

There is no question at all that CEOs today are spending far more time dealing with environmental issues than did their predecessors. Not only are they spending more time on environmental matters, but the nature of the environmental forces which are of concern to them has altered dramatically.

The range of time is from 25 to 50 per cent, on the average, with a high of 80–90 per cent on particular occasions. Many of the CEOs in this study said that 10–15 and certainly 20 years ago their predecessors spent very little and in some instances practically no time at all on external affairs.

The list of priorities for the CEOs attention has changed significantly and varies, of course, from CEO to CEO and time to time. All CEOs interviewed would agree that the environmental forces of most concern to them and occupying most of their time, relate to government actions and the impact of public opinion on public policy.

Two New Underlying Strategies

Paralleling the increasing expenditure of time by the typical CEO on environmental forces has been a significant modification of perceived CEO responsibilities. Underlying this change are two new strategies. One is a strategy of active CEO involvement in external socio/political processes. The other is a new and deepening concern for the legitimate interests of major constituencies of the enterprise.

A Strategy of Involvement in Socio/Political Processes
Traditionally, the strategy of the majority of top executives in the United States has been one of maintaining a low profile in the public forum and an intractable position against any governmental initiatives. Even casual consideration of the current mountain of government regulations over business and the low level of creditability which business enjoys attests convincingly to the disastrous consequences of that strategy.

Today, the strategy is just the reverse. It is one of active involvement in the public policy processes and new programs to communicate with constituents. This is not meant to say that business leaders in the past did not get involved in the political and social processes. They did, but there was no general conscious and purposeful strategy to do so as there is today.

The Strategy of Positive Response to Legitimate Constituent Interests
The second major strategic change of CEOs in dealing with environmental forces is a recognition of their need to respond positively to legitimate constituent interests. In the past, many CEOs of large companies said clearly that they were trustees for major constituent interests and they and their companies had a responsibility which went beyond the strictly economic one of seeking to optimize only the short-term wealth of their common stockholders.

CEOs giving the annual McKinsey lectures at Columbia University from 1956 to 1967 clearly enunciated the trustee concept. It was framed primarily in terms of balancing the interests of three constituents—consumers, shareowners and employees. Today's CEO sees a long list of constituencies, in addition to these three. Furthermore, the demands of all constituent groups have enormously expanded in recent years. These two considerations add a major new dimension to the trustee idea.

There is no question at all about the fact that CEOs of the largest corporations have formulated a strategy to be responsive to the non-economic as well as the economic forces operating in their environment. By their words and actions they conclude that the non-economic forces are as potent in fashioning corporate behavior as are the economic forces. They believe that they must respond as best they can to legitimate public demands.

They would accept the view that the worst possible strategy would be one that is perceived by the public generally as being non-responsive, if not in opposition to, important interests of society. A society with the ultimate power over the conditions under which business functions would not today receive sympathetically such a strategy of the largest companies.

Today's CEOs believe that a strong and viable business system will not exist in a society where a majority of the public perceives the private interests of people in business as being opposed to public interests.

Top managers of our corporations believe, and rightly so, that the corporation is and should be fundamentally an economic institution. The drive for increased profits is a dominant motivating objective. Profit consciousness, however, does not deny social consciousness. The two, rather, are closely related. One of the questions which I put to many CEOs was whether they found any important conflicts between their economic drives and the assumption of social responsibilities. The response was no. They had little trouble, they said, in reconciling the two.

It should be repeated that this report concerns the views of CEOs sampled for this survey. There are many CEOs, even of some large corporations, who believe that they are discharging completely their social responsibilities when they manage their companies efficiently in producing products and services that the public will buy. The CEOs of this sample would accept the idea that a company is being socially responsible when it operates efficiently. But they go beyond that. They believe that as corporations grow larger social programs which they undertake voluntarily become more and more necessary and important. Indeed, as many of them were quoted as saying, they will not be able to optimize long-range stockholder returns unless they do so. They realize that there is, however, a limit to what they can and should be doing in the social area. They all recognize that today and in the foreseeable future the great bulk of the social programs which they do undertake are and will be mandated by government. So, while they talk about responding positively to legitimate constituent interests they are addressing only a small part of their total social responsibilities. Nevertheless, the philosophical difference between their accepting voluntarily constituent pressures to pursue social programs and their denying that they have any obligations to do so is very great and important.

These two strategies have led to the necessity for CEOs to have characteristics not thought too important in the past. When added to traditional qualities needed by CEOs the result is a new model of CEO to which I now turn.

Changing CEO Required Managerial Qualities

Many of the CEOs who were interviewed were asked what qualities they believe their successors should possess. In mind, of course, are those qualities required in CEOs of large corporations to meet the challenges facing their organizations in such a way as to assure the most effective operations of their companies and the survival of the business institution. The following is a composite of their responses, plus the thinking of some CEOs expressed in their speeches and written materials, and my personal observations.

It will be readily seen that some of the qualities are not new, and some of them add new dimensions to old qualities. Some of them, however, are new.

The fourteen qualities presented are not discrete. Many of them are linked and can be classified as subsets of others. Many of them can, of course, be further subdivided. I will give more attention to the newer characteristics although time limitations force me to be very brief for all. The listing is in no particular order of importance.

(1) The CEO must have a thorough knowledge of the economic and technical characteristics of the business. This is, of course, a traditional quality needed by CEOs and I shall not further elaborate.

(2) The CEO must be an astute administrator. This, too, is a traditional needed skill, but it has new dimensions today because of the new forces focused on the CEO. The managerial task is much more complicated now than yesterday. CEOs must grapple with more forces as evidenced by the many new constituent interests with which they must be concerned. Managers must make more important decisions in a shorter period of time and with less information than ever before. Astute administration today involves an ability to integrate traditional decision-making criteria (principally economic and technical) with new qualitative solutions to environmental demands (for example, social responsibilities). In sum, the CEO must be able to 'run the store' efficiently and effectively.

(3) The CEO must be a leader. By leadership, among other things, is meant a capability of influencing people in the organization to follow the CEO willingly and enthusiastically in achieving the objectives of the enterprise, in becoming more sensitive to social and political factors affecting them and the enterprise, and in participating in community and political processes. Most of the CEOs in the sample for this study would accept the view that CEOs must not only be able to inspire their employees but also be influential on the public platform. In short the CEO must have charisma.

(4) The CEO must be sensitive to social and political forces which impact on the company. The strategy to be concerned about environmental forces other than the strictly economic and technical ones was discussed previously. More will be said about it later, but a few more dimensions might be noted here. At the Bank of America one major criteria for promotion

of managers is sensitivity to the environment in which the bank operates. CEOs recognize that the environment poses both threats and opportunities so sensitivity refers to both phenomenon.

(5) The CEO must have the ability to balance appropriately the legitimate interests of major constituents of the business. It is one thing to be sensitive to environmental forces. It is quite another to balance in the decision-making processes the traditional economic/technical considerations with the non-economic interests of constituents, external as well as internal to the company. This skill is daily becoming more and more important for the typical CEO and is dramatically changing the managerial task. This capability was discussed before but I might add a few dimensions.
The balancing act has few if any ready-made problem-solving formulas for the CEO. It is complicated by the need for making many different trade-offs, cost/benefit analyses and weighing many different constituent demands and company obligations. The stakes in doing a good job, however, are substantial. As one CEO put it: 'Only as he gets good 'passing grades' in these areas can he hope to maintain the company's legitimacy; and without that, the company is ultimately headed for costly, if not fatal, trouble. So his responsibility to his directors and shareholders will be as great in this area as in production, marketing and finance.'[1]
But as I noted before, while difficult, the CEOs do not perceive the balancing task as embodying mind-boggling contradictions, although the process demands dealing with contradictions, nor any major inconsistency with the striving for profits.

(6) The CEO must assume a personal responsibility for advocacy, activism and outspokenness and must discharge this responsibility effectively. This is a major new role for most CEOs. It means they must become a public figure, a spokesman for both a company as well as the business institution. To be effective the CEO must present articulately and coherently the company and industry position on the public platform. This means departure from the comfort of the board room and plunging into the seas of controversy in the public forum, the hearing room, the press room, and the class room. There are risks, of course, but they must be assumed.

(7) The CEO must be a good communicator. To perform well in the public arena a CEO must be a good communicator but the need goes beyond that. Managers must exchange ideas, facts, opinions, and so on, with other managers, staff, the board of directors, shareholders, government agencies, and so on. Communications is a means of leading, administering, informing and persuading. It is a unifying force in an organization. Managers today have more techniques for communications than ever before but using them effectively remains a difficult art. More than ever before business executives find it necessary to communicate better with the media. Many companies are literally sending their managers to professionals to learn better how to communicate in general and especially with the media and through the media to the general public.

(8) The CEO must be able to swim in political waters with as much ease as in the traditional economic and technical environments of the corporation. They need greater political sophistication in this politicized economy. As one CEO put it: 'I question whether anyone in a major corporation should be entrusted with top executive responsibilities unless his involvement in government affairs is strong, informed and broadly based. Business—and the nation—deserve no less.'[2]
Political activities can cover a wide spectrum from the legislative halls in Washington to local regulatory agencies. They can range from concentrated work on major pieces of legislation to encouraging employees to register to vote. They can include participation in trade associations which in turn seek to influence public policies, educational campaigns to influence public policy, performing services for politicians, and urging executives to serve as elected officials in communities where plants are located.
Involvement in the political processes requires special skills if a CEO is to be effective. For example, to be effective in Washington, D.C. the CEO must understand the political and decision-making processes, how a politician thinks and is motivated, and how regulators think and are motivated. The CEO must know how to prepare a solid case, how to develop and organize staff to help prepare the case, and how to present it persuasively. This by no means covers the requirements for effectiveness in the political arena, but it serves to underscore the point that the skills needed are considerably different from those required by CEOs just to run the business.

(9) The CEO is becoming more of a strategist than his predecessors. It follows from what has gone before that the CEO must spend relatively more time on strategic matters and cannot devote as much time to tactical administrative affairs as in the past. The CEO thereby becomes more of a strategist than in the past in terms of total managerial tasks.

(10) The CEO must have a global perspective. Both CEOs of multinational corporations as

well as those whose companies do business only in the United States must be much more sensitive to and respond appropriately to what is going on in other parts of the world. This world is becoming much more complex and interrelated. Today, a producer of speciality high technology can go bankrupt or face serious cash flow problems because of a move by a foreign country which is suddenly opposed by the United States government. So many things can happen in so many parts of the world that companies which might be vulnerable to potential adverse impacts must maintain surveillance of these areas and forces. CEOs feel the need today to understand the political, social, as well as the economic changes which are taking place in other parts of the world. With global intelligence, decision-making can be global; that is, movements of capital and products can be made where the cost is least, but decisions can be modified as social and political factors dictate.

(11) The CEO must be broadly gauged intellectually. As one CEO puts it: 'To deal with the delicate and divergent internal and external forces of the day, the top manager will have to be a 'generalist', in the very best sense of the word—with a feel for history, politics, literature, current events and the arts; in addition to being a highly qualified professional manager.'[3] If the CEO is to be a skilled communicator, an articulate and persuasive spokesman for his company and the business institution, wide-ranging intellectual interests will be invaluable in strengthening these talents. Top business executives must be able to think clearly about many complex issues and communicate with a wide range of people and groups.

(12) The CEO must set a high moral tone for the company. As one CEO observed when talking about codes of ethics: 'It is important to see the rules in writing, but it seems to me that constraints against dishonest and unethical behavior can be institutionalized only up to a point. All who work in a corporation must also be guided by example. The examples set at the top set the moral tone for the corporation, or any large organization for that matter, and perhaps speak more clearly than any code about how the corporation sees itself, about the standards to which it adheres, and the practices it will and will not tolerate. Setting the moral tone is plainly the job of the chief executive and his associates.'[4]

(13) The CEO must be profit conscious. All CEOs in the sample for this report reaffirm the position that the corporation is basically an economic institution. The fundamental purpose is economic, not social nor political. Its vitality and viability depends upon its economic performance and its ability to protect, sustain, and improve profitability. In this light the CEO is and must be profit oriented. But this thrust for economic efficiency and consequent profit does not mean, as pointed out previously, any reduced attention to legitimate social and political demands on the corporation. A proper balancing of these forces can be made by a still predominant economic institution which will maximize over time all legitimate interests focused on the corporation.

(14) Finally, the CEO must maintain poise amid a bewildering variety and range of forces in the environment and the many frustrations to be encountered in discharging the managerial tasks which must be assumed. The less poise the less effective will likely be the managerial performance.

In sum, these qualities add up to a new model for the CEO of a large corporation. Acquiring the requisite skills in all of these areas is certainly a formidable task. But it can be done. The CEOs interviewed for the study possessed the qualities described in the model.

The Infra-structure and Internal Decisions Processes

As to the infra-structure and internal decision-making processes—the focus is on the way in which organization and decision-making processes have developed as a result of the impact of environment on the management task of the CEO. It is recognized, however, that internal changes in companies result from many forces so all of the new developments noted here cannot be attributed solely to alterations in the management task of the CEO.

During the past 10–15 years new relationships have developed between the CEO and line managers, new staff groups have been formed and old ones have found their functions significantly expanded. The types of decisions and the ways in which they are made are significantly different from the past. Space does not permit any detailed examination of these changes but a few highlights will make the point that the environment has dramatically altered the internal organization and operation of the typical large corporation.

The Board of Directors

We can begin at the top of the corporate pyramid—the board of directors. Corporate boards of directors are becoming much more aggressive in discharging what they perceive to be their responsibilities and are working more closely with the board chairman. This new posture is the result of increasing criticism of board behavior which in turn has led not only to new regulations, particularly those of the Securities and Exchange Commission, but to liability suits brought and won by stockholders.

Not many years ago the typical board meeting dealt only with operational and financial matters. Today the territory covered is far wider and the probing is more penetrating. Boards are far more involved in company strategic planning, are concerned about how the company is affecting its environment, and how management is reacting to all important environmental forces.

Board organization has changed importantly. There are many more outside directors on boards. All boards have audit committees whose responsibilities are expanding from traditional narrow accounting and financial audit functions to management controls and ethics. In 1970 the General Motors Corporation set up the first public policy committee in a large company. Now most large companies have a committee with a title such as Corporate Responsibility, Social Responsibility, Public Responsibility, Public Issues, Public Affairs, Ethics, Public Interest, Corporate Ethics and Social Responsibility, and so on. The names indicate that these committees focus on the social and political programs of a company.

The CEO and Company Operations

It is generally conceded that the CEOs of large companies cannot discharge effectively their external responsibilities and, at the same time, deal with the details of their business as did the CEO of the past. The result is that they are dividing the job. Many companies have a top chief executive officer and an operating officer who might be given the title of chief operating officer (COO), or president. The CEO is mostly concerned with the outside environment and the president or COO is concerned principally with the detailed operation of the business. The CEOs in my sample believe that a good bit of the internal management job should be delegated but the CEO should still be responsible for the entire operation of the company.

CEO Relationships With Other Line Managers

Many important changes have taken place in the relationships of the CEO with other line managers growing out of the environmental impacts on the CEO. We have time to note only a few. To begin with, both centralization and decentralization of authority has taken place. As a result of the rapid growth of government regulations in a wide range of areas (e.g. environment, product, services, pensions and work place conditions), together with difficult problems in compliance, larger companies have centralized direction over such matters in one or more departments located at central headquarters. In the mid-1960s many of the new laws were administered by divisions but in recent years there has been a tendency to administer them from central headquarters.

At the same time authority concerning certain external affairs has been decentralized. CEOs do not believe that they alone are responsible for interfacing with the external social and political environment. They believe that dealing with this environment is a responsibility which is shared with their line managers and other employees of the enterprise.

All CEOs to whom the issue was addressed believe that it is very important that managers and employees, throughout the organization, become more sensitized to the changing environment, particularly the social and political environment, externally and internally. This is high on the agenda of most companies because CEOs believe that the more attuned are the managers, staff, and employees to the environment the easier will be the CEOs task in adapting appropriately to the changing environment. Furthermore, they believe that the better informed people are, the better decisions they will make.

The list of methods to sensitize managers to environmental forces is long. An important technique in many companies is for the CEO to deal with such matters in face-to-face meetings with line managers at regular management meetings. Most companies also employ a wide range of 'educational' programs. For example, among the more frequently found programs are: internal management development programs having environmental concerns as part of the curriculum, company developed and continuing education programs in Washington, DC to teach managers about government functions, company publications, attendance at outside institutes or university seminars and conferences, management retreats and seminars, participation in professional societies or industry trade association meetings, forums at which invited university faculty make presentations, and encouragement to participate in social and political processes in communities in which managers live.

More and more companies are appraising the performance of their managers in the social and political area and are using the results in determining rewards. An example is an evaluation of how well a manager is implementing the policy of the company concerned with equal opportunity, pollution, worker health and safety, community relations, relations with employees, political activity, and so on. There is no uniformity among company practices in this area except to say that while such considerations are a part of the managerial evaluation process the predominant standards of performance are still economic, as they should be.

The CEO and Staff

There is no way a CEO can keep abreast of environmental forces which he should know about without adequate staff help. This help is needed to formulate appropriate policies for the company in light of environmental forces, to devise strategies to implement policies, to work out plans to implement strategies, and to exercise the needed control over the organization to make sure that goals are achieved and policies are carried out.

The CEO also needs much help when venturing into the public arena. He must be armed with accurate information about the political, social, and economic aspects of the issues which he chooses to address. He may want help in developing a company program to deal with public issues including the building of constituencies to support his position. Failure to do the necessary homework in the public policy area may not only result in losing the battle, while making the CEO and the company look foolish, but may further erode the decling creditibility of business in the popular mind.

There are great variations in changes in staff organization and relationships with CEOs among companies. Also, any extended description of these changes requires more time than can be devoted to the subject. Thus, I shall merely try to hit some of the high points.

The Public Affairs Function. In the past, a typical public relations function covered two subjects: publicizing the products of the company and building its image. The task was fairly low-key and simple. Today this older function is a very small part of a much larger public affairs function which includes the following responsibilities:

- ☆ monitor the social and political environment to identify forces which may have a potential significant impact on company operations;
- ☆ coordinate the analysis of environmental forces throughout the company;
- ☆ identify the forces in the environment which are most likely to have the most important impact on the company and transmit that information to top management and other staff;
- ☆ help top management in the selection of those public policy issues on which the company will concentrate attention;
- ☆ prepare appropriate analyses of public policy issues which top management chooses to address;
- ☆ contribute to and participate in the injection of social and political projections in the strategic planning processes;
- ☆ develop communications programs aimed at various company publics of the enterprise and framed within policies of the company;
- ☆ develop programs to advance the interests of the company in the political processes of federal, state and local governments;
- ☆ develop programs by means of which the company may respond appropriately to the interests of the people in the communities in which it does business.

In a number of companies these functions are distributed among different staff groups, but in more and more companies the organizational approach is to integrate them in one department or have staff groups report to one individual.

To pursue these functions obviously requires a close working relationship not only with the CEO but with other line managers and other staffs. New talents are required. Needed, for example, are skilled observers of social and political forces, people who understand the different publics of the company, competent public policy analysts, effective lobbyists, good communicators and writers, and those with a thorough knowledge of the way in which the company operates.

Public Policy Issues Programs. Additional comment should be made about so-called key public policy issues programs. Most large companies today, as noted previously, are involved in public policy issues. Some confine themselves to issues which are of direct concern to the company and others expand coverage to include broad public policy issues of general importance. Companies that get involved in issues of a general nature usually select a limited number—four or five—for intensive corporate activity in any year.

The key issues are chosen in many different ways. In some companies the CEO alone will decide, but in more companies the CEO gets advice and counsel from other managers and staff. Once chosen, an intensive program would entail the development of position papers; dissemination of documents to the general public, legislators, stockholders, employees, and so on.

Public Policy Research Staff. Some companies have a public policy research staff to help the CEO deal with public policy issues. In other companies *ad hoc* groups may be formed to deal with specific issues, or the work may be done in one or more staff groups.

Corporate Social Policy Committee. A number of companies have corporate social policy committees in addition to board public policy committees and key public policy issue programs. The corporate social policy committees have different functions, but generally they bring people together to identify emerging social policy issues and make recommendations about proper company response to them.

The Government Relations Function. As might be expected from what has been said previously the government relations function in the typical large company these days is of major significance. It involves many people and covers much territory—providing information, lobbying, encouraging employees to become involved in the political processes, and administering political action committees.

About 500 corporations today have offices in Washington compared with from 100 to 200 in the late 1960s. Along with this growth in numbers there has been an expansion of responsibilities. The typical Washington office is a warning-post for a company to identify forces which should be dealt with. It is a center for communications about political activities. It provides services for visiting personnel. It is a source of expertise on who the CEO and others in the company should see, what should be presented, how to be persuasive, and so on. It represents the company among members of the Congress. It engages in analysis and research on public policy issues. And, of course, it engages in lobbying.

It soon became apparent, once executives decided to become deeply involved in the political processes, that various constituents of the company who had an interest comparable to that of management could be valuable allies in the legislative seats of government. So companies have developed so-called 'grass roots' programs to enlist the aid of different constituents, such as employees, stockholders, people in communities where plants are located, retirees, suppliers and customers.

Grass roots programs operate in different ways but fundamentally they are efforts to organize personnel in a company to help the company make its point of view heard in seats of government; to stimulate employees to monitor, be sensitive to, and communicate to company executives information about impending or proposed government action which will be of interest to the company; and to stimulate employees to become generally politically involved. Care is taken to be sure that no employee is forced to be involved in any action where the point of view of the employee differs from that of the corporation.

A survey of 211 companies by the NICB revealed that 54 per cent had grass roots programs. Although there were a few programs introduced as far back as 1940, most of them were formed after 1975.[5]

Corporations were permitted to form political action committees (PACs) in 1975 to make contributions to candidates for office and to political parties. Not many were created in 1975 and 1976 and then in 1977–1978 a large number were formed. After that the growth decidedly slowed. Today there are about 920 PACs in individual companies of which only about 680 are active. Many companies, including many *Fortune* 500 companies, do not have PACs and do not intend to have any. While the purpose of helping to elect business-oriented legislators is the dominant objective sought by companies in distributing PAC funds there are other purposes. For example, many companies believe a basic objective of their PAC should be to promote political awareness among their employees.

Other Staffs. Many other staffs have found their functions and decision-making processes changed as a result of environmental impacts. Time permits only a brief note about them. Many companies dealing directly with consumers have created consumer advocates within the companies. There is no question at all about the fact that legal departments have grown significantly in number and the subject matter with which they are concerned. Marketing departments in many companies have assumed a number of the functions, or parts of them, noted above and have, thereby, expanded their purview. Generally speaking when the CEO is active in the public policy area he looks to all relevant staff functions for help. Therefore, each department must be prepared to deal with those aspects of its discipline connected with the public policy dealt with by the CEO. Finance, for instance, will be obliged to develop expertise in tax policy if the CEO decides to become involved in that area. Production and manufacturing may have to become knowledgable about productivity in the United States if the CEO gets involved in that area, and so on.

This by no means exhausts the ways in which environmental forces have influenced changes in the organization, decision-making processes, behavior, and attitudes within corporations, especially the larger ones. But it does illustrate the profound changes which have taken place.

The Future

The conclusion is obvious: the management task of the typical CEO of our largest corporations has changed dramatically from that which was usual only a decade ago. This development, together with other forces affecting the corporation, has significantly changed the internal line and staff functioning and decision-making processes. These facts raise a number of important questions concerning the future, a few of which are now presented.

(1) Will the business environment continue to be turbulent, complex, threatening, and of major concern to CEOs of the large corporation? There is every reason to believe that the answer is an unequivocal yes.

(2) Will the basic strategies of business corporations of involvement in the political processes

and sensitivity to the legitimate demands of corporate constituents be followed in the future? The answer clearly is yes. The domination of government gives every indication of increasing rather than decreasing and the pressures on government by special interest groups will expand rather than contract. In such a setting the very survival of the business institution could be at stake with a passive political posture assumed by business managers.

(3) Will the typical CEO of the future large corporation need the skills which have been displayed by the executives in the sample to be effective in discharging his responsibilities? There is no doubt about an affirmative answer to this question in the minds of the executives sampled in this study.

(4) An important question is: how rapidly will this model be followed by CEOs in the future? Executives sampled for this study believe that its expansion will be slow, but it will spread. One of them ventured the belief that 20–30 years from now it will be unusual to find a manager in a corporation of any size who is not involved in social and political activities.

(5) Are the CEOs surveyed satisfied with the internal organization and decision-making processes that are designed to help them and their companies deal properly with the business environment? The answer is no, but it is improving.

(6) Will the changes in the managerial task of CEOs and internal organization and processes found in this study among large corporations be effective, especially if they spread among other corporations, in preserving the best of the business institutions? I believe the answer to this is a clear and unequivocal yes. I believe also that the executives in the sample would agree.

(7) Will our schools of business/management/administration modify their curricula to reflect the great changes taking placed in the management task, and in the internal operations of companies, which have resulted from environmental forces? Many modifications have been made in curricula but the question is: are they as penetrating and as widespread as necessary to develop in managers and staffs the kind of skill and understanding which they will need and should have?

References

(1) L. Lundborg, interview with author.

(2) J.W. McSwiney, Let Charlie do it? An address to the Government Affairs Committee Workshop, American Paper Institute, Pebble Beach, California, 3 August (1972).

(3) D. Rockefeller, The chief executive in the year 2000, Remarks at the Commonwealth Club of California, San Francisco, California, 2 November (1979).

(4) W. S. Sneath, Framework for a business ethic, Remarks at the 22nd Southern Assembly, Biloxi, MIssissippi, 5 January (1978).

(5) P. S. McGrath, *Redefining Corporate-Federal Relations*, p. 37. The Conference Board, New York (1979).

Appendix

Chief Executive Officers Interviewed

Dr. James G. Affleck
Chairman
American Cyanamid Company
Wayne, NJ

Mr. Joseph F. Alibrandi
President & Chief Executive Officer
Whittaker Corp.
Los Angeles, CA

Mr. Roy L. Ash
Chairman
AM International, Inc.
Los Angeles, CA

Mr. Charles L. Brown
Chairman
American Telephone & Telegraph Co.
New York, NY

Mr. Fletcher L. Byrom
Chairman
Koppers Company, Inc.
Pittsburgh, PA

Mr. Alden W. Clausen
President & Chief Executive Officer
Bank of America
San Francisco, CA

Mr. Charles R. Dahl
President & Chief Executive Officer
Crown Zellerbach Corporation
San Francisco, CA

Mr. Richard L. Gelb
Chairman
Bristol-Myers Company
New York, NY

Mr. Walter B. Gerken
Chairman and Chief Executive
Pacific Mutual Life Insurance Co.
Los Angeles, CA

Mr. Fred L. Hartley
Chairman, President and Chief Executive
Union Oil Company of California
Los Angeles, CA

Mr. Robert S. Hatfield
Chairman
The Continental Group, Inc.
Stamford, CO

Mr. Philip M. Hawley
President and Chief Executive Officer
Carter Hawley Hale Stores, Inc.
Los Angeles, CA

Mr. Wayne M. Hoffman
Chairman and Chief Executive
Tiger International, Inc.
Los Angeles, CA

Mr. Jack K. Horton
Chairman
Southern California Edison Co.
Los Angeles, CA

Mr. Reginald H. Jones
Chairman
General Electric Company
Fairfield, CO

Mr. Richard G. Landis
Chairman
Del Monte Corp.
San Francisco, CA

Mr. E. W. Littlefield
Chairman
Utah International, Inc.
San Francisco, CA

Mr. Louis B. Lundborg
Chairman of the Board (Retired)
Bank of America
San Francisco, CA

Mr. Cornell C. Maier
Chairman, President and Chief Executive
Kaiser Aluminium & Chemical Corp.
Oakland, CA

Dr. Franklin D. Murphy
Chairman of the Board
Times-Mirror Co.
Los Angeles, CA

Mr. Fred W. O'Green
President
Litton Industries, Inc.
Los Angeles, CA

Mr. David Rockefeller
Chairman
Chase Manhattan Bank
New York, NY

Mr. Donald V. Seibert
Chairman
J. C. Penney & Co., Inc.
New York, NY

Mr. Richard R. Shinn
President and Chief Executive Officer
Metropolitan Life Insurance Co
New York, NY

Mr. William S. Sneath
Chairman
Union Carbide Corporation
New York, NY

Other Executives Interviewed

Mr. Charles E. Bangert
Attorney
Randall, Bouget & Thelan
Washington, DC

Mr. Richard Clark
Vice President & Special Assistant to the Chairman
Pacific Gas & Electric Co.
San Francisco, CA

Mr. Arthur W. Cowles
Vice President Public Affairs
Koppers Company
Pittsburgh, PA

Mr. Robert L. Fegley
Chief Executive Director—Communications
General Electric Company
Fairfield, CO

Mr. Steve Gavin
Vice President Corporate Relations
Pacific Mutual Life Insurance Co.
Los Angeles, CA

Mr. Richard D. Godnow
Assistant Director, Business Roundtable
The Business Roundtable
Washington, DC

Mr. William G. Greif
Vice President
Bristol-Myers
Washington, DC

Mr. Emmett W. Hines
Director of Government Relations
Armstrong Cork
Washington, DC

Mr. Robert W. Irelans
Manager Corporate Relations
Kaiser Aluminium and Chemical Corp.
Oakland, CA

Mr. James Johnston
Director of Government Relations
General Motors Corp.
Washington, DC

Mr. Steven Markowitz
General Manager Government Relations
The Continental Group, Inc.
Stamford, CO

Ms. Julia Norrell
Assistant Executive Director
Business Roundtable
Washington, DC

Mr. John Post
Executive Director, Business Roundtable
The Business Roundtable
Washington, DC

Mr. J. Robert Roe
Vice President Corporate Communications
Litton Industries, Inc.
Los Angeles, CA

Mr. Michael P. Roudnev
Vice President Public Affairs
Del Monte Corporation
San Francisco, CA

Mr. Wayne H. Smithey
Vice President of Washington Affairs
Ford Motor Co.
Washington, DC

Mr. Steven Stamas
Vice President Public Affairs
Exxon
New York, NY

Mr. Thomas S. Thompson
Vice President—Public Affairs
The Continental Group, Inc.
Stamford, CO

Mr. Jack O. Vance
Managing Director
McKinsey & Company
Los Angeles, CA.

Dr. Donald Watson
Manager, Public Issues Research
General Electric Company
Fairfield, CO

Mr. William E. Wickert, Jr.
Manager, Federal Government Affairs Division
Public Affairs Department
Bethlehem Steel Corp.
Washington, DC

Mr. Ian H. Wilson
Consultant, Public Policy Research
General Electric Company
Fairfield, CO

PART TWO

The Role and Responsibilities of the Board

What is The Board of Directors Good For?

Dan Bavly, Horwath Bavly Millner & Co., Tel-Aviv

The history of corporate crisis in recent years indicates that the present method of operation of boards of directors is inadequate to deal with crises or influence events. Whether the remedies lie within the present structure or whether they should be found by establishing a new system is the challenge facing the corporate world and the academic business school. If, however, remedies are difficult or impossible to find, then at least the limitations of the boards of directors should be made clear.

'When Boards were conceived . . . nobody envisioned the world in which they misfunction today.'[1]

How often does the Board of Directors fulfil the tasks set it by law and expected of it by the owners of the business, the shareholders or the public in general? Can its members truly aid their Chief Executive Officer and his senior staff, advising and supporting them through thick and thin? Do they contribute to the success of their company?

There is a growing school of thought which is increasingly sceptical about the efficacy of most Boards. These businessmen and onlookers believe that, as they accumulate, statistics will show that the institution has fallen far short of expectations and that the answer to the question of what is the board of directors good for is summed up in the clearly negative results of a recent survey: the Board 'is not fulfilling the role for which it was purportedly designed.' (The survey, which covered the Chief Executive Officers of 2235 corporations, was conducted by the Egon Zehnder International Consulting Firm. It is referred to by Stuart I. Greenbaum in his article 'Boards and the crisis in banking' published in '*Directors & Boards*' by MLR Enterprises, Inc., 229 S. 18th Street, Philadelphia, 19103.) Worse, 'the Board has become,' in the words of Peter F. Drucker, ". . . an impotent ceremonial and legal fiction. It certainly does not conduct the affairs of the enterprise".[2]

Of course, there are exceptions and some Boards have been known to rise to the challenge of a crisis but failure to act when necessary seems to be the more frequent phenomenon. Contrary to the common image, there is little reason to think of board members as well-informed about the activities and problems of their company; or as capable of fulfilling their brief adequately and promptly. 'In every major business catastrophe . . . (since the Great Depression) . . down to . . . recent debacles . . . the Board members were apparently the last people to be told that anything was awry. . . And it is futile to blame men. It is the institution that malfunctions.'[3]

There is a virtually non-ending amount of business literature on the workings of the board. Few analysts are neutral. There is a clear line that divides those who discuss this institution in a positive manner from those who show it little respect. Theoreticians, especially those connected with schools of business administration, discuss the Board in great detail. They often furnish statistics of how boards work and how to improve their performance. There are two characteristic approaches: one is a wide-ranging discussion of data collected in an attempt to quantify the qualities of the board member or the type of corporate meeting he attends; the other, to which even more space is devoted, covers the theoretical role and responsibilities of the outside director and how he should discharge his duty to the shareholders. Among the most respected thinkers in this group and one of the clearest is Myles L. Mace, distinguished retired professor of Harvard Business School who, in his study '*Directors: Myth and Reality*'[4] stated that while:

The author is Executive Partner in one of the larger firms of Certified Public Accountants in Israel, Horwath Bavly Millner & Co., and is currently a member of the Advisory Committee to the Banking Commissioner.

☆ The Board provides advice and counsel

☆ The Board serves as some sort of discipline

☆ The Board acts in crisis situations

☆ it often does *not* have primary influence nor does it

☆ establish the basic objectives, corporate strategies or broad policies of the company

☆ ask discerning questions or even

☆ select the president.

But Mace was unusual in his criticism. Most academics treat the Board with far greater tolerance.

Businessmen, with practical experience, have either nothing or little good to say about the operations of the boards of directors they know. The Zehnder survey found that in general, day-to-day life, the board has little influence over the activities of the company. 'Boards of Directors are surprisingly unimportant . . . A solid majority of bank boards are *not* active contributors to the strategic success of their banks'. And the author goes on the note that only one of fifty-five CEOs of the largest banks views his boards as a 'critical contributor to his bank's success'.

In one of the few recently published books that takes a long, hard look at the role of the Board, Robert Townsend[5] comments that "most companies have turned their boards of directors into non-boards. The Chief Executive has put his back-seat drivers to sleep." he goes on to add that, "In the years I spent on various boards I never heard a single suggestion from a director (made as a director at a board meeting) that produced any result at all."

Similarly, Harold S. Geneen, retired Chief of ITT, said: "Among the Board of Directors of Fortune 500 companies, I estimate that 95 percent are not fully doing what they are legally, morally and ethically supposed to do. And they couldn't, even if they wanted to."[6] And Drucker adds, in agreement: "The Board cannot do what the law says it should do, that is, to 'manage' . . . Board meetings rarely go beyond . . . trivia".[7]

Senior executives will rarely criticize their boards in public. Why should they? They invariably take the attitude expressed by Townsend: "Directors . . . spend very little time studying and worrying about your company . . . they know far less than you give them credit for . . ."

Accordingly, John Naisbitt in *Megatrends* relates to the Board only briefly, while both Ira Magaziner and Robert Reich in *Minding America's Business* and Thomas Peters and Robert Waterman in *In Search of Excellence* and, as might be expected, Mark McCormack in *What They Don't Teach You at Harvard Business School* totally ignore the existence of this institution. All succeed in describing 'Lessons from America's Best-Run Corporations' without ever noticing that, at the top of each 'chart of organization' there sits a Board. The omission is quite an eye-opener.

It might be a very negative statement to make but boards of directors have, in the past-generation, been totally ineffective. Can they be improved? Should or can an alternative be found?

These are certainly difficult questions, probably as yet unanswered. But ignoring the fact that the board as it functions today is close to useless might be even more costly.

When the Board Could have Been of Help

To understand how disappointing their performance has been, we have only to consider how little use boards have proved to be when it came to identifying, isolating and dealing with crisis situations.

Experience gained in the past decade would indicate that business today should be prepared for far greater trade fluctuations than it saw in the thirty years following World War II. From the increase in the number of enterprises going out of business in recent years, we can learn that crisis situations are increasingly common. 1984, for instance, saw the largest number of bank collapses since the Great Depression. Also, business has become more diversified and geographically far-reaching. Multinationals are exposed to the threat of bombings and worse on the part of terrorist organizations ranging from the Japanese Red Army, the PLO, the Italian Red Brigades and the Irish Republican Army to various Latin American anti-U.S.A. forces.

It is in crisis situations that the value of the Board is tested. Yet, most last-minute corporate rescues have been the work of a capable chief executive officer or the main outside financing body. It has been very rare for the board to help save the corporation. Most companies do not have serious contingency plans for crisis situations. When they do, they refer to a limited set of possibilities.[8] Less than half the companies (47 per cent) with less than $500m in annual sales 'have a plan that would enable them to communicate quickly and effectively in a crisis'. Not surprising that, while these do not occur overnight, we have much anecdotal evidence that they often come as an unexpected shock to both management and the board of directors.

Aware of the need to produce ever higher quarterly results, officers and directors too easily are capable of 'crisis denial'[9], complacently accepting the assurance of their CEO that there is no need for action as the crisis will disappear. Actually, it is here where independent help might be needed but where boards so rarely rise to the occasion.

In the early 1980s, increased attention was devoted to corporate crisis management. Many publications, mainly articles, were published on the subject, ranging from 'Are you Ready to Meet a Disaster', by Virgil M. Dissmeyer, in the *Harvard Business Review* for June 1983, to 'Terrorists vs. the Multinational Corporations', published by Michael G. Harvey in the *Public Relations Journal* for October 1983. Like the books mentioned above, all these have one omission in common: they ignore the existence of the board of directors or of their individual members.

Whether management proved successful or less so, there is little evidence to indicate how boards contributed to ameliorating the conditions of their respective companies.

What is Expected of the Board Members?

It is all very well for Harold Geneen to recommend, from the safety of his retirement, that boards of directors should play a far more active role in management. While he knows that 'the Board's responsibility is to sit in judgement on the management, especially on the performance of the Chief Executive, and to reward, punish or replace the management as the Board sees fit. . It doesn't', and he never encouraged his board to do so when he was orchestrating the growth of ITT. Now, in the post-Geneen age, when the performance of the group is far less impressive, one still hears little about any possible increase in the influence of the Board.

According to the law, the work of a board member carries serious, indeed intimidating, responsibilities. Had the directors fully understood the degree of responsibility they were undertaking and feared the relevant laws, most would never have accepted the honor. One important reason why they do agree to serve on the Board is that so far courts have interpreted their responsibility as fiduciaries to shareholders very leniently. (This consideration could change if the recent ruling of the Supreme Court of Delaware that the Directors of Trans Union Corp. indeed violated the interests of shareholders is accepted by the Supreme Court in Washington.) Another factor was the insurance coverage. Not much attention was paid to this factor until recently. But in the mid-1980s the cost of insuring corporate officers and directors jumped sharply. If tariffs continue to rise it 'could lead to the exodus of outside directors.'[10] In spite of the increased expectations of directors themselves, there is no broad reassessment of the risks or attractions of directorship. As in the past, directors seem to regard their office as a sinecure and devote far too little time to learning what is going on in their corporations. 'Directors run virtually no personal risk for any amount of complacency, cronyism or outright neglect of their duties', contends Geneen.

It is not that the qualifications of the Board member are necessarily substandard. Most corporations follow in principle the twelve guidelines[11] used by Northern Illinois Gas Company in their choice of directors.

What these guidelines do not include is a description of what the candidate thinks of the company and how he intends to serve it. Research has shown that, exemplary though the character of the board member may be, he often proves to be far less active in his role as a board member than he was in the career which first made him successful and prominent enough to be invited to serve on the board.

When the Board Member is Expected to Act

If terminal crises are beyond the arena in which they can operate effectively, the main test to the Board comes when it is expected to act because the company is faced with a drop in profits, is incurring losses or losing markets and must take painful decisions. Is the Board informed of the danger of impairment of equity in good time, does it take preventive steps, ultimately perhaps causing a change in its CEO before the situation deteriorates to the point of outside intervention?

Eli Ginzburg quotes Dayton Hudson who wrote in the *Harvard Business Review* published in January/February 1984, 'Every time you find a business in trouble, you find a board of directors either unwilling or unable to fulfil its responsibilities . . .'. Yet, with the rare exception, such as that of the Continental Illinois Board members, they remain immune to the corporate and their own shortcomings.

The failure, in 1984, of Continental Illinois National Bank and Trust Co. and its Board of Directors came as a surprise, not only to the general public but in particular to the Board itself, in spite of the repeated warnings since the early 1970s that it was essential for boards of directors to brace up to the age in which they found themselves. And yet, there is still little evidence that other boards have taken seriously to heart the public display of accountability exacted by the Federal Deposit Insurance Corp. when, as the price of the Government bail-out, ten of the sixteen board members of Continental Illinois were forced to retire.

So far, the warning has not been heeded. Even in the recession of the early 1980s and during later pressure from the financial institutions, there is little sign that directors have read the plethora of publications on

PANEL 1. *Guidelines of Northern Illinois Gas Company for Choice of Board Members*

(1) Has outstanding business, administrative, or other valuable experience, proven ability and significant accomplishment.

(2) Holds position of high responsibility (preferably chief executive officer, currently or prospectively) with a major organization. If it is a business corporation, volume of business should not be too small in relation to NI-Gas and preferably should be greater (unless other compelling reasons override).

(3) Has no present or visible potential for conflict of interest. Is not connected with any organization presently serving or that might serve the company, such as institutions engaged in commercial banking, investment banking, law, or management consulting. Is not an officer or director of any (a) major supplier to competitors of the company, (b) other sizeable Illinois utilities or (c) rivals or companies represented on our board. Is not the CEO or a top administrator of an organization that has the NI-Gas CEO on its board.

(4) Contributes to the collective experience of the board, so that a diversity of age, business, geographical location, area of endeavor, and viewpoint is represented, all of which are significant to the company's opportunities and responsibilities.

(5) Has shown a willingness and is connected with an organization that has shown a willingness to serve the community in civic, social, and charitable activities.

(6) Possesses self-confidence and is at ease with persons of distinguished attainment.

(7) Is articulate, but not garrulous, and commands respect from peers.

(8) Possesses maturity, but also displays youthful initiative, enthusiasm and a progressive attitude.

(9) Is independent of recent past or present directors.

(9) Is an existing or potential stockholder.

(11) Is enthusiastic about the prospect of serving, and can devote the necessary time.

(12) Is neither chosen nor excluded solely because of race, color or sex.

what is expected of them and have risen to today's business challenges.

The case of Continental Illinois, where the board did not act fast enough to prevent crisis, supports the premise that boards often lack the determination to act when most needed. Geneen relates this to the fact that "Nominally, outside directors are elected by the stockholders. Actually, in most instances they serve at the pleasure of the Chief Executive." And Townsend gives his reasons for the failure when he writes[5] that 'Directors have one (function) . . . they can and must judge the chief executive officer, and throw him out when the time comes. Since this task is painful, it is rarely performed even when all the directors know it is long overdue.'

The Inevitable Drudgery

It can be instructive to study the agendas of board meetings, which give an indication of corporate priorities and the time devoted to them over any given period. During the height of the energy crisis, more than a decade ago, for instance, when it was not clear from where Israel would get her oil supply and there were threats to its sources of energy, the boards of Israel's three oil-distribution companies were intensely busy modernizing their gas-stations. Much time was being devoted to discussing which colors they were to be painted, while hardly any time was spent on ascertaining where future oil requirements would be purchased from. While the climate was peculiar to this country, there was nothing unusual in the emphasis chosen by the Israeli corporations. Rather, it was typical of the way in which boards take their decisions and draw up their order of priorities. The agenda is invariably prepared by the Chief Executive Officer, often in consultation with the Chairman of the Board. It is their prerogative and the outside director rarely has a say.

The outside, non-executive, board member is expected to give relatively little time to the company he is serving. This minimizes the effectiveness of the contribution he is, in theory at least, expected to make. The average chief executive officer spends well over one hundred and fifty, often two hundred, hours per month working for his corporation; the chief operating officer and the chief financial officer put in just as much time, if not more. But it is rare for the outside board member to spend more than ten hours per month. Eight is probably nearer the average. And almost all the time the outside board member devotes is in the form of committee work. Accepting the time constraints, is it reasonable and fair to expect wise and independent counsel from the board member? The CEO or another executive prepares the material to be studied and discussed. The board member is very much dependent on what knowledge the company, through the senior officers, provides. It is unusual for the board member to have an independent source of relevant information. Not surprisingly, it is almost impossible for him in his capacity as a board member to form a truly independent opinion.

In a way, it follows that the board member will prefer to consult on macro- rather than micro-problems. He is more comfortable relating to long-term questions, where results will not be promptly evaluated, rather than addressing himself to immediate challenges. He rarely has the patience to deal on a quarterly basis with the small, tedious, dull aspects of finances, accounting and other such humdrum aspects of business management, and hopes other corporate officers or directors will assume responsibility. And yet, more often than in the past, the outside director is expected to spend at least some time on these subjects. A case in point is the audit committee. Among the most enthusiastic supporters of this institution were the second-tier accountants who, in the 1960s, began to be worried about their lack of contact with the board.

They believed that an audit committee would offset, in part at least, their dependence on the Chief Executive Officer. Soon after their canvassing proved a success and such committees were introduced, however, the auditors discovered that, quite often, their members showed disappointingly little curiosity in the workings and findings of the audit. They preferred the comfort of detachment which the long-term strategic committees afforded them. Rather than involving themselves in the minutiae of the company and judging the work of the accountant, they were known to cut the Gordian knot by pressing for a change of auditor and urging an appointment from one from the larger, image-wise safer, better-known firms from among the Big Eight. There is no evidence that, in the following years, audit committees helped strengthen controls over the corporation or helped improve their management and executive systems.

Indeed, since June 1978, the board of every company listed on the New York stock exchange has been required to have an audit committee of independent directors.

The theory is that the board member is instrumental in the planning of long-range strategies. It is only reasonable to expect any chief executive officer to establish long-term targets and to develop the means of reaching them, within the context of the possible options, the state of the market in general and the company's resources in particular.

Peter F. Drucker doubts even that. "The Boards of Directors cannot work out a company's strategy . . . but it is the duty of the Board to make sure that a company . . . has adequate strategies . . .".[12]

But what, then, can the board member's contribution really be expected to be? The question of whether the concept of long-range strategic planning is a valid management instrument, in which the board member's experience can be exploited, a high-falutin exercise in futility or purely a cop-out to allay the doubts of the board members as to their usefulness, remains (empirically) unanswered.

So Who are Today's Directors?

There is an apparent inherent contradiction in the task of board member. Board members are generally expected to be the best, most experienced and highly trained representatives of the business world. It is almost impossible to find such persons who are not, at the same time, very ambitious and active. And yet, on the board, they are expected to be part of a supportive group, offering wise but basically passive counsel while the executives carry out the corporate management tasks.

In their role as board members, most people behave very differently from their daily character in their main line of business. Very often, they accept the different behavioral requirements of the board member out of loyalty to the chief executive officer and radically change the nature of their performance from their everyday business lives. This, together with the small amount of the time they devote to the company, means that, in fact, they have limited value as board members.

It is probably not practical to try, in the foreseeable future, to change the role of the board significantly but the expectations of how they will perform might be up-dated.

Why this gap between theory and practice? Probably one reason is that, as a theoretical model, boards are perceived as a neat operation. They answer needs and offer comfort. It is the academics, rather than the businessman with practical experience, who gives the most emphasis to the importance of the board. They almost certainly believe that it is the exception rather than the rule for the board to fail. Frustrated would-be executives at heart that they are, their academic objectivity is somewhat clouded by the less than secret hope and ambition of most professors in MBA schools from Harvard through Wharton to Stanford, London and Tel-Aviv to be invited to join one or more glamorous-sounding boards themselves. It helps their standing on campus and the added directors' fees should not be underestimated. There are some signs that indicate that the professors have been careful not to bite the hand that might offer them this status. They rarely interfere in the day-to-day operations of the company, and some believe they are gullible and ready to cooperate with the corporate officers. This often makes them popular with the senior executives and improves their chances of being asked to stay on the board.

There is an ongoing debate as to whether outside directors are preferable to inside directors. There is a clear indication of the increased average number, from eight to nine in thirteen, of outside members in the mid-1980s. And the pressure to reduce the presence of management on the board is growing more powerful. Peter F. Drucker quotes Professor Harold Williams, ex-Chairman of the Securities Exchange Commission, who argues to make the Board totally independent of management in composition, with the Chief Executive Officer as the sole member of the Board.[13] *Fortune,* however, quotes Myles Mace, who summed it all up by saying that:

> "There have been some cosmetic approaches by many companies to create the impression that directors have a lot more to do on the board . . . But there has been no real improvement in what directors do or don't do. Directors do not perceive themselves as representing the shareholders except at the annual meeting."[14]

In his article, Stuart Greenbaum is clearly dissatisfied and recommends that, to enhance performance, "an air of respectful tension between the board and management should be cultivated (and) the unimpeded and unfiltered flow of information to the board should be protected and fostered". While both recommendations are sound, they carry an aura of wishful thinking rather than the weight of an operational brief.

That does not mean that recruiting new directors to boards is a simple matter. Modern stress has reached the board room and, while not acutely worried about the exposure to litigation, "a surprising number of those invited to sit on boards politely decline to do so", says Lester B. Korn (Chairman of the executive search firm of Korn/Ferry International).[15] They would rather avoid the risk of being placed in the public spotlight, and they recognize that to fulfil their job as they should they will have to devote more time than they feel they can afford. It is premature, however, to expect a critical imbalance between demand and supply of directors. Not to be underestimated is the compensation they receive. Remuneration has risen substantially in recent years (directors of companies with annual revenues of more than $1bn get an average of $30,000) and we are likely to see more increases in fees and perks', says Korn towards the end of his article.

By their very structure, boards are passive and inevitably weak. In this age of high technology and the need for instant decisions relating to complicated professional data, their contribution will, at best, be marginal.

It is probably not practical to try, in the foreseeable future, to change the role of the board significantly but the expectations of members might just be updated. As important as having them spend, say, 12 days a year on company activities, a way should be found to afford them far more extensive knowledge and information on the operations and product of the corporation, its ethical and legal standards, etc.

The history of corporate crisis in recent years indicates that the present methods of operation of the board of directors make their capacity insignificant as a means of influencing events. How, if at all, can their standing be improved to offer due protection to shareholders is a question that must be seriously studied by both businessmen and academics. Whether the remedies lie within the present structure or whether they should be sought by establishing a new system is one of the challenging subjects facing the corporate world in general but, not least, schools of administration and their distinguished professors!

PANEL 2. *What are Directors For?*

As early as 1971, *Businessweek*[16] wrote:

'There was a time when a corporate director could regard his appointment as just an agreeable tribute to his wealth and his connections, a sign that he had entered the inner circle of the business community. If any director still thinks of his job that way, the proliferation of stockholder suits, the drumfire criticism of the militant consumerists, and the mounting complaints of minority groups should make him think again.

The problem of the modern director is to define his role so that he does not meddle with day-to-day management but nevertheless knows what is going on and makes his influence felt in the determination of broad policy. It is not a problem that lends itself to easy answers. Each company is a separate case and it is fair to ask whether a man who serves on a dozen or more boards really is doing his job on any of them.

In too many recent cases (Penn Central, for example) no one has been more surprised than the directors when the management finally admitted that the company was in deep trouble. And in too many cases, consumer groups or spokesmen for minorities have hit home when they charged that no one on the corporate board was thinking about them. As a result, business today is more vulnerable to punitive legislation and regulation than it has been at any time since the 1930s.

If corporate management is to survive in anything like its present form, directors will have to take on new responsibilities. They must make sure that corporate goals are consistent with the larger goals of U.S. society. And they must monitor management to see that it pursues these goals effectively, including the basic objective of earning a reasonable income and keeping the company out of the bankruptcy courts.'

If, however, after such a serious examination is carried out, it is ascertained that not much can be done to enhance their position, then, rather than encourage expectations, steps should be taken to make limitations clearer to the public in general and to those directly interested in particular. Not least, this would mean considering whether and how to adapt what at times appears in parts to be a radical and punitive set of laws to the far more modest role directors actually play on today's Board.

References

(1) Peter F. Drucker, The bored board, in *Towards The Next Economics And Other Essays, 1981,* p. 107, Heinemann. First published in Wharton Magazine, Autumn (1986).

(2) Ibid., p. 108.

(3) Ibid., pp. 108 and 110.

(4) Myles L. Mace, *Directors: Myth and Reality,* Division of Research, Graduate School of Business Administration, Harvard University, Boston (1971).

(5) Robert Townsend, *Further Up The Organization,* p. 56.

(6) Harold S. Geneen, Why directors can't protect the shareholders, *Fortune,* p. 28, 17 September (1984).

(7) Peter F. Drucker, The bored board, in *Towards The Next Economics And Other Essays, 1981,* pp. 110 and 112, Heinemann.

(8) Daniel C. Brown, Revealed: lack of crisis plans, *Business Marketing,* p. 10, September, 1984, in which the writer refers to a Western Union Corporation survey published in July (1984).

(9) Stuart St. P. Slatter, The impàct of crisis on managerial behavior, *Business Horizons,* pp. 65–68, May/Juñe (1984).

(10) David B. Hilder, Liability insurance is difficult to find now for directors, officers, *The Wall Street Journal,* 10 July (1985).

(11) Marvin Chandler, It's time to clean up the boardroom, *Harvard Business Review,* p. 10, September/October (1985). See Panel 2.

(12) Peter F. Drucker, The real duties of a director, *The Changing World of the Executive,* p. 33, Heinemann (1982, 1985).

(13) Ibid., p. 34.

(14) Myles L. Mace, *Fortune,* pp. 9–10, 7 January (1985).

(15) Lester B. Korn, *Fortune,* pp. 209–210, 29 April (1985).

(16) What are directors for?, *Businessweek,* p. 90, 22 May (1971).

The British Boardroom: Time for a Revolution?

David Norburn, Franklin D. Schurz, Professor in Strategic Management, Notre Dame

This paper establishes a profile of executive directors who control and implement strategy within the boardroom of Britain's largest companies. It will argue that many of the observed characteristics fail to match those necessary to effect successful economic performance within a scenario of low market growth and structural change.

Introduction

It is remarkable how little we know about who decides what strategy should be adopted when compared to the plethora of learned articles prescribing normative strategic responses. Whereas the origin of strategic options at various hierarchical points within the corporate organizational structure is frequently debated, it would be hard to refute that the primary focus for strategic accountability is the Boardroom. Shareholder intervention in removing directors responsible for 'failed' strategies is markedly increasing: 'golden handshakes' abound: rapid efforts to improve the professionalism of directors through the representative corporate bodies are to be seen on both sides of the Atlantic.

Yet the Division of research at the Harvard Business School commented recently that 'difficulties of access to sensitive data have hitherto confined students of boards mostly to their own experience and to hearsay evidence'. Very little rigorous research, especially doctoral research, has been published.

This paper will review what is known about decision-making within the Boardroom; what prescriptions have been recommended, and whether these are realistic when compared to the characteristics of the executive director.

The author is Franklin D. Schurz, Professor in Strategic Management at the University of Notre Dame, Indiana.

Summary of Boardroom Research

Both normative articles and empirical studies concentrate their efforts upon four main headings, but frequently fail to agree.

Boards Should Approve Strategy

According to Andrews,[1] 'a responsible and effective board should require that company management develop a unique corporate strategy . . . and share with management the risks associated with its adoption'. 'Effective board participation in strategic processes could make an important long-term difference in a company's performance.' Lauenstein[2] states 'the board must have a clear notion of what constitutes an adequate strategy'. Wommack[3] stresses a more positive role: 'the board of directors' most important function is to approve or send back for amendment management's recommendations about the future direction of the corporation'. McAdam[4] goes even further towards the establishment of corporate direction and policy formation. '(Boards) should establish the longer term objective of the company and the basic strategies by which these are to be obtained. They should define the specific policies (but not tactics) that are to be followed in implementing strategy.' This position is supported by Cary[5] who considers that top level management should 'have some discretion but in general are deemed to execute policies formulated by the board'. Even the Director General of the British Institute of Directors, Walter Goldsmith[6] states that 'the board, being concerned with the direction of the business would determine longer term strategy and see that the management was running the business properly'.

But is this what boards actually do? Despite the prescriptions above, considerable doubt exists. Worsley[7] reminds us that 'What is crucially missing is any account of actual decision-making at the top (intrinsically difficult to obtain access to, of course), except usually long after the event'. McDougall[8] in his analysis of 64 Canadian companies raises the question as to whether the boards participate in corporate decision-making and policy at all, and noted 'in many companies directors come to meetings unprepared and with inadequate information both on current operations and on special projects. The directors' meeting, then, becomes a place where the director learns from the management what's going on'. This position is supported strongly by Mueller,[9] when he recommends that boards should set objectives, directions and goals in some systematic context. 'Too few directors raise their sights above the lowest plane in the hierarchy of corporate governance, the ordering and implementing of some action, to the second and higher plane of objective-setting.' In his study of 21 British boards the author[10] found substantial disagreement in the establishment of corporate direction. 'The entire picture of objective setting is one of confusion and is in marked contrast to the recommendations of the academic and consultancy world.' In an overlapping sample, in an attempt to establish causality, Birley[11] supported the findings 2 years further on: Boards could not agree on objective-setting, but Bourgeois[12] found that those which did were likely to perform better.

Little appears to have changed since the earlier studies. Douglas[13] (1934) blasted at 'directors who do not direct'. Baker[14] (1945) found that directors were criticized as being 'rubber stamps', 'back-scratchers', 'logrollers' and 'incompetent managers who do not know what their duties are'! Smith[14] (1958) described the board in most companies to be a 'legal fiction'.

Boards Should be Adequately Informed to Evaluate Strategy

It seems axiomatic that in order to fulfil its recommended role of endorsing or setting the strategy, directors should have the information flow to support their decisions. Harding[16], for example, considers that at the very least 'Directors must be prepared in advance for the matters to be discussed at the meeting'. Koontz[17] emphasizes that 'the reach of the executive is determined by the information system at his command'. Ross[16] insists that 'it is up to the directors to satisfy themselves that the management information system is adequate'.

Yet a drastic skew exists between model and practice. Even at the simplest level it is very doubtful whether the board can fulfil its imperative task of endorsing strategy. A survey by the Conference Board[18] of 454 corporations, showed that 45 per cent of boards met less than six times a year. Time must constrain effective policy. In 1970, Heidrick and Struggles[19] endorsed this view and revealed that of the 474 companies surveyed, a mere 6 per cent issued an agenda for board meetings, and 11 per cent pre-issued no information at all. In the author's[20] study of boardroom information systems, 36 per cent even of those items received were viewed as irrelevant. Further, both Heidrick and Struggles, and the Conference Board results hint at covert hostility towards directors, in that 20 per cent of executives below board level responded that directors should not have unrestricted access to company plans and operating data. Even presuming that directors could identify pertinent information items, Mace's[21] study revealed that 'it is regarded as improper—"just plain bad manners"—to ask executives challenging questions at board meetings. Much information is edited well before it reaches the boardroom. Norburn[22] found that 'important decision-making is informal and political. Performance is more likely to be improved by fostering more informal communication than by expending a lot of effort on designing formal procedures in planning mannuals'. Hall[23] notes that 'work and agreements take place in the private and informal settings'.

Boards Should be Independent of the Executive

In political and sociological contexts, much has been written to separate '*de facto*' power from '*de jure*' authority. In the university world, the relative powers of the administration versus departmental chairmen! In Britain, the Cabinet and the Civil Service was described by Bagehot[24] as 'the dignified and the efficient'. Should the board of directors be separate from the executive? Three basic models have emerged, reflecting the legal and political response to business regulation in three geographic areas. The British and Commonwealth model tends to be a single broad pattern with a majority of internal executive directors. Recent surveys put the minority of non-executive directors at 30 per cent, although this number could be argued to be inflated as to its independence in that a large number of retiring executive directors join this category.

In Europe a two-tier system has evolved. In West Germany the system is statutory, with other countries—Austria, Holland, Sweden, France—moving strongly in that direction. The top tier is a supervisory board and fulfils the strategic function. It is composed of elected employees, and outside professionals, e.g. bankers. No internal executive may be elected. The second tier comprises the management board and is entirely executive.

In the United States, a combination of the two above models exists. Whereas the board is dominated by a majority of external directors, with the chairman of the board being frequently a former president, an executive committee normally exists comprising of the internal vice-presidents under the leadership of the chief executive officer.

With all three models, the major argument centers

around the issue of corporate governance. The role of business is now considered far wider than an economic unit striving to add-value for the benefit of its shareholders. Increasingly the impact of commercial decisions is evaluated against a social cost–benefit criterion incorporated within political legislation. Who best should make these decisions?

Little support exists for a majority of inside executive directors within the boardroom. Gustavesen[25] suggests that in Norway 'boards ideally would be made up largely of outsiders to obtain psychological and social freedom needed for competent decision-making'. Williams[26] states that 'shareholder elections (of directors) are almost invariably routine affirmations of management's will' and that 'the board often insulates management rather than holding it accountable'. As the recent chairman of the U.S. Securities and Exchange Commission he concludes that 'management should not be represented on the board by other than the chief executive'. Douglas[27] supports this view when he urged that 'the board should be divorced from management'. Greanias and Windsor[28] put it far more strongly—'the dilution of shareholding permits management to elect itself, and, in turn, the directors . . . this situation is intolerable'. As long ago as 1776, Adam Smith[29] forewarned of the problem: '(internal) directors, being the managers of other people's money than of their own, it cannot be well expected that they would watch over it with the same anxious vigilance with which the partners in private companies watch over their own. . . . Negligence and profusion, therefore, must always prevail'.

Opposition to non-independent directors is almost uniform and it is remarkable in this barrage that the role of the executive director is still so strong within the board. Indeed, in his investigation of 80 American corporations Pfeffer[30] (1972) showed that the greater the proportion of outside directors, the better the financial performance relative to the performance of that industrial sector although Vance's[31] earlier (1964) work showed the reverse relationship.

The Board Should Hire and Fire the Chief Executive Officer

Should the board appoint the CEO? Conventional wisdom would agree, for in his study of Irish directors Moran[32] found that 70 per cent of his sample thought that they should, yet interestingly, did not state that this is what they did do. In his review on what constitutes an effective board Beevor[33] pronounces 'the board has only one supreme executive act to perform; to hire or fire the chief executive'. Despite the attraction of these statements, no support exists as to their implementation. In his analysis of leadership in 155 large corporations, Gordon[34] concluded that the boards active in this procedure was atypical, and that the most common source was the preceding chief executive. Mace's[35] study highlighted that the appointment of external directors was determined predominantly by the president and that there were therefore few appointments of 'boat-rockers' or 'wave-makers'. The board's arms-length relationship in selecting and firing the president was 'rare'. He found that presidents, through *de facto* powers of control, select new members of the board, and determine what those boards do and do not do. In summary, it is the president who is in the driving-seat, not his peers.

The Research Study

Thus we are left with a fascinating situation of normative dialogue and empirical disagreement. But in all the excitement, very little evidence exists which attempts to determine the characteristics of the director himself. Mace[35], in his stimulating list of questions unanswered by his data base, raised the issue—'what *should* directors actually do?' The author would argue that what directors will do is very much a function of their educational background, managerial grooming, and their experience of managing controlled growth. What are these characteristics? With the exception of Copeland,[36] who investigated the background of some British, German and American CEO's, and Sturdivant and Adler,[37] who traced the origins of U.S. senior executives, little is known.

Contrary to the United States, the majority of most boards in the United Kingdom are composed of executive directors. For reasons stated above, it was considered that executive directors would be more directly concerned with Policy/Strategy formation than non-executive directors. Access to Executive directors posed a major problem, for from the Times 1000 list [similar to the Fortune 500] which catalogues British companies in order of sales turnover, many companies fail to identify the director's function. However, the *Financial Times Yearbook* did list the name of the Managing Director, and combining the two tabulations, a sample of 450 of Britain's largest companies were asked to participate.

Each Managing Director received a letter explaining the aims of the project together with four questionnaires. He was asked to complete one and to pass on the others to three internal executive directors. Of the total 1800 questionnaires sent, 418 executives (23 per cent) participated in the analysis. Although industrial sectors were coded, individuals and their companies remained unidentifiable.

The major objective in the design of the questionnaire was to establish what commonality existed amongst top executives of important British companies; which factors contribute to the success of British business and industrial leaders; and which attributes brought them to positions of prominence. Having established common characteristics, would they be consistent with the four boardroom tasks described by the literature?

Research Results

Three broad categories emerged from the analysis: those relating to their experience within the corporate environment; those relating to social and educational influences; and those which relate to their personal benefits.

Corporate Influence
1. *Age, Tenure Mobility.* The British director is unlikely to have moved companies for a considerable period of time. The director had an average company tenure of 18 years, and was 50 years old. Gaining experience from employment in many different companies, particularly at the strategic level, was little in evidence.

Table 1. Age, tenure and inter-company mobility

	Age	Tenure	Company mobility
Mean	50 years	18 years	3 times
range	<35->65	1->35	1->5

It is frequently recommended that senior executives should switch companies in order to achieve a seat in the Boardroom, but the evidence refutes this position quite emphatically. Only 15 per cent of the participants achieved their directorship by changing companies, and most had worked for less than three organizations. Advice to young managers as to career planning would probably be:

☆ If you consider cross-company experience is desirable, do it early in your career.

☆ Sit tight after you pass the age of 45! Company 'hopping' tends not to be rewarded.

For those directors who had worked for more than one company (a surprisingly low 78 per cent), Table 2 shows the high and low-key triggers for moving from one company to another.

Again, the contrast between perceived trigger and empirical results was sharp. Whereas tests of personal traits underlined self-motivation, and therefore probably a perception of insufficient career progression, financial reward ranked but

Table 2. Mobility triggers

Most frequent rankings	Least frequent rankings
1. Challenge	1. Creativity
2. Responsibility	2. Location
3. Income	3. Status

third. Curiously, status through job-titles ranked lowly and moving geographical area was not seen to be the barrier to mobility so frequently stated. The least important trigger was a lack of opportunity to exercise creativity (3 per cent) adding weight to the arguments of myopia and lack of lateral thinking within the British Boardroom.

2. *The Importance of Functions.* The second area investigated concerns career patterns within functional disciplines. How mobile within corporations would directors have been, and which functions would be seen as the 'fastrack'? What advice would they give to rising executives in order to achieve a boardroom position in the 1990s?

In absolute terms, the entry point of a corporate career leading to the Boardroom is dominated by the Financial/Accounting function, with Technical/Professional also showing prominence. The chances of promotion to being an executive director from a start in accounting are three times that of production and twice that of a start in Marketing. This seems curious given the numerical equation of these functions within the boardroom but perhaps reflects the importance placed upon an externally validated qualification by the recruiting company. When they started their careers some 30 years previously, accounting and professional examinations existed: marketing, production, and personnel examinations did not.

Table 3. Functions of directors

	Percentage response				
	Started	Majority career	Current	Fastest route	Fastest in 10 years
Finance/accounting	32	21	14	33	21
Technical/professional	24	8	2	4	14
Marketing/sales	16	13	5	27	23
Production/manufacturing	10	8	3	2	4
General management	6	41	69	24	23
International	2	4	4	4	9
Personnel	2	2	2	0	1
Other	6	3	1	1	1
No response	2	0	0	0	5

But these comments relate to the absolute numbers at entry and do not reflect 'conversion ' from the entry function. By comparing the percentages of functional entry points to that of current functional responsibility it can be observed that a professional/technical qualification was a better starting point to become a director. Further, this entry point ensures faster mobility and greater inter-functional experience. Table 4 illustrates.

Table 4. Career mobility

	Majority career/entry function (%)
Professional/technical	31
Financial/accounting	66
Marketing/sales	80
Production/manufacturing	80
Personnel	143

An entry at either function of Marketing or Production provides mainly single functional experience. Most managers stay within that function and have little cross-functional decision-making before becoming a director. The least attractive entry point is that of Personnel: not only from the absolute numbers was it more difficult to make the Boardroom, but this function was the least mobile of all. This 'Cinderella-like' position of the Personnel function is worrying in that strategic success or failure is carried out through people, not strategic boxes. If less emphasis is continued to be placed upon management development, it could well be argued that major competitive disadvantage will be experienced when trading against those organizations who give this function particular emphasis, for example, Japanese companies.

When asked which functional area was the fastest route to becoming a director, the responses contrasted strongly with that function within which they had spent the majority of their working career. Currently Accounting and Marketing were thought to be the swiftest paths, whereas General Management responsibility was less significant. But the more interesting responses came when directors were asked to identify those functions which would be the fastest route in the 1990's. Here Accounting was demoted strongly, whereas a technical, and international responsibility was upgraded in importance.

These results provide a fascinating commentary on the change in trading conditions over the last two decades. Whereas a major skill had been the ability to administer controlled growth, which reflects the importance of the Accounting function, we now see the impact of turbulence. Zero and negative growth prospects give rise to a demand for different skills. In Hall's[38] analysis of financial success in declining industries, two strategies were identified. Either maximize product differentiation commensurate with an acceptable delivered cost, or have the lowest delivered cost commensurate with an acceptable product differentiation. Given the need to focus more sharply on market segmentation, particularly in the export market, directors now strongly increase the value of international experience. Given constraints upon the degrees of freedom in improving profit margins, the importance of production rises, probably reflecting the increased emphasis upon cost-reduction programmes through value-analysis. Given the increased importance of product differentiation in the face of declining demand, technical skills, particular research and development, are more valued.

3. Working Habitat. As careers progress, directors perceive that working hours increase and that trips away from home become more frequent. But the oft-held image of the Director as an over-worked, over-stressed, jet-setting executive is totally unsupportable. Directors do work about 25 per cent longer than the average working week, and spend one night in ten away from home on business, but they still manage to take four weeks holiday, usually abroad. The view of sacrificing domestic locational choice in order to march up the corporate ladder similarly has little support. Twenty-seven per cent of directors had never moved house for the sake of their business career: indeed, only 28 per cent had moved more than four times. Nor had many experienced much of an international grooming, since 65 per cent had never worked away from Britain. Surprisingly, since their previous comments indicated that an International experience would increase in value in accelerating progress up the 'fast-track' for the next 10 years, only half the sample considered that an overseas posting had proved valuable for those who had this experience. A mere 19 per cent used a language other than English for business, and of these, fluency was minimal.

In summary, the corporate habitat is one of moderately hard work, locational inertia, and a national commercial emphasis. Given that imports have now reached 33 per cent of U.K. domestic consumption, this perceived habitat seems far too cozy. This comment is given additional support when directors were asked to describe the status of their own companies, shown in Table 5.

Table 5. Corporate status

	% Low	High
Growing	15	77
Declining	3	5

A massive 92 per cent considered the status of their company to be growing, with 82 per cent considering their company to be of high status. Despite the fact that the sample represented the *Times 1000*, and therefore by definition, the largest U.K. corporations, this view seems both indefensible myopic and wildly optimistic. If British directors measure status relative to other domestic companies, accusations of 'Little Englanders' seem well founded. If status is to be measured in terms of international market competitiveness, their view is very unrealistic when one considers the rapid decline in the U.K. share of OECD exports, or the massive increase of imports for domestic consumption. If profit is the criterion, 'real' margins have been inadequate to replace assets on a current-cost basis for a number of years. A situation of growing status simply fails to exist. Is this because inadequate information is enshrined in formal systems reaching the Boardroom,[20] or is it more likely that Mintzberg's[43] observation applies in that CEO's appear to spend little time 'thinking'?

Education and Family Background

1. *Secondary Education.* Almost 90 per cent of directors experienced a secondary education where the ratio of pupils to teachers was significantly lower than the national average. Fifty-one per cent received a grammar-school education, and 38 per cent that from a fee-paying public school. This result contradicts the frequent jibe that privileged, public school-boys dominate the boardrooms of British Industry. The majority of British directors have achieved their position from a basis of competitive meritocracy: entry to the grammar schools was on the basis of intellectual ability, not on income. It will be fascinating to see at the end of this century whether output from the system of comprehensive secondary education begun in the mid-1960s will dominate the boardroom, or whether the private system will succeed now that the grammar schools have been abolished.

2. *Tertiary Education.* After secondary school, 43 per cent achieved a degree from an accredited university, of which 36 per cent were awarded a post-graduate qualification. Almost half of these were MBA's. By classifying accounting qualifications (28 per cent) and other professional qualifications as tertiary, nearly 90 per cent of directors had passed at least one major examination of national recognition. Of those attending university, the view of Oxbridge domination is weaker than conventional wisdom. Table 6 illustrates the most favoured universities.

Given the average age of the British director (50), it is not surprising that the newer universities, who were given their charter in the mid 1960s, were sparsely represented. But it is noteworthy that the achievement of an MBA degree, first instituted in the U.K. in 1967, has resulted in such a quick payoff.

Table 6. Universities attended

	%
Cambridge	24
London	21
Oxford	12
Manchester	7
Glasgow	5
Birmingham	4
Other (<4%)	27

3. *Gender.* Of the 418 directors in the study, only one was female. Despite equal opportunity legislation of the previous decade, very strong evidence exists to support the charge of both overt and covert discrimination. Woman's place is clearly in the living-room, *not* the boardroom. Given that men and women attend British universities in roughly equal proportions, the opportunity-cost of this situation is massive. The same unsupportable percentages exist in most European countries, but in the United States[39] the number of female directors is increasing rapidly, albeit from a very small base.

4. *Childhood Environment.* The location of childhood environment coincided with the demographic location of British industry headquarters, suggesting evidence of geographic immobility of employment. As expected, the South-East of the United Kingdom predominated. By segmenting further, almost half of the sample spent their childhood in the suburbs rather than in an urban or rural environment.

Family background was very stable during childhood for only 3 per cent of their parents had divorced. Typically, mother stayed at home (86 per cent), whilst father (58 per cent) exercised his managerial discretion at work. Interestingly, only 5 per cent of current directors had fathers the occupation of whom could be categorized as semi- or unskilled manual, which again reinforces the view that socio-economic income group mobility is particularly slow. Few directors were single children (16 per cent): most had siblings but were markedly the more likely to be the first or the last child in the family.

5. *Marriage.* Similarity with their parents shown in Table 7 is remarkable.

Table 7. Directors and marriage

	Parents	Current directors (%)
Married once	89	89
Divorced	2	3
No. of children (median)	2	2
Working wives (full-time)	10	5

Marriage 'patterning' is identical and is the more surprising when compared to current forecasts that one in two marriages will end in divorce. Despite the results reflecting the two decades of 1930 (parents marriage) and 1950 (their marriage), it is quite clear that the marital background of directors is atypically stable relative to the national position. British directors do not come from, nor do their children experience, a broken home. The trend in the likelihood of wives being employed is notable for its direction, for it would appear that as the manager ascends the ladder of socio-economic income grouping towards his directorship, the less likely is his wife to work. Of the very small proportion of wives who did work, no wife earned the husband's equivalent income and most earned less than 15 per cent of the director's remuneration.

Personal Beliefs

This section analyses responses as to how the director feels about his employment and independence, his attitude to success traits within the organization, how he considers his managerial style, and his social environment.

1. Ambition and Independence. Most directors aspired to be no higher than their current position and would continue to conduct their present occupation even if they were financially independent. Eighty-three per cent stated that they would choose the same, or a similar career, if they could begin their working life again. Despite this, 46 per cent wished to retire before the age of 60, with only 12 per cent wishing to continue their current job for as long as possible. The picture is therefore one of quiet satisfaction with their working career, reinforcing their belief in having made correct choices at an earlier stage. Putting it more harshly, it could be argued that these results indicate a desire to duplicate historic achievement and to vacate the job as quickly as possible.

Job satisfaction also mirrored the directors' attitude towards occupational independence. Whereas nearly half the sample had considered running their own business, only 16 per cent had actually done so and of these, most had lost this independence by being acquired by their current company. Current U.S. research[40] indicates that two-thirds of gross new jobs created originate from companies whose payroll is less than 25 employees. If this were true for Britain, this negative attitude from our corporate leaders towards occupational independence can but exacerbate the national unemployment position. In the boardroom, the need to be exposed to occupational risk is definitely subordinate to job security.

2. Career Advancement Determinants. It is frequently proposed that careers are advanced by 'who you know' rather than 'what you know'. The British director rejects this emphatically. Despite the fact that 38 per cent received a fee-paying, public-school secondary education, about which popular prejudice holds as a lifetime exclusive club, directors believe that they have been promoted through personal performance. Conversely, the majority of directors do believe that their first boss exerted a significant and positive influence upon their corporate careers. It is not too difficult to reconcile these views, but quite clearly they impinge upon issues of corporate patronage, upon matching the characteristics of management trainees to their reporting supervisory managers, and upon management development and selection.

Having achieved their corporate Valhalla, Table 8 illustrates their view of preferred traits to enhance the managerial success of executives.

It is curious that those success traits rated the highest were those appearing to be inward-looking, personal to that individual's self-esteem, and almost machismo. Those rated badly were those which were considered external to the existing set of frameworks and were mainly empathetic. The emphasis upon achieving what were essentially short-term budgeted results contrasts strongly with both the managerial attitude of foreign competition; e.g. the Japanese (McMillan,[41] Wheelwright[42]) who appear to have overcome the isolation of the boardroom from both shop-floor and operational strategies, and to the lengthy time period taken to achieve a positive pay-off (Biggadike[43]). Continuation to identify this characteristic as the primary success trait must lead to charges of corporate sub-optimisation in the medium-term. Of the remaining traits which were well regarded for rising executives, it is noteworthy that they appear inconsistent with their own current beliefs and characteristics. For example, senior managers should be ambitious, but when they achieve the boardroom, they themselves were ambitious no longer.

Table 8. Success traits

Ranking of top 5	Weighting (%)	Ranking of bottom 5	Weighting (%)
Achieving results	26	Creativity	8
Intelligence	17	Concern for people	4
Desire for responsibility	16	Lateral thinking	0·5
Ambition	16	Social adaptability	0·2
Integrity	11	Loyalty	0·2

Of those traits considered unimportant, the most concerning are the poor rating of creativity and lateral-thinking. Since the trading conditions for the next decade are likely to be quite dissimilar from those of the decade previous, it is these characteristics which appear to be even more needed than when Mintzberg[44] first raised them as top management requirements in 1976. Additionally, the low rating of concern for people, and social adaptability seems remarkable short-sighted.

3. Managerial Style. A central requirement in successful strategy implementation, is to pursue that strongly through an opposite organizational structure with an appropriate managerial style: the '3 S's'. Several authors—Handy,[45] Hosmer,[46] Leontiaides[47] and Norburn and Miller[48]—have advised that a mismatch will constrain performance. Table 9 illustrates how directors perceive their own style to be when managing subordinates.

Given that most companies of the directors in the sample were in zero-growth, or decline positions, the bi-polar distribution is particularly interesting. Although it has never been proven that one style of management is better than another, a move towards autocracy is often recommended for post-mature sectors. Why then should we see two distinct preferences when faced with crisis trading conditions? Should there be 'horses for courses'?

Table 9. Style of management

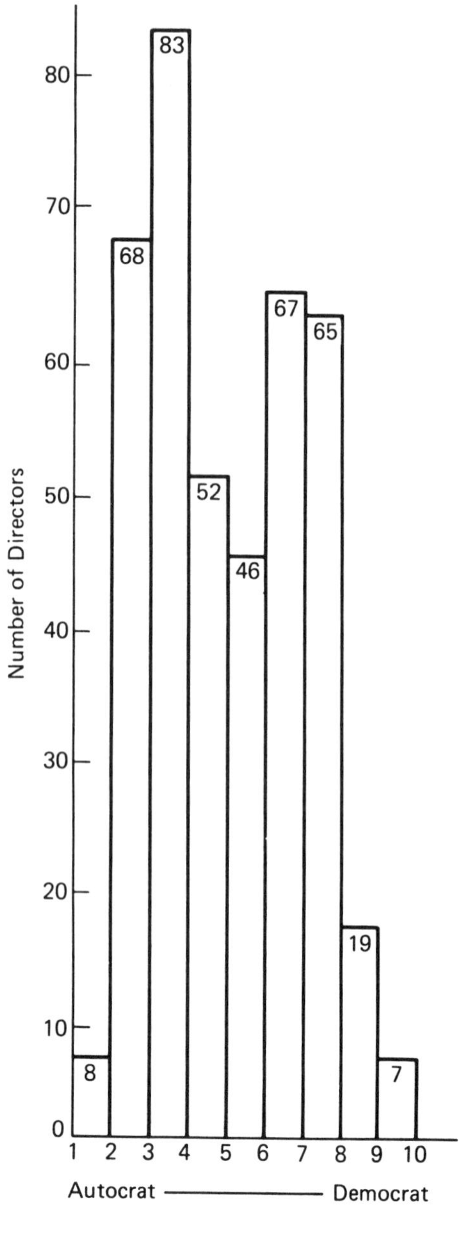

4. Social Environment. Most directors (60 per cent) believe themselves to have adequate time to spend with their families, this being consistent with the earlier results of locational satisfaction, holiday, marital security and the choice of conducting the same career again. They are also predominantly 'heathen'. In contrast to his American counterpart,[49] only 16 per cent considered religion to be of significant importance in their lives, although 60 per cent considered themselves to ascribe to the views of the Church of England. Seven per cent were Catholic and 5 per cent Jewish. Nearly 90 per cent voted Conservative, thus supporting the free enterprise system politically. Only 1 per cent of directors voted for the Socialist party. Taking the majority as representative of the sample, directors both drink and exercise 'moderately', suffer from stress 'seldom' and 'never' smoke! They sleep 7 hours a night: only 6 per cent needing less than 6 hours. The British director is a contented, domesticated, family man!

Conclusions

In summary, the composite British Director has had little inter-company experience; likes a 'challenge', but despises creativity; is most likely to have been an accountant, and least likely to have had production, or international experience; and considers (falsely) that his company status is growing. He is educated, male, suburban, and maritally stable. He is no longer ambitious but is content with his lot. He does not ascribe his success to patronage, but to hard work and concern for achieving his budget. He is more likely to be authoritarian, and does not consider social adaptability, concern for people, loyalty, and lateral thinking, are likely to enhance executive success.

The critical question is whether these characteristics are those which are likely to lead to corporate renaissance, or whether they are those more likely to accelerate non-competitiveness in the arena of world trading.

The literature described earlier in this article reached consensus on four board requirements for directors. The first of which is that they *should endorse strategy*. But the formation of any strategy is forward-looking, and given the short-term orientation of directors from this data, it really does seem that they will find this to be a very difficult task to perform. Secondly, directors should be *adequately informed* to evaluate strategy. Since the British director has been promoted through the corporate hierarchy up the route of single functional experience it seems unlikely that even if an adequate information system exists, that the director is sufficiently multi-disciplined to evaluate its strategic implications. Thirdly, directors should be *independent of the executive*; quite clearly, they are not. Lastly, boards should *hire and fire the Chief Executive Officer*. Given the uniform endorsement of success traits of an inward-looking nature, directors could be correctly described as 'corporate clones' or 'modular managers'. Consensus certainty exists, but are they looking in the right direction?

Perhaps the most serious problem is not so much our basic recessionary condition, but the lack of adaptability to it in the managerial response of our top executives. If it can be argued that psychological behaviour is strongly influenced by social experience at childhood and at adult levels, it must be considered that the ways of strategic thinking will have been conditioned by that which was successful during their rise up the corporate managerial ladder. If economic conditions for the next decade were likely to be similar to those of the previous two, our top executives would be honed to perfection. Who better to direct then those with a proven record of success? But it is quite evident that the trading conditions of the decade ahead are outside historical experience, and that given this atypicality we should no longer promote to the Board on the basis of ability to administer controlled growth rates of bygone years. For the British director, it is a case of 'right place, wrong time'.

References

(1) K. R. Andrews, Directors' responsibility for corporate strategy, *Harvard Business review*, November/December (1980).

(2) M. Lauenstein, Organizing to develop effective strategy, *Journal of Business Strategy*, Winter (1981).

(3) W. W. Wommack, The Board's most important function, *Harvard Business Review*, September/October (1979).

(4) P. Macadam, How much authority should a Chief Executive delegate?, *Chief Executive Magazine* (1979).

(5) W. Cary, *Corporations—Cases and Materials*, 4th Edn (1969).

(6) R. I. Tricker, Misdirected directors, *Special University of London Lecture*, p. 6, November (1980).

(7) P. M. Worlsey, The distribution of power in industrial society, *Sociological Review Monograph*, No. 8 (1964).

(8) W. J. McDougal, *Corporate Boards in Canada*, University of Western Ontario research series, April (1968).

(9) R. K. Mueller, *The Incomplete Board*, Lexington (1981).

(10) D. Norburn and P. Grinyer, Directors without direction, *Journal of General Management*, (2) (1974).

(11) S. Birley, Acquisition strategy or acquisition anarchy?, *Journal of General Management*, **3** (3), Spring (1976).

(12) L. J. Bourgeois, Performance and concensus, *Strategic Management Journal*, **1** (1980).

(13) W. O. Douglas, Directors who do not direct, *Harvard Law Review*, June (1934).

(14) J. C. Baker, *Directors and their functions*, Harvard Universiy School of Business Administration (1945).

(15) E. E. Smith, *Management's least used asset: the Board of Directors*, From The Dynamics of Management. Report No. 14, American Management Association (1958).

(16) W. J. McDougal (Ed.), *The Effective Director*, Monograph, University of Western Ontario, pp. 29 and 41 (1969).

(17) H. Koontz, *The Board of Directors and Effective Management*, McGraw-Hill (1967).

(18) Conference Board Survey (1967).

(19) Heidrick and Struggles, Profile of the Board of Directors, **5** (1971).

(20) P. Grinyer and D. Norburn, Planning for existing markets. Perceptions of Executives, *Journal of the Royal Statistical Society*, **138**, Part 1 (1975).

(21) M. Mace, *Directors. Myth and Reality*, Division of Research: Harvard Business School (1971).

(22) P. Grinyer and D. Norburn, Strategic planning in 21 U.K. companies, *Journal of Long-Range Planning*, August (1974).

(23) P. M. Hall, A symbolic interactionist analysis of politics, *Sociological Inquiry*, **42** (3–4) (1972).

(24) W. Bagehot, *The English Constitution*, Watts, London (1964).

(25) B. Gustavesen, Redefining the role of the Board, *Journal of General Management*, Spring (1975).

(26) H. M. Williams, To create public trust, make Boards freer, stronger, *Financier*, February (1978).

(27) *Ibid.*, 13.

(28) G. C. Greanias and D. Windsor, *The Changing Boardroom*, Gulf (1982).

(29) A. Smith, *Wealth of Nations*, Modern Library, Inc., New York (1937).

(30) J. Pfeffer, Size and composition of corporate Boards of Directors, *Administrative Science Quarterly*, June (1972).

(31) S. C. Vance, *Boards of Directors: Structure and Performance*, University of Oregon Press (1964).

(32) B. Moran, The relevance of Boards of Directors, *Irish Journal of Business and Administrative Research*, Spring (1978).

(33) J. G. Beevor, *The Effective Board: a Chairman's View*, Occasional paper, British Institute of Management (1975).

(34) R. A. Gordon, *Business Leadership in the large corporation*, Brooking Institution (1945).

(35) *Ibid.*, 21.

(36) G. Copeman, *The Chief Executive*, Leviathan House (1971).

(37) F. D. Sturdivant and R. D. Adler, Executive origins: still a gray flannel world, *Harvard Business Review*, November/December (1976).

(38) W. Hall, Survival strategies in a hostile environment, *Harvard Business Review*, September/October (1980).

(39) S. P. Sethi, Women directors on corporate boards, Working paper, 1981. *Center for Research in Business and Social Policy*, Univ. of Texas at Dallas.

(40) J. Naisbitt, *Megatrends*, Warner (1982).

(41) C. McMillan, Is Japanese management so different?, *Business Quarterly*, Spring (1982).

(42) S. Wheelwright, Japan—where operations really are strategic, *Harvard Business Review*, July/August (1981).

(43) R. Biggadike, The risky business of diversification, *Harvard Business Review,* May/June (1979).

(44) H. Mintzberg, Planning on the left side and managing on the right, *Harvard Business Review,* July/August (1976).

(45) C. Handy, *The Gods of Management,* Souvenir Press (1978).

(46) L. T. Hosmer, The importance of strategic leȃdership, *Journal of Business Strategy,* **3** (2), Fall (1982).

(47) M. Leontiaides, Choosing the right manager to fit the strategy, *Journal of Business Strategy,* **3** (2), Fall (1982).

(48) D. Norburn and P. Miller, Strategy and executive reward, The mismatch in the strategic process, *Journal of General Management,* **6** (4) (1981).

(49) J. Sussman, *Korn/Ferry Internatuional's Executive Profile: A Survey of Corporate leaders* (1979).

PART THREE

Strategic Control

Strategic Control: A New Task for Top Management

*J. H. Horovitz**†

This paper examines the important question of the relationship between strategic planning processes and strategic control instruments. The author examines planning and control methods as practised at top management level in three European countries and shows that whilst planning has evolved from short to long term, from operational to strategic concern, control systems at top management level still tend to focus on monitoring short term operational performance. This paper draws together this analysis and presents a set of propositions for the attention of top management which can ensure that long range and strategic plans are effectively controlled through the direct monitoring of strategic performance.

Introduction

In the last decade, efforts and emphasis have been put in long range and strategic planning at top managerial levels. However, companies have had increasingly, some doubts about the ineffectiveness of such planning activities. Partly, reasons for such doubts can be found in the swiftness of changes and the turbulences of the environment in the past 5 years. Partly however, lack of effectiveness may be found in the lack of control and monitoring of long-run and strategic planning by top management. As with other types of plans, developing objectives without monitoring achievements may render such planning ineffective.

In fact, an empirical assessment of the different kinds of planning and control practices at top management levels in three European countries—Great Britain, Germany and France—show that whereas planning has evolved from short term to long term, from operational to strategic, control at top management level still focuses on monitoring short term operational performance rather than directly monitoring achievement of long range and strategic plans.

This article presents the planning activities currently practiced in medium to large French, British and German comparable companies, as well as top management control practices. As a conclusion, a set of propositions for top managerial attention are presented. If long range and strategic plans are to be effective, the author proposes that involvement of top management in control of short term performance should be reduced whereas new tools and tasks be set up so that the chief executive can monitor directly his strategic performance.

Current Concepts on Planning and Control Systems

Planning as a necessary managerial task is not new in concept. Early classical management theorists[1] had noted the necessity for managers to look at the future, all the more that one reaches top positions. However, the emergence of different types of planning is much more recent. In the 1950s or early 1960s, both practitioners and scholars for instance have focused their attention on the development of long range planning as opposed to short range planning or budgeting.[2] When defining the different dimensions of planning, Steiner[3] mentions that plans can encompass different elements: strategy, policies, operational, plans, programmes, budgets, procedures . . . showing the large diversity of types of plans.

In fact, many companies have moved from a single person or department dealing with short range planning (such as budgeting) to two separate departments and phases ('long range' planning and budgeting). Some companies have even separated at least in scope if not in functions, the strategic planning activities, from the long range planning activities. By and large, in fact, authors today agree that a *long range plan* is not necessarily a *strategic plan*: whereas the first one deals mainly with predicting the consequences of decisions taken today on current operations, the second deals with one defining the basic orientations of the firm, its key moves and its key areas of competence for the future.

It is also implicitly or explicitly recognized in current management concepts that control is the necessary counterpart of planning. As such, control is often defined

*ESSEC Boite Postale 105, 95001 Cergy, Cedex, France.
†Dr. Jacques Horovitz is Associate Professor of Business Policy and management at the Ecole Supérieure des Sciences Economiques et Commerciales, France.
Reprinted from *International Studies of Management and Organization,* Vol. III, No. 4, 1979, pp. 96–112, by permission of M. E. Sharpe, Inc., Armonk, New York 10504.

as 'the process which ensures that performance is as near as practical to plan'.[4] Stated differently, as a guiding instrument, the objective of control is to help take corrective action when objectives defined by planning are different from performance, either by changing performance or by modifying plans, as depicted in the following Figure 1.

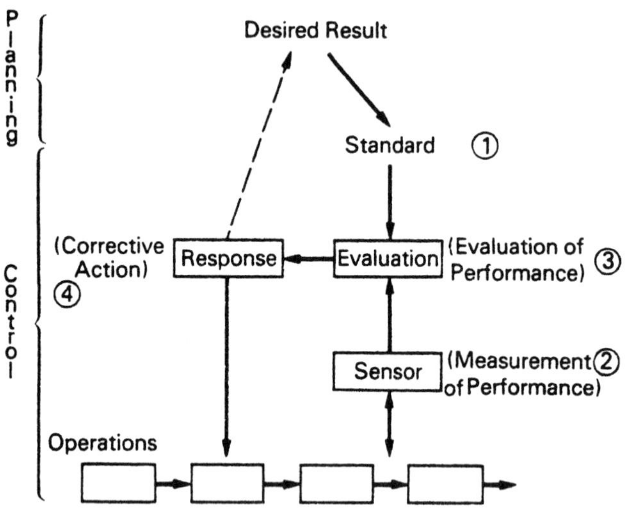

Figure 1. The control process

The question then arises as to whether different types of planning and plans require different types or the same type of control tools and emphasis.

In practice, for instance, budgetary control deals mainly with setting financial norms or standards, measuring performance through accounting and analysing variances. For a different kind of plan such as programming, in which key tasks and dates are set, control deals more with monitoring time and completion of tasks; for procedures, internal audit is the key tool.

An in-depth exploratory study of management control practices across countries was made by the author.* It involved 52 comparable firms in Great Britain, France and Germany, belonging to electronics, mechanical engineering and textiles to get an array of conditions in technology and market stability. Personal interviews with 175 executives (chief executives, controllers, production and marketing and line managers), were carried out. Planning and control documents were, in addition, content analysed as part of this empirical study, questions dealing with planning activities were asked as well as on top management control (i.e. what top managers look at, when and how). The results are reported below. One issue was to assess whether in practice different kinds of control were used for different kinds of plans; and specifically for firms which had embarked on strategic planning, to see whether they were using specific control tools for such planning.

*Local independent companies in comparable business and size range were selected. Not in the first hundred in their country, all were in the top five hundred in three sectors: textile, mechanical engineering, electrical equipment and electronics. The full study will be published shortly by MacMillan Press Ltd.

Empirical Findings

Current Long Range and Strategic Planning Activities

Table 1 below reports how many firms have a written long range plan.

Most British firms have been doing long range planning for 6 years or more and many have set up a special department at the corporate level to collect individual plans coming from each subsidiary, the holding being the most current organization form found. Starting 6 months ahead of time or even before, it is essentially a bottom-up process whereby each individual managing director submits a 5 years plan every year which will be discussed individually at the corporate level with the chief executive and central staff, and then reshaped at the subsidiary level before being submitted again. An aggregate plan follows and is written before the budgetary sessions start. This process, which lasts about 4–5 months, involves about 100 people per firm* and planning procedures and content requirements are usually issued on a standard planning manual by the planning department. The plan deals with all facets of the unit and is not solely concerned with operations but is also strategic in nature.

Most German firms investigated have also engaged in long range planning but not for as long a time as the British ones. As in Great Britain, it is most of the time a bottom-up approach. The process usually starts a little bit later than in Great Britain (4 months before its application), and people do not work on it for as an extensive period of time. Shorter in horizon (3 years), it is much more oriented towards operations than towards strategy or strategic thinking. The only standard manuals that may exist focus upon financial forecasts. This happens all

*Out of an average of 10,000 people.

Table 1. Number of firms engaging in long range planning annually

	Great Britain		Germany		France	
		(%)		(%)		(%)
Number of chief executives who report having a written long range plan	13	73	14	78	5	31
Number of chief executives who do *not* have a written long range plan	5	27	4	22	11	69
Total	18	100	18	100	16	100

the more as quite frequently there is no separate department for long range planning: the controller is responsible for both long range planning, budgeting and controlling at the corporate level. As a result of this organization for planning, it sometimes happens that long range plans are done together with, or even after, the budget or annual plan. Usually ,fewer people than in Great Britain participate in it (70 people).*

Few French companies (5 out of 16) engage in long range planning, annually. For those who do it, it often looks like 3 years financial forecasting so as to look at what is coming rather than taking decisions today which can change the normal course of actions for tomorrow. The 1973 crisis seems to have disgusted some planners, and they have either stopped or become more suspicious about it. Thus, some firms have reduced the horizon (from 5 to 2 or 3 years), others abandoned planning altogether; finally, two firms—not included in the five in Table 1—do it only every 5 years. Few people participate in the effort (50 people) and there is no planning manual to fix procedures or content requirements. As a result the effort is short (work on it lasts for 2 months) and half of the companies who do it prefer to do it after the budget which means the first year of application has already started.

Turning now to strategic planning, for those who have written long range plans, Table 2 below shows the number of firms in which 'strategic considerations' are present.

Table 2. Number of firms considering strategic dimensions

	Great Britain		Germany		France	
		(%)		(%)		(%)
Long range plans have some sort of strategic analysis imbedded	8	62	6	43	3	43
Does not have it	5	38	8	57	4	57
Total	13	100	14	100	7†	100

†Including two firms who plan every 5 years only.

Since in most cases, long range planning is a bottom-up activity, those strategic considerations are mostly provided by operational units (product-market subsidiaries in the case of Great Britain and divisions in the case of Germany). The corporate strategic plan is thus very often an aggregate of units' plans after they have been probed, discussed and tested through planning sessions with headquarters (involving the chief executive, the central controller, planning director when present . . .).

Thus, Tables 1 and 2 show that today long range planning exists in many firms. Some firms have even gone further by including strategic dimensions in those plans, although in the range of companies investigated such efforts are most bottom-up.

*For the same average size of 10,000 people.

Current Top Management Control Practices

Turning now to control activities at top managerial levels, overall control is short term, operations oriented and sometimes very detailed and in no way matching those recently developed planning activities which have just been described.

To assess the link of planning with control, chief executives were asked to state what information they look at to monitor their business, what they focused their attention on; in addition they were asked to state what they considered the critical factors for success in their business(es), and how these were monitored in their reporting systems. Finally, the main recurring reports they received were content analysed. The analysis shows the following results.

Information is Mostly Detailed, Short Term, Dealing mostly with Operations and Internal. Chief executives appear to receive information on short term performance more than long run issues. Content analysis of daily, weekly and monthly reports sent to chief executives show that information deals predominantly with sales, profit, personnel, cash, deliveries, costs, output and balance sheet information (see Appendix 1).

It is all the more detailed and frequent that firms are less decentralized (France and Germany) that control and planning departments are unseparated (Germany and France) and that planning is less sophisticated (i.e. dealing less with strategic matters, more with short run than long run operations), that is for Germany and France. Finally, most of the information is provided by internal sources (i.e. control or accounting departments) and not by special sources to match planning studies.

In fact, Tables 3, 4 and 5 below show that in the case of Germany—where planning is less strategic—and France —where long range planning is not so much used—information to the chief executive is more frequent, that

Table 3. Frequency of top manager's information

	Great Britain	Germany	France
Number of chief executives looking at daily information	5	12	8
Number of chief executives looking at weekly information	11	13	10
Number of chief executives looking at monthly information	18	18	16

Table 4. Type of information provided

	Great Britain		Germany		France	
		(%)		(%)		(%)
Performance only	2	11	4	22	5	31
Plan and performance	7	39	10	56	8	51
Plan and performance and now expected	9	50	4	22	3	18
Total	18	100	18	100	16	100

Table 5. Number of monthly reports to chief executives which include detailed costs

	Great Britain		Germany		France	
		(%)		(%)		(%)
No detailed costs	13	73	0	0	1	6
Detailed costs	5	27	18	100	14	94
Total	18	100	18	100	15	100

most of it deals with ex-post control (i.e. performance only or plan and performance) rather than information about the performance expected to the end of the year; it also shows that for these two countries, control is detailed such as costs reports which are provided to top management.

Information is Biased by Cultural Factors. Not only chief executives use short term, often detailed, information to monitor performance, but also the focus of analysis is biased by country: thus British chief executives put predominantly emphasis on *finance* whereas French and German chief executives put first emphasis on production, matching well educational backgrounds of managers (accountants vs engineers).

Had any strategic control been present, one would have thought that the five key functions of the firm—i.e. finance, marketing, production, personnel and research development—would have been differentially focused depending on main objectives and/or market and technology. A fact which was not found during the study. Whatever the sector, functional emphasis was biased by country.

For instance one would have thought that in a fast changing environment such as electronics, marketing would have come first. However there was no evidence of such differential emphasis by strategy or by sector.

Key Factors for Success are not Monitored. All chief executives were asked what they considered the key factors for success in their businesses. Answers varied per country: whereas over half of British chief executives could answer that question, most German chief executives did not understand it and their answers were mostly on what they were doing. French chief executives' answers were trivial in all three sectors: quality, price, delivery. Although this reinforces the idea of more firms in Great Britain using strategic analysis than in the two other countries, when it comes however, for those who listed such factors, as to how they were monitored, in all three countries, answers were negative. No specific information system was present for such matters. Top management looked at operational results rather than monitoring directly whether a strategy was well implemented.

Propositions

Analysis of current practices has shown that long range and in some cases strategic planning exist. However when one looks at chief executive control, empirical evidence suggests that there is no control system to match such planning.

As a result, chief executives continue to monitor their business mostly through short term operational sometimes very detailed culturally biased accounting information.

Our opinion is that a control system specifically designed to long range and match strategic planning is necessary and vital for success in strategic thinking.

It is necessary because no matter how automated and fast current internal information arrives at the top, it does not provide an adequate basis for evaluating strategic moves, which are often proposed by the line. What purpose in guiding the overall orientation of the firm can control serve when it provides to the top daily sales, deliveries...? What kind of corrective action can it generate which has some long term relevance? However, strategic control is vital, especially when the firm diversifies in activity and/or is situated in rapidly changing and complex environments. In such firms, top management cannot stay on top of things with such monitoring devices as the ones witnessed largely because of the mere scope of activities and of the complexity of technology which demands that strategic moves be proposed by the line. Short term performance can in fact hide strategic depletion. Top management needs direct monitoring of critical elements of strategic success.

In one British electronics company investigated, top management has in fact put emphasis on a critical element in control. Whereas usual performance (i.e. financial results) is only reported every quarter, top management closely monitors—daily if needed—customer satisfaction, explicitly defined to be its major strategic strength: no equipment sold to a customer shall be down for more than 12 hours. To check on this, every morning and afternoon the chief executive is warned when an equipment has been down for more than 12 hours and corrective action is immediately taken at the highest level to replace or send a part or equipment to the customer. A systematic procedure has been set up whereby a service man unable to repair equipment within 2 hours notifies his superior, who in turn notifies his superior after 2 more hours (and so on up to the chief executive) in order to allow close control over what has been defined as a distinctive competence by the company: no down time whatever the costs.

What would such strategic control at the top involve? In order to answer that question, one has to go back to the planning process witnessed.

Although refinements are quite numerous in this field, strategic analysis—as witnessed in the firms investigated at unit levels—basically involves:

☆ Analysing the environment to determine trends, opportunities and threats and key factors for success in each market segment.

☆ Analysing the firm to determine key resources, competitive strengths and weaknesses.

☆ Analysing and defining key objectives and aspirations, both long run and short term, qualitative and quantitative. A strategic plan then chooses for the future:

the product market portfolio;

the distinctive competences to be developed;

the basic means to achieve stated objectives;

and the key priorities.

The choice among several alternatives relies on a set of *assumptions* concerning the evolution of the environment as well as of the resources of the firm. From there on, long range operational plans, policies, action programmes and budgets are defined.

Following the control steps defined earlier (setting standards, measuring performance, evaluating and taking corrective action) strategic control could focus on the following areas:

☆ Key assumptions concerning the evolution of the environment and of the internal resources of the firm: are the trends hypothesized when choosing a plan evolving as defined? Are the crucial factors for success still the same? Are the internal resources defined as necessary to carry out the key strategy evolving as defined?

☆ Key areas of competence: are the distinctive competences what they were supposed to be?

☆ Key performance results and priorities.

For each of the three above areas (external and internal assumptions; distinctive competence, key results) standards would be set. Except for key results, these standards would mostly be predictors with pars set for each by top management. Measurement would not usually come from internal usual accounting information. For instance, if a firm decides it wants to compete by being a leader in technology this could involve setting predictors such as number of new product introductions, presence in professional meetings, deposit of *X* number of licences, presence in known-to-be technologically advanced customers. . . . These would be the areas to be monitored by top management; these would constitute the bulk of the reports read by top management. Table 6 below summarizes the questions to be answered in such control reports.[5]

Table 6. Strategic control points

What are the three of four fundamental hypotheses on which my strategy(ies) is (are) based?
measure how they move at a certain frequency
define a limit above which I take corrective action

What are the three or four critical factors for success for my firm
(or for each product market area)
define norms for my firm
check regularly if the firm still possesses those factors

What are my key distinctive(s) competence(s)?
define norms
measure regularly if I still have them

What are my key priorities and performance results
define norms
measure completion of phases and key performance

Conclusion

An empirical investigation of management control practices in France, Great Britain, Germany has shown that although planning does not deal only with short term financial matters but has gotten sophisticated by dealing, also with long range, strategic matters, control is still essentially short term, operations oriented as shown in the following Figure 2.

Degree of Sophistication →

Types of Plans Witnessed	Annual Budgets Yes	Action Programs Some	Long-range and Strategic Plans Some
Types of Control Witnessed	Budgetary Control Yes	Program Control Some	Strategic Control ?

Figure 2. Evolution of planning and control practices

Especially in firms engaged in diversification in fast changing and complex environments, top management control based on such short term detailed information is not adequate. It calls for new tools—strategic control—focused on setting standards, measuring and evaluating performance in the following areas: key assumptions concerning the evolution of the environment and the resources of the firm, the constance of crucial factors for success, the development of distinctive competences and key results. Such a control system can hardly be provided through control channels currently used (i.e. accounting information). However it is deemed necessary in order for strategic planning to be effective: a plan is worthless without control.

References

(1) H. Fayol, *General and Industrial Management* (London: Pitman, 1949).

(2) W. H. Newman, C. E. Summer and E. Kirby Warren, *The Process of Management*, 3rd Ed. (Englewoods Cliffs, N.J.: Prentice Hall, 1972).

(3) W. H. Newman, *Constructive Control* (Englewood Cliffs, N.J.: Prentice Hall, 1975).

(4) G. A. Steiner, *Top Management Planning* (New York: Mcmillan, 1969).

(5) Adapted from J. H. Horovitz and D. Xardel, *Diriger une Entreprise Moyenne, Les Leçons de l'Expérience* (Paris, France: Les Editions d'Organisation, 1976).

Appendix 1

Content analysis of weekly report to chief executives

	Great Britain				Germany				France			
	daily	%	weekly	%	daily	%	weekly	%	daily	%	weekly	%
Sales	0	0	3	37	7	58	9	69	2	25	4	40
Orders	3	50	6	54	6	50	6	46	2	25	6	60
Production	1	17	2	18	6	50	6	46	3	38	3	10
Personnel	0	0	0	0	0	0	1	8	2	25	2	20
Cash	2	33	8	73	7	58	11	85	3	38	5	50
Mail	3	50	—	—	1	8	—	—	2	25	—	—
Delivery	0	0	1	9	3	25	3	23	2	25	4	40

Appendix 2

Content analysis of monthly report to chief executives

Does the monthly report emcompass	Great Britain	%	Germany	%	France	%
Outlook for the future (qualitative reports and/or projected figures	12	67	4	22	6	37
Overall group balance sheet	10	56	4	22	4	25
Unit balance sheet (subsidiary, division, sub-division)	13	72	2	11	0	0
Overall group income statement. Profit and loss statement	15	83	8	44	8	50
Unit income statement	18	100	17	94	13	81
Personnel statement (direct, indirect; ratios, etc. . . .)	10	56	15	83	11	73
Inventory ($)	15	83	15	83	14	93
Receivables	15	83	11	61	7	47
Orders	15	83	11	61	10	67
Return on capital	9	50	3	17	3	20
Capital expenditures	11	61	8	47	5	33
Detailed costs	5	28	18	100	14	93
Quantities produced	0	0	15	83	12	80

The Directors' Role in Planning: What Information Do They Need?

John D. Aram and Scott S. Cowen

The primary role of a corporate board of directors is to assist management in increasing the economic value of the firm. Yet, the nature of management practices at the board level and the character of director information often do not permit directors to perform these functions adequately.
This paper describes information requirements of boards in the context of how directors intersect with planning and control systems. The discussion summarizes studies of three companies identified as having board-management relationships capable of contributing to the economic value of the firm. General and specific conditions for implementing effective director information systems are discussed, and the importance of the motivations of CEOs and directors in developing value-creating boards is identified.

The role of the corporate board has been intensively examined over the last decade. Criticism of corporate governance has focused on the business and personal ties of directors to the firm,[1] on the independence of the firm's public accountants,[2] and on the duty and loyalty of legal counsel to the corporate entity.[3] During this time period changes in corporate board practices have occurred: disclosure requirements for directors have become more stringent[4] and audit committees are required of all companies traded on the New York Stock Exchange.[5] However, during the same time, board reforms have been soundly criticized,[6] SEC requirements for disclosure concerning auditor independence have been rescinded,[7] and proposed reforms in legal ethics have been rejected.[8] These events appear to indicate that the roles of directors, auditors and corporate lawyers are disputable issues and that only modest change has resulted from a decade of controversy.

Recently, the role of the board and the representation of shareholder's interests surfaced in the context of controversial conglomerate acquisitions. For example, in regard to the Bendix–Martin Marietta–United Technologies–Allied Corporation struggle for corporate control, one noted management analyst states:

> Within and without [the corporation] the credibility of American business management has been undermined. The very legitimacy of the mechanism by which our corporations are governed is opened to attack. If the caretakers of shareholders—managers and boards—do not accept their responsibility who should shareholders turn to? The Government?[9]

This observer, as most others, is not questioning the basic premises of the free enterprise system—private property, economic decentralization, or capital mobility. On the contrary, he is asking whether adequate mechanisms exist for making professional managers accountable to the firm's owners to permit the full realization of these values. Does the structure of corporate decision making give confidence that management will act to create economic value for owners and comply with society's laws, norms and expectations? Or, if management does not act in these ways, can owners realistically expect that they can act to select new management personnel?

The field of institutional economics brings a valuable analytic perspective to the issue of the performance of corporate boards. In his treatise, *Markets and Hierarchies,*[10] Oliver Williamson raises the question whether economic efficiency is better served by more numerous small-scale producers of single products than by fewer and larger multiproduct firms. He notes high transaction costs associated with decentralized organizations as well as costs imposed by the opportunistic behavior of individuals. Larger multiproduct firms overcome such costs and thereby may improve economic

The authors are at the Weatherhead School of Management, Case Western Reserve University, Cleveland, Ohio.

efficiency. Williamson places great reliance on the internal capital market of diversified, divisionalized firms for efficient allocation of capital. In addition, he assigns considerable importance to the effectiveness of internal management controls, such as internal auditing, to maintain intra-firm economic efficiency.

Corporate directors must play a crucial role in the management practices of planning and control which Williamson identifies as vital to economic efficiency in large diversified firms. Yet this role is not consistently and explicitly defined. The role of the board is important, moreover, from the standpoint of corporate governance; assuring effective procedures of planning and control are the means of fulfilling the fiduciary responsibility of directors to shareholders. Attention given to director affiliations and the roles of auditors and lawyers are simply ways of attempting to increase director oversight and involvement in the economic decisions of the firm. From both economic efficiency and corporate accountability standpoints, then, key questions are: How well equipped is the board to ensure internal efficiency and maximum return on shareholders' investments? What board–management relationship is required to meet these standards? What management practices are necessary? What information is needed by the board?

These questions direct our attention to internal organizational and management practices which are necessary for efficient capital markets and for optimal performance of the private, for-profit sector. They are also questions that need to be answered to resolve the continuing tension between public calls for managerial accountability and general practices of the corporate board. The ability to develop knowledge in these areas is the first step toward implementing a system of board practices that both preserves the private and decentralized character of the economy and establishes a credible system of corporate governance. This knowledge needs to be developed independent of questions of director affiliations, the auditor's role, and a legal code of ethics; if a predominant mode of corporate organization today is the multiproduct, diversified firm, the entire society has an interest in management practices which maintain internal firm efficiency.

Study Description

This paper reports results from an exploratory study of board practices and board–management relationships in three publicly held companies.[11] These three companies were identified by participants in an initial survey of 13 professional directors and chief executive officers of large firms. Individuals were asked to identify firms with board–management relationships having the greatest likelihood of creating and maintaining shareholder value. Three such companies were identified and agreed to cooperate in the study.

Key directors were interviewed in each of the companies; however, the major focus of the research involved close examination of the policies, procedures, practices and information developed in the company to support director decision-making. Consequently, senior managers in each company provided the major point of contact for evaluating the concrete manifestation of board policies and practices. Brief outlines of the businesses and performance of each of the three companies at the time of the study are presented in Table 1.

This paper presents a model of effective board information and decision-making for optimizing economic efficiency in the diversified firm. The model draws upon practices in each firm; it does not represent the actual system utilized in any of the three. The intent of the exploratory study is to draw a general model of good board practice from intensive company studies, rather than to evaluate the strengths of one or another of the companies.

The discussion is intended to identify concrete directions and means for board improvement. The role of the board is managerial planning, and control is the process by which managers' efforts, incentives, and decisions need to promote the economic value of the firm. As the ultimate body accountable for management's actions, information used by directors assumes major significance. The three case studies illuminate the information required of directors in the managerial process of the firm.

Director Involvement in Planning and Control

The involvement of directors in the central managerial process of the firm was analyzed in terms of the three basic elements of planning and control: goal and strategy formulation, management control and executive compensation. Table 2 summarizes the role of directors in each of these elements. This perspective relates director involvement to specific items of information: directors are involved in each element only as they receive relevant and useful information pertaining to that aspect of management. This framework also makes clear that the board cannot exercise its responsibility for the economic efficiency and value of the firm in ways different from the managerial process of company officers.

Goal and Strategy Formulation

Owing to differences in sizes, industries, and unique company traditions, director involvement in goal and strategy formulation assumes different formats. The process of goal formulation results in specification of the organization's long-term financial and non-financial goals. All three firms are similar

Table 1. Descriptions of three company studies

Company A
Company A is a $2bn producer in the paint and coatings industry with recent diversification in the retail drug sector. The firm ran into serious financial difficulties in the mid-1970s, including a substantial loss of market share and a decline in earnings beginning in 1975 that led to a deficit for the company in its 1977 fiscal year. A new management was appointed by the board in January of 1979 which implemented a new philosophy, revised management practices, and aided restructuring of the board. From 1978 the company increased net income per share over 800 per cent, reduced long-term debt as a percentage of equity over 13 per cent, and increased return on equity nearly 16 per cent. The firm can safely be termed a 'turnaround' case.

Company B
Company B is a diversified financial services firm with business lines in investment and financial services, insurance and real estate. Its compound net earnings and earnings per share growth from 1977 through to 1978 were 47 per cent and 43 per cent, respectively. In 1977, the company achieved a return on equity of 6·8 per cent; by 1981 this return had increased to 19·1 per cent.

The composition and functions of the board of this company have changed over the years as the company moved from partnership to a privately-held corporation to a publicly-held firm. The firm has adopted an aggressive growth and diversification stance in the light of the turbulence in the financial services industry, and has correspondingly sought to implement a strong board–management relationship and advanced practices of strategic planning and control.

Company C
Company C is a leader in the design and manufacture of office furnishings, concentrating in the rapidly growing market for modular office systems. It is a medium-sized company with 1982 sales of $135m. The company's financial performance has been strong: since 1978 the company had a 250 per cent increase in revenues and a 600 per cent increase in earnings per share. The 5-year average return on equity between 1978 and 1982 was 17·4 per cent. This company is an instructive case in the role of the board because the firm is family controlled. The CEO and major family representative has sought to gain constructive, critical assistance from the board. The CEO appears to use the discretion available to him about the role of the board to challenge and thereby improve his direction of the firm.

quantitative measures of corporate performance: return on investment, return on net worth and cash flow. Specific targets for achievement are based on past company trends, current competitor data, and general economic conditions. For example, Company B relies heavily on alternative market returns generated by the capital asset pricing model in setting its goals; corporate and divisional financial targets are established based on historical trends and stock price performance of independent and publicly-held competitors. Targeted rates of return depend on the risk-free rate of return, a market risk premium, and a risk premium unique to the business unit. The corporate board will have responsibility for reviewing the adequacy and appropriateness of rate-of-return goals. Companies A and C rely on historical trends in the company's performance and on market opportunity analysis.

Table 2. Role of directors in the planning and control process

Goal and strategy formulation
- ☆ Discuss, probe, test and evaluate the appropriateness and reasonableness of management's goals and strategies
- ☆ Approve or disapprove management's proposals for the realization of these goals and strategies
- ☆ Periodically compare management performance with goals and strategies

Management control
- ☆ Discuss and review corporate objectives (financial and non-financial) for the coming year
- ☆ Periodically review actual vs planned financial performance of the corporate entity and its major business segments.

Executive compensation
- ☆ Review and approve the company's executive incentive and bonus plans
- ☆ Review and approve the CEO's recommendations for incentive, bonus and salary payments to key executives
- ☆ Determine the salary, bonus and incentive compensation of the Chairman of the Board and CEO
- ☆ Review CEO's plans for management succession

Goal setting in Company A involves setting quantitative and qualitative targets for major operational areas in each division-marketing, technical development, manufacturing, materials management, cost reductions, administrative, human resources, and acquisitions and divestitures. In addition, multiple financial targets are set for each division, including annual income and expense, inter-division transfers, cost of sales, 2-year quarterly budgeted income and expense, 5-year sales, profit, net assets employed and cash flow, and analysis of profit before tax change. Each divisional plan is available to directors in the annual board review of the division's strategy, operating plan, and financial goals.

The most extensive involvement of directors in strategy formulation in any of the firms occurs in Company C through the use of a board executive committee. This committee, comprised of four of the board's five unaffiliated directors and the firm's CEO, meets at least quarterly for a full half-day. The CEO uses these meetings to obtain a critical evaluation of the company strategies and plans and to gain an in-depth review of its problems. The CEO asks executive committee members to review and advise on major issues, and the committee chairman regularly reports the nature and general substance of these discussions to the whole board for review.

Company B annually uses a team of managers drawn from its divisions to form 'strategy boards'. Appointed groups conduct extensive analyses of three or four primary strategic topics each year drawn from issues recommended by the firm's business units. Sample topics in the last several years have concerned human resource strategies, impact of technological innovations on the company, cross-selling strategies, and the internationalization of the industry. Each strategy board analyzes an issue and makes recommendations, which with management and director modifications, are inputs into the annual planning process in the operating units.

Company A follows a more typical pattern of annual presentation of each major business unit's strategy to the corporate board each year. Sometimes presented at a special director–officer retreat, and sometimes reviewed within the regular board meeting schedule, the board is involved with strategy review of every division each year.

This brief discussion shows that each firm studied uses a custom-designed approach to goal and strategy development. Nevertheless, the three firms share certain commonalities. First, directors in each firm participate in reviewing business strategies of the corporation and its major divisions. Information for this review may be personally communicated (Company C), prepared in extensive reports (Company B), or presented verbally and in written plans by heads of strategic business units (Company A). In each case, senior officers and managers jointly evaluate strategic issues.

Similarly, extensive and detailed corporate and divisional goals are reviewed at the board in each company. While the format and method of presentation vary, each firm provides a means for meaningful director oversight and review of this process. Table 3 presents a listing of many of the specific items of goal and strategy information considered in one or another of the three companies studied. The goals established in this phase of the managerial process provide the basis for an operating and financial control system, the subject of the next section.

Table 3. Goal and strategy formulation: specific director information

Types of goals established

Return on sales
- Profit before taxes as a percentage of net sales
- Gross profit to net sales
- Operating profit to net sales
- Net Income after taxes to net sales

Asset utilization
- Inventory turnover
- Cash flow
- Accounts-receivable collection
- Working capital
- Fixed asset turnover

Leverage
- Long-term debt as a percentage of total capital
- Total debt to total assets
- Debt as a percentage of debt plus equity
- Accounts-payable turnover

Overall measures
- Return on equity
- Return on investment
- Earnings per share
- Profits after taxes
- Cash flow generated
- Dividend payout values
- Market price of stock
- Book value of stock

Review of goals based on
- Historical trends in corporate performance
- Competitor performance
- Economic and industry conditions: present and future
- Risk-reward review of company and its major segments through use of capital asset pricing model.

Planning information provided
- Definitions of businesses, customers and markets
- Specification of corporate and segment goals
- Analysis of competitors; estimates of market shares and market sizes
- Evaluation of strengths and weaknesses of each business segment
- Financial projections by segment for strategic plan period (to include pro forma financial statements and impact of strategies on goals)
- Capital expenditure projections
- Specifications and definition of strategic priorities in each functional area
- Plan for improving net-asset turnover
- Improvement plans for improving productivity, human resources, and product development
- Pricing strategies
- Acquisition possibilities

Management Control

Table 4 presents summary information received by directors at Company A on a monthly basis. Backup information for the major items in this table are provided in the report and figures are broken out for each of the divisions. The availability of such extensive information provides a good basis for director involvement in assessing management's performance. The firm's CEO reviews this information in each regular quarterly meeting of the board on an exception basis identifying and discussing major variations from targeted goals.

Management control at Companies B and C also flows from goals established in the planning process. Monthly summary information in Company B focuses on earnings, per share data, key financial ratios, and balance sheet changes. Figures at Company C involve similarly extensive financial and operating data; the large order aspect of this business has lead to the development of monthly reporting for work-in-process inventory as well as shipments.

Management control information in each company provides several ways to evaluate current information. Year-to-date information is presented in each case on a current year and past year basis. In addition, monthly and 3, 6 or 9 month figures are presented for current and past years. Each company also presents current performance vs planned budget performance for key financial ratios, financial goals and budget items.

Director involvement does not necessarily occur on the basis of monthly reports. However, in each case quarterly reports are discussed at a full board meeting in each company. In every case, materials are distributed to directors between 1 and 2 weeks prior to the board meeting.

Executive Compensation
Financial goals established in the goal setting process and reviewed in management control reports are the starting point for executive compensation. In each company an executive cash bonus depends on performance against these goals. However, in each company cash bonuses also depend on achievement of individual qualitative goals set with each senior manager. In Company A these often involve personnel development, research and development progress, and new product development. In Company B they are called the manager's 'critical few' and pertain to current year activities that will improve business profitability in later years. In Company C they are called 'key actions', and they serve a similar purpose. In the CEO's words, key actions are "the things that will determine if managers achieve their strategic plans".

Across the three companies, quantitative financial measures of performance were reported to account for two thirds to three fourths of an executive's evaluation for an annual cash bonus, and more qualitative objectives account for the remainder. In each case, recommendations for awards for senior managers are made to the compensation committee of the board by the CEO, and the committee establishes the amount of the CEO's annual bonus.

In addition to this method of establishing annual bonuses, two of the companies have executive stock option plans designed to reward long-term executive performance, Company B has a program in which performance shares, equal to the market value of the company's stock, is awarded annually based on achievement of return-on-equity targets. Performance shares vest after 5 years.

Company C awards company stock to key managers based upon growth in earnings per share above the rate of inflation. This plan is tied to a stock subscription program in which the bonus is used to repay the company for earlier stock subscription loans.

As an additional effort to emphasize long-term performance by executives, Company B has a final plan that ties stock awards to a percentage of the executive's salary. These awards are 50 per cent vested after 5 years and 100 per cent vested after 10 years.

Summarizing the executive compensation plans of the three companies, each firm ties a major portion of annual incentive bonus to performance targets which are established in the planning process and which are reviewed on a monthly basis. This process is critical to establish an integrated planning and control process, and is essential to director involvement in goal setting and control, thereby influencing executive compensation.

Each company has a compensation committee of the board which reviews bonus awards and makes recommendation to the whole board. Thus, directors are involved in the development and administration of executive compensation through board committees.

Discussion of Company Studies: Conditions for Implementation

General Conditions
The previous section presented specific elements of planning and control in three companies identified as having management–board relationships likely to enhance the economic value of the firm. Each company seeks to integrate goal and strategy formulation, management reporting and control, and executive evaluation and compensation, and each appears to provide meaningful procedures for director information and involvement. The means for ensuring economic efficiency in large diversified firms are available; fiduciary responsibility of directors is possible at a high level of performance. However, the attainment of director involvement may be another matter. The main question is, 'On what factors does realization of this board role depend?' In general, factors necessary to realize this board role depend on development of particular people, organizational roles, skills, and timely and relevant information. The critical aspects of each can be summarized by a series of questions:

☆ People: Do both the senior officers and the directors *understand* the concept of a value-creating board and do they *desire* to build a value-creating board?

  Are specific needed skills present in the organization and management?

☆ Roles: Do the persons in the key roles of CEO, CFO and directors have a clear statement of their own roles and also understand one another's roles?

  Are the interface relationships among these persons and other important parties well developed?

☆ Information: Have policies and practices been

Table 4. Summary of Company A's managing report format

Division:	Adjustments	Monthly summary Calendar year-to-date to 30 April 1982			Issued 17 May 1982	Supplementary and explanatory	
	Current month actual	Variance from favorable (unfavorable) Budget	Prior month	Prior year	Year-to-date Actual	Variance from favorable (unfavorable) Budget	Prior year
External sales							
Internal sales							
Total sales							
Standard profit							
Standard profit %							
Factory operations							
Other cost of sales items							
Provisions for LIFO (Last in/first out)							
Gross profit							
Gross profit %							
Selling (general and administrative)							
Operating profit							
Corporation charge							
Other (income) expense							
Balance sheet conversion (Gain loss)							
Profit before tax							
Net cash flow							
Capital expenditures							
Cost reduction							
Administrative employees							
Marketing employees							
Technical employees							
Manufacturing and distribution employees —hourly							
Manufacturing and distribution employees —salaried							
Total employment							
Net assets employed							
Past due receivables							
Total receivables							
Raw material and in process							
Finished goods							
Last in/first out reserve							
Other reserves							
Total inventory							
Payables							
Allocated working capital							
Working capital							
Net fixed assets							
Capital leases/ Allocated assets							
Net assets employed							
Ratio analysis	Month actual budget			Year to date actual		Budget	Year
Profit before taxes to net sales %							
Gross profit to net sales %							
Operating profit to net sales %							
Net assets employed to net sales %							
Return on net assets employed %							
Flow through %							
Receivable days							
Receivable days overdue							
Inventory days— first in/first out							
Accounts payable days							

developed to assure the integrity of financial and operating information?

Are specific procedures of the managerial process, planning and control, defined and executed, and are directors informed and involved at each stage of the process?

Neither people nor roles nor information alone can lead to a value-creating process; each of these elements of board effectiveness must be well developed individually and must act in concert with the others. Adequate information, *per se,* cannot lead to an effective board in the absence of appropriate goals and skills for key people or in the presence of confusion over roles and responsibilities. Moreover, it is not necessary for people, roles, or information to develop in a specified order. Rather, improvement in each is likely to be both a cause and a consequence of improvement in the others. The process of general management involves working with multifaceted problems; approaching the ideal of a value-creating board requires development of a complex managerial system.

Specific Conditions
Will the right combination of people, roles, and information result in a value-creating board? In theory—yes, but in practice these general conditions must be supported by specific conditions if a company is to be successful developing a value-creating board. To develop an effective board, management and directors must be committed to this goal and willing to make the effort necessary for its accomplishment. The study indicates the importance of time and place, board agenda, and systems for achieving a value-creating board role, given a complete director information system.

Time and Place. Adequate time must be structured for directors to prepare themselves on key issues facing the company and to know the firm's major products, facilities, customers and key employees. This may involve holding board meetings at field locations, it may imply regular director residencies, and it invariably means exposure of senior managers to directors. Increasing the utility of planning and control information to directors means giving them personal and qualitative knowledge that serves to help them interpret quantitative and regular planning and control information. Of course, achieving a high level of knowledge and ability to contribute by directors implies a substantial commitment of time and energy by the individuals involved. Company systems can only go so far; director performance also involves having the right individuals as directors who are willing to invest their personal time to assist management.

Board Agenda. The primary means of director contribution to the firm on an ongoing basis is regular board and committee meetings. In this process the intent and nature of the meeting agendas are critical determinants of director contributions. Agendas can be structured and managed to evade or to encourage discussion of problems and issues. Information *per se* is relatively useless without creating a setting and a pattern of norms that allows its utilization. The agenda process is a key determinant in realizing the value of director information.

Systems. Value-creating boards exist in companies where management has spent the time and effort to develop effective planning and control processes, has obtained director involvement in these processes and has designed information systems to support management and directors decision making processes. Director involvement in goal and strategy formulation, management control and executive evaluation and compensation is critical in the achievement of an effective board because it provides a focus and structure to board decision-making. The research indicates that the director's role in executive evaluation and compensation is an area in which specific board practices and conditions can spell the difference between value-creating and other types of corporate boards. Time, place and agenda are again critical; however, as the basis for the financial reward system that drives the economic performance of the firm, the board's personnel and compensation functions assume heightened importance in the ability of the board to integrate managerial performance and shareholder interests over the long term. Specific challenges to the board or its compensation committee are (1) to ensure that reward systems designed to balance short- and long-term performance actually function toward the desired balance and (2) to ensure that financial rewards are given to senior managers only on the basis of actual performance against predetermined objectives. Fulfilment of these standards requires an unusually high level of board or committee decision-making ability.

This discussion of specific conditions for implementing a director information system in a value-creating board indicates that director contributions depend importantly on several personal and relatively intangible qualities. The intent, motivation and willingness of directors and senior managers to make the board information system aid the process of value-creation is critical. Information and procedures described in the company studies are valuable examples of systems that can assist director contribution to the firm, but like all systems, board information depends significantly on the human purposes to which it is applied.

Conclusions

The company studies described in this research outline specific elements of the planning and control process which can support effective director involvement in the economic efficiency of the firm. Detailed board-management procedures and information used by directors were presented to illustrate the management process by which value-creation *can* occur at the board. However, the effective implementation of planning and control information depends on more intangible personal attitudes and skills and the ability to fulfil necessary organizational roles. Whether or not such systems are actually used to fulfil the promise of economic performance in the diversified firm depends on much more than development of planning and control systems.

Of course, effective planning and control may be implemented in the large diversified firm with no board involvement whatsoever. However, in the publicly-held firm, institutional mechanisms that act to protect shareholder interests in the economic performance of the firm become vitally important. Consequently, the role of the board in planning and control assumes major significance. The present research identifies the procedural elements of meaningful director involvement in the internal economic processes of the firm. Further research hopefully can address the motivational aspects of this process and identify the means to achieve full managerial accountability within a private and decentralized economic system.

References

(1) Senate Subcommittee on Citizens and Shareholders' Rights and Remedies, *The Role of the Shareholder in the Corporate World: Hearings before the Subcommittee on Citizen and Shareholder Rights and Remedies of the Senate Committee on the Judiciary*, 95th Cong., 1st Sess., pt. 1 at 98–118 (1977).

(2) Securities and Exchange Commission, 'Disclosure of Relationships with Independent Public Accountants', Accounting Series Release 250, 29 June 1978. Securities and Exchange Commission, 'Scope of Services by Independent Accountants', Accounting Series Release 264, 14 June (1979).

(3) The American Law Institute, *Principles of Corporate Governance and Structure: Restatement and Recommendations.* Tentative Draft No. 1, 1 April (1982). American Bar Association, Commission on Evaluation of Professional Standards, 'Model Rules of Professional Conduct', draft as amended by the House of Delegates at the 1982 Annual Meeting, 30 June (1982).

(4) Securities and Exchange Commission, 'Shareholder Communications, Shareholder Participation in the corporate Electoral Process and Corporate Governance Generally', *Federal Register*, 14 December, 588522–588534 (1978).

(5) *Audit Committee Policy of the New York Stock Exchange*, January (1977)

(6) K. R. Andrews, Rigid rules will not make good boards, *Harvard Business Review*, November–December, 34–46 (1982).

(7) Securities and Exchange Commission, Accounting Series Release No. 296, 'Relationships between Registrants and Independent Accountants', *Federal Securities Law Reporter*, No. 72, 318, 20 August (1981) and Accounting Series Release No. 304, 'Relationships Between Registrants and Independent Accountants, *Federal Securities Law Reporter*, No. 72, 326, 28 January (1982).

(8) Meeting the whistle: ABA debates Kutak ethics rules, *ABA Journal*, 69 (April), 421–423 (1983).

(9) R. H. Hayes, The undermining of business credibility, *The New York Times*, 10 October (1982).

(10) O. E. Williamson, *Markets and Hierarchies: Analysis and AntiTrust Implications.* The Free Press, New York (1975).

(11) J. D. Aram and S. S. Cowen, *Information Requirements of Corporate Directors: The Role of the Board in the Process of Management.* Final Report to the National Association of Accountants, April (1983).

PART FOUR

Using Strategy to Control the Business

Corporate Self Renewal

P. E. Haggerty, President, Texas Instruments Inc., Dallas, Texas, U.S.A.

In this article President Haggerty of Texas Instruments discusses the problem: How can an organization become older and yet stay flexible and adaptable. He explains how at Texas Instruments he has tried to develop a system or framework within which continuous innovation, renewal and rebirth can occur. The system involves innovation in research and development, in production and in marketing, and means that "at Texas Instruments, the long range planning system is fundamentally a system for managing innovation". The inception of formal planning to identify and state succinctly in writing the strategies required for growth and development, has produced a sizable increase in the production of Major Impact Strategies with a potential pay-off of $50 million net sales over five years.

BY ITS VERY NATURE THE PROFIT-EARNING privately or publicly owned corporation is meant to be long-lived. If not nominally eternal, at least its lifetime is presumed to extend with vigour and usefulness through a multitude of generations of managers and owners. The corporate form was indeed a brilliant legal invention to provide for the possibility of such long life and independence from the life spans of individual family owners and managers. But, while the corporate legal framework can provide the form for such long-lived institutions, it cannot provide the substance.

Surely, a principal responsibility of corporate general management must be to ensure corporate self-renewal. And yet, if corporate self-renewal is a principal responsibility for general management, in my opinion it is *the* principal responsibility of a corporation's board of directors.

No one has written more usefully on this subject than John W. Gardner, president of the Carnegie Foundation and now, of course, Secretary of Health, Education, and Welfare, in his book, *Self-Renewal—The Individual and the Innovative Society*. Here are a few paragraphs from his book which are most expressive of these problems.

"When organizations and societies are young, they are flexible, fluid, not yet paralysed by rigid specialization and willing to try anything once. As the organization or society ages, vitality diminishes, flexibility gives way to rigidity, creativity fades and there is a loss of capacity to meet challenges from unexpected directions. Call to mind the adaptability of youth, and the way in which that adaptability diminishes with the years. Call to mind the vigour and recklessness of some new organizations and societies —our own frontier settlements, for example—and reflect on how frequently these qualities are buried under the weight of tradition and history.

"All of this seems to suggest that the critical question is how to stay young. But youth implies immaturity. And though everyone wants to be young, no one wants to be immature. Unfortunately, as many a youth-seeker has learned, the two are intertwined.

"Most of the processes that reduce the initial flexibility and adaptiveness of societies and individuals are, in fact, processes of maturing. As such they are not only inevitable but, in their early stages, desirable. The process of maturing may have made our frontier communities less vigorous and venturesome, but it also made them more livable, more orderly and in important respects stronger. Everyone who has ever shared in the founding of an organization looks back with nostalgia on the early days of confusion and high morale, but few would really enjoy a return to that primitive level of functioning. Babies are charming but no one would wish to keep them forever at that stage of growth.

"In short, we would not want to stop the process of maturing even though it narrows potentialities and reduces adaptability.

"The reader may ask, 'Is there no possibility, then, that an individual (or an organization or society) might advance toward maturity without advancing toward rigidity and senility? Isn't it a question of knowing the difference between the two and stopping short of the latter?' Unfortunately, it isn't that simple. There may be a point at which raw young vitality and mature competence and wisdom reach a kind of ideal balance, but there is no possibility of freezing change at that point, as one might stop the motion in a home movie. There is nothing static in these processes."

Nor is there anything static about corporate self-renewal. It is a difficult

This paper was originally prepared for presentation at the American Society of Corporate Secretaries, at the Homestead, Hot Springs, Virginia.

and complex subject, and I would not pretend that my treatment of it will be exhaustive. Also I may refer unduly to the company with which I have the good fortune to be associated. If this discussion is to be useful, I think it must contain specific concepts and ideas, and since the

> **Texas Instruments *exists* to create, make and market useful products and services to satisfy the needs of its customers throughout the world**

last 22 years of my professional life have been spent with Texas Instruments, inevitably most of the ideas, illustrations and concepts will come from my experience there.

> **The *opportunity* to make a profit is TI's *incentive* to create, make and market useful products and services**

Any examination of corporate self-renewal must begin with the principles which control organizational structure and purpose, and, for me, the first of these is that in the complex world in which we live today, brought into being by the expanding technological revolution, a technologically based company such as Texas Instruments exists to create, make and market useful products and services to satisfy the needs of its customers throughout the world.

> **Self-Renewal begins with innovation and innovation is the key to**
> **1) useful products and services**
> **2) profitability**

The second vital principle is that it is the opportunity to make a profit which provides the incentive for Texas Instruments to create, make and market such useful products and services. We do not exist to make a profit, but the *opportunity* to operate at a profit is the *incentive* to create, make and market useful products and services for our society. Furthermore, if TI is to prosper, to grow, to broaden and to improve the products and services we offer, it must be so managed as to ensure a high level of long term profitability. For the privilege of the incentive, in the form of profits, to create, make and market useful products, our economic system in the West requires that we operate at a profit or disappear. The requirement that we make sufficient profit to attract the necessary investment or cease to exist provides the discipline we need to ensure that we operate effectively.

We are convinced that corporate self-renewal begins with innovation, and that both useful products and services and long-term profitability are the result of innovation and that, as a matter of fact, profitability at a level above the bare fee for the use of assets results only from the innovation advantage and disappears as soon as the innovation has become routine.

First, I must make clear the breadth of innovation we have in mind. Too often in this technological age we associate innovation automatically with research and development based on the physical sciences, but the fact is that critical innovation—regardless of the field—may occur in the make and market functions as well as in the create function. Further, the effective innovation is the integral (that is, the sum total) of the innovation in all three of the categories: create, make and market. *A company which is outstanding in research and development and truly creates useful products and services, but which is relatively weak in innovation in making and marketing may well be out-performed, both in terms of product and service contributions and profitability, by another organization less outstanding in product and service research and development, but better balanced, with a high level of innovation in all three of the categories—create, make and market.*

Let me illustrate the importance of innovation in each of the three categories with these more specific examples.

TECHNOLOGICAL INNOVATION

Texas Instruments entered the semiconductor business in the spring of 1952, four years after the invention of the transistor by Bardeen and Brattain of the Bell Telephone Laboratories. Almost at once we reached several important conclusions: (1) that the inherent characteristics of semiconductor devices were such as to make them broadly useful in military equipment, but that the temperature limitations of germanium, from which metal all devices were then being made, would severely limit widespread applications; (2) that a dramatic semiconductor device accomplishment by TI was needed to stimulate their use then, not some

FIGURE 1. TRANSISTOR AND INTEGRATED CIRCUIT
Courtesy of Texas Instruments

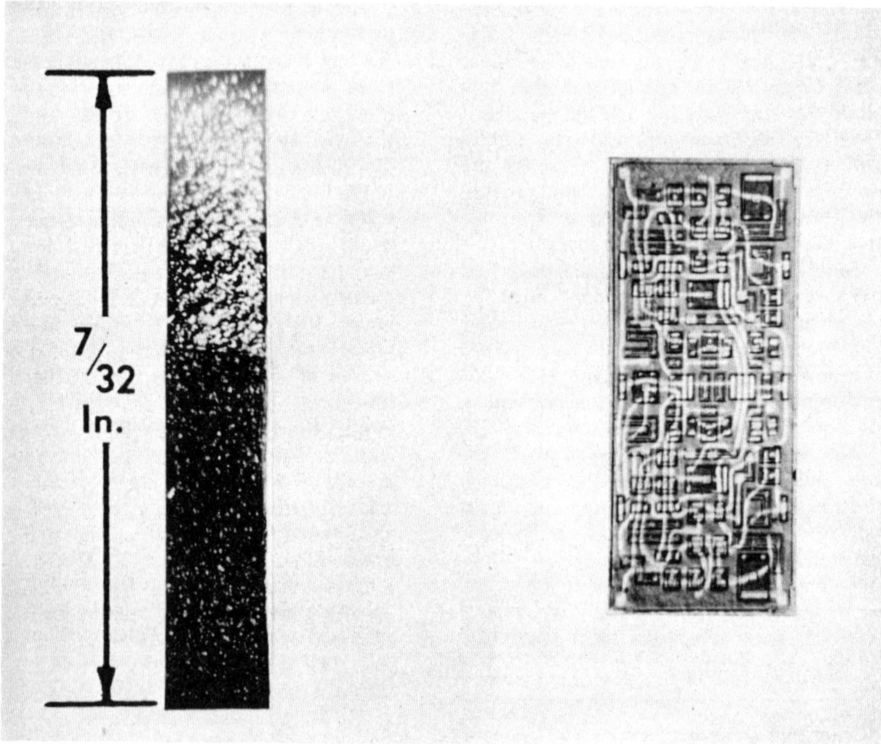

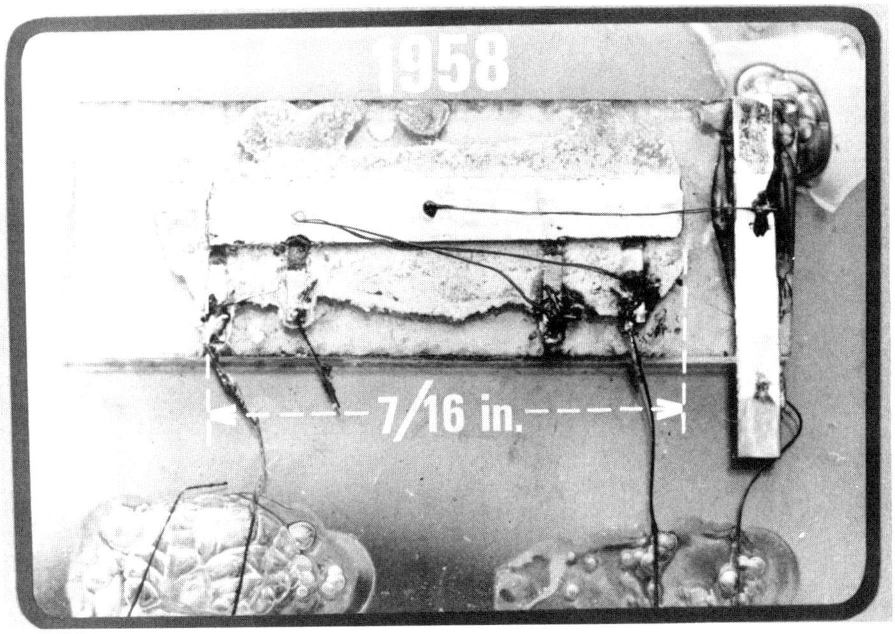

FIGURE 2. PHOTOMICROGRAPH OF INTEGRATED CIRCUIT
Courtesy of Texas Instruments

years in the future, and to convince potential customers that TI was ready, willing and able to supply usable semiconductor devices.

Early in 1953 we began work to develop a small signal transistor which would meet military environmental conditions. We chose silicon as the material for the device and, based on the state of the art at the time, we chose junction technology as the likeliest with which to produce a usable device immediately. By early 1954 we had achieved our product goal, and in the early spring of 1954, while others were predicting another two-to-three year development cycle, we announced the commercial availability of TI silicon transistors.

We had the market so created substantially to ourselves for over three years. Unquestionably, this innovation in the "create" category was one of the principal reasons our then small company seized leadership in the semiconductor market from other electronics industry leaders which more logically might have attained such a position.

On the left of Figure 1 is shown one of the first silicon grown junction transistor bars, inherently the heart of that transistor which was introduced in the spring of 1954 and which was such a very important first both for Texas Instruments and for the electronics industry.

On the right of the illustration is another technical innovation and even more remarkable accomplishment, an integrated circuit which performs the same kind of function as the collection of vacuum tubes, transistors and other electronic components you have seen in your radio or TV sets, but which by a generally accepted definition, is "the physical realization of a number of circuit elements inseparably associated on or within a continuous body of material to perform the function of a circuit." The particular one illustrated, appreciably smaller than the 1954 grown junction bar which made a single transistor, contains the equivalent of 69 components—38 transistors, 5 capacitors and 26 resistors.

Figure 2 shows a photomicrograph of what is one of the very first integrated circuits ever made. This device was developed in our TI laboratories in the summer of 1958, just ten years after the transistor itself was invented at Bell Telephone Laboratories.

The impact of that innovation in semiconductors and upon the evolution of electronic equipment has been dramatic. In Figure 3 on the left of this illustration are three generations of development in electronic circuitry. The vacuum tube assembly in the background, the transistor circuit board in the centre, and the integrated circuit in the circle at the bottom left of the illustration—all perform exactly the same computer circuit function.

Impressive as this change is—and the entire evolution took place in barely a decade—even greater accomplishments lie ahead. In our laboratories are semiconductor products involving much higher levels of complexity in electronic circuits. The technology that is developing is called "Large-scale Integration." Products made through use of this new technology we call "Integrated Equipment Components," or IEC's.

The right half of the illustration shows an IEC, which is representative of the next, or fourth, generation of change in electronics. What you see illustrated are the packaging and the top layer of interconnection of 247 complete circuits contained within a one-and-one-quarter-inch-diameter silicon slice.

We can expect this development to make major changes in the way we work with our customers and organize to operate our business.

FIGURE 3. THE DEVELOPMENT OF ELECTRONIC CIRCUITRY
Courtesy of Texas Instruments

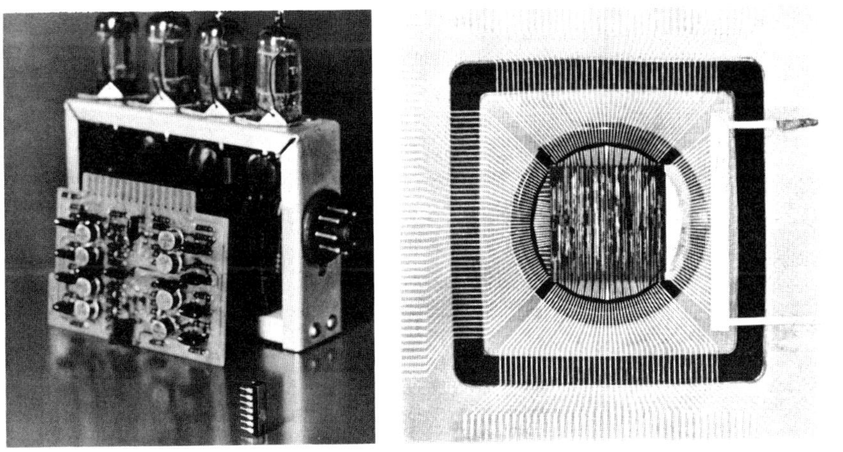

FIGURE 4. A MANUFACTURING LANDMARK, FORD MECHANIZATION, 1915
Courtesy of Texas Instruments

For example, we can characterize our semiconductor business today as that of selling large numbers of more-or-less standard devices.

With Large-Scale Integration, we must work much more closely with our customers to translate their particular system and design problems into special solutions and in much less time than it now requires. Design automation techniques become essential. And the equipment for manufacturing these integrated equipment components must not only be highly automated, but what is somewhat contradictory, extremely flexible at the same time.

MANUFACTURING INNOVATION

Innovation in the "make" category can be no more dramatically illustrated than with the first use of mass assembly and mechanized assembly methods at the Ford Motor Company. The concept of moving assembly which spread through Ford in the years 1914 through 1915 from one magneto line to chassis assembly and thence to the assembly of body and chassis is illustrated in Figure 4. Continuous movement through assembly operations is one of the milestones in manufacturing history, and though this body drop operation now looks quaint, it was top-notch innovation in 1915. Labour time in assembly dropped from 12 hr. and 28 min. per chassis to 84 min. per chassis in just seven months. It is unnecessary, I think, to elaborate on the impact of this innovation in bringing about mass marketing of automobiles and, hence, the creation of the automobile industry in the United States as we know it, as well as extensions from that industry to all industry everywhere in the world.

As a result of this kind of manufacturing innovation which, in turn, developed from Henry Ford's market innovation, based on the high-volumed, low-priced, single-style Model T, plus some contribution from the low-volumed, high-priced Lincoln, the Ford Motor Company possessed well more than 50 per cent of the automobile market in 1921.

MARKETING INNOVATION

Yet, in that same year, General Motors Corporation formulated a product policy, based on marketing innovation, which was to play a principal part in its seizing through the years the very position then occupied by Ford. The innovation involved can be no better described than by Alfred Sloan, long-time chief executive officer of General Motors. I quote from his book, *My Years with General Motors.*

> "The product policy we proposed is the one for which General Motors has now long been known. We said first that the corporation should produce a line of cars in each price area, from the lowest price up to one for a strictly high-grade, quantity production car, but we would not get into the fancy-price field with small production; second, that the price steps should not be such as to leave wide gaps in the line, and yet should be great enough to keep their number within reason, so that the greatest advantage of quantity production could be secured; and third, that there should be no duplication by the corporation in the price fields or steps.
>
> "These new policies never materialized precisely in this form—for example, we always have had in fact duplication and competition between the divisions—yet essentially the new product policy differentiated the new General Motors from the old, and the new General Motors from the Ford organization of the time and from other car manufacturers."

General Motors thus took a course radically different from Mr. Ford's, a course based on a new concept of the automobile market, a concept involving regular upgrading of the product and recognition of a growing desire for a variety of models to meet the needs of most buyers across a broad price spectrum.

The results of this marketing innovation

can again best be expressed in Mr. Sloan's own words.

"It was not difficult to see in 1925 and 1926 that Chevrolet was closing in on Ford. In 1925 Chevrolet had about 481,000 U.S. factory sales of cars and trucks, while Ford had approximately two million factory sales. In 1926 Chevrolet moved up to about 692,000 factory sales of cars and trucks, while Ford moved down to about 1,550,000. His precious volume, which was the foundation of his position, was fast disappearing. He could not continue losing sales and maintain his profits. And so, for engineering and market reasons, the Model T fell. And yet not many observers expected so catastrophic and almost whimsical a fall as Mr. Ford chose to take in May 1927 when he shut down his great River Rouge plant completely and kept it shut down for nearly a year to retool, leaving the field to Chevrolet unopposed and opening it up for Mr. Chrysler's Plymouth. Mr. Ford regained sales leadership again in 1929, 1930, and 1935, but, speaking in terms of generalities, he had lost the lead to General Motors. Mr. Ford, who had had so many brilliant insights in earlier years, seemed never to understand how completely the market had changed from the one in which he made his name and to which he was accustomed . . . Mr. Ford failed to realize that it was not necessary for new cars to meet the need for basic transportation. On this basis alone Mr. Ford's concept of the American market did not adequately fit the realities after 1923. The basic-transportation market in the United States (unlike Europe) since then has been met mainly by the used car."

From these examples in two such widely different industries as automotive and electronics, it seems to me the impetus toward self-renewal generated by the innovating company, not just for the company involved, but for an entire industry and its customers, is self-evident.

These examples, I believe, also make clear why *corporate self-renewal begins with innovation, and this is why at Texas Instruments our long-range planning system is fundamentally a system for managing innovation.*

The TI examples were all in electronics, but on a completely comparable level I could have described the result of another extremely successful breakthrough strategy which has given us a truly new approach to seismic exploration for petroleum. The key to this innovation is the application of statistical communications theory to seismic data processing. This new approach has really revolutionized seismic exploration for petroleum and unquestionably broadened markedly the geographic areas in which petroleum based on sound geophysics can be conducted.

I could also have illustrated TI innovation in materials. Our *materials systems concept*, for example, brings about the integration of two or more materials, usually metals, and sets of useful properties not otherwise available in new layered materials.

The products evolving from this innovation which are most familiar to the reader undoubtedly are the new U.S. clad-metal quarters and dimes.

The process of creating change at TI is one of deliberate innovation in the create, make and market functions—and of managing this innovation to provide continuing stimulus to the company's growth in usefulness to society

The point is that self-renewal at TI begins with deliberate, planned innovation in each of the basic areas of industrial life—creating, making and marketing in all product and service areas—and with our long-range planning system, we attempt so to manage this innovation as to provide continuing stimulus to the company's growth in usefulness to society and as a business institution.

With our system we attempt to make innovation more manageable by stating in some detail our various business objectives and then endeavouring to set strategies and tactics which will allow us to meet those long-term business objectives.

By strategy I mean the general course of action the executive responsible intends his organization to pursue in achieving company goals. By tactics I mean the specific programmes which must be carried out to implement the strategy successfully.

Strategies, of course, come in all shapes and sizes. There can be "hold the line" strategies, "modest gain" strategies, and "breakthrough" strategies. They all have their proper place in the management of a business, but it is highly unlikely that any of them will have a major impact on the company unless at the outset the strategy specifically is designed to do so. In other words, it can be a breakthrough strategy only if one's answer is yes to the question: "Will this strategy, if it succeeds, have a major impact on the growth and prosperity of my company?" Of course, a prime problem is that most strategies of this kind consume many years from time to conception to the point at which one can state with certainty that the strategy is working and the profits produced from it are adequate to justify the time and effort expended.

TI's great success in semi-conductors was the result of a breakthrough strategy accomplished through successful tactical R & D programmes. Establishment of our materials-oriented central research laboratories on 1st January, 1953; our introduction of the first silicon transistor in the spring of 1954, which I described earlier as an example of innovation; the additional device development which led to the first all-transistor pocket radio in October, 1954; the development of a process for making pure silicon, with our first production plant going on stream in 1956—all were successful tactics in pursuit of a strategy which resulted in our seizing the lead in the semiconductor industry from other much larger companies which might more logically have been expected to be out in front.

However, it was only about seven years ago that we began to recognize that our great TI successes had resulted from well-conceived strategies and well-carried out tactics in support of these strategies. About six years ago I finally began to comprehend more clearly the pattern which had existed in these successful strategic programmes. At that time we detached one of our senior officers from his other duties to spend full time in study and implementation of a formal system for accomplishing these innovative successes.

A year later we initiated a formal system to identify and state succinctly, yet completely, in writing the strategies we would follow for growth and development throughout our company. We also identified the tactics we would pursue in order to implement the strategies. In effect, we are now in our fifth year with the system, and, while we still have much to learn about the management of innovation and much to improve in our long-range planning system, there is little question but that we have succeeded in diffusing throughout our management, both corporate and divisional, not just a recognition of responsibility for initiating innovative programs, but an improved ability to conceive, describe and pursue such programs.

Today, each division, as shown in Figure 5, has its own formally identified strategies and tactical action programs to implement them. There are additional intracompany strategies and tactical action programs . . . TAPS. We now have a total of 77 different strategies and 591 tactical action programs being carried out in pursuit of these strategies. Of even greater significance, perhaps, are the 23 strategies we identify as of potentially major impact on the corporation if successful. We define a major impact strategy as one which will generate at least $50m. a year of net sales billed over a period of at least five years. By contrast, five years ago there were only four major impact strategies.

Our Objectives-Strategies-Tactics (OST) System is an essential part of our ability to manage change innovatively and is the fundamental tool we have used thus far to assure corporate self-renewal.

Activity	Strategies	TAPS
Intracompany	19	124
Divisions		
Materials	10	75
Semiconductor-Components	22	194
Apparatus	12	113
Science Services	8	56
TI Supply	6	29
TOTAL	77	591
MAJOR IMPACT STRATEGIES ($50M/YR for 5 YEARS)	23	

FIGURE 5. SUMMARY OF TI STRATEGIES AND TACTICAL ACTION PROGRAMMES—APRIL, 1967

FIGURE 6. GROWTH OF TI NET SALES BILLED 1946-66 AND PROJECTION TO 1976

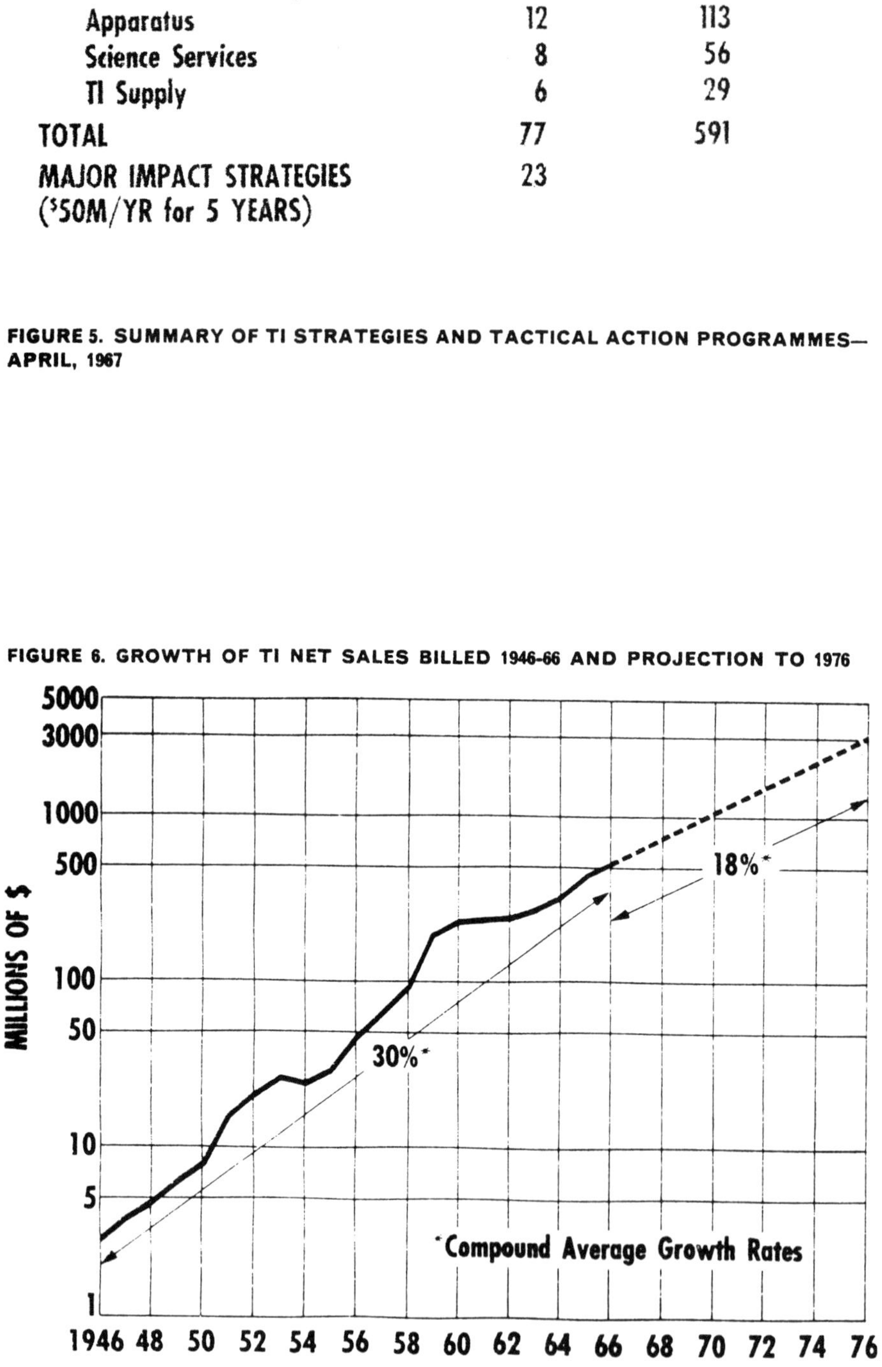

COMPANY RESULTS

The measure of a corporation's success in self-renewal is clearly complex, but undoubtedly, its long-term record of sales billed and earnings expresses best its accomplishment as its goals for the long-term future express its intentions.

Texas Instruments has grown at an average compound rate of 30 per cent per year, from just over $2m. in 1946 to just under $600m. in 1966. Our earnings after taxes have followed a similar if slightly more erratic curve and have actually grown at a slightly higher compound rate of 31 per cent per year since 1946. Our goal in net sales billed in the general time period expressed by the year 1976 is $3b. with a corresponding increase in earnings. This will require a compound growth rate of 18 per cent from 1967 on and while the policies and practices we have pursued have been sufficient to achieve our present size and capability, the growth we must still accomplish in terms of absolute dollars is much larger. And it is in the terms of this long-term goal, and even more generally for the years beyond 1976, that our Board of Directors at Texas Instruments has been examining its responsibilities, structures and practices. We recognize keenly that as a board, our responsibilities include not just attaining the corporation's long-range objectives but responsibility for what kind of corporation we are and become while our goals are being attained. Our deliberations have convinced us that our prime responsibility as a board of directors is to ensure our corporate self-renewal.

In specific terms, this means that as a board we must prepare not only to attain a multi-billion dollar level in the 1970's, but to govern an institution of that size and to ensure that it continues to be a viable, constructive, self-renewing corporation dedicated to changing the world around it—not change for the sake of change, but change for the creating, making and marketing of really useful products and services to satisfy needs and solve problems for customers around the world.

THE CHANGING ENVIRONMENT

I think it is clear from my discussion of innovation and the resultant products and services that our internal environment at TI is changing rapidly. The external environment, to a considerable extent, because of our own actions but to an even greater extent through influences outside of our control, is changing even more rapidly. It is these changes, of course, with which we are much less prepared to comprehend, cope and take advantage.

For example:

1. Consider the increasing complexity of our society, which inevitably will be compounded by rapidly increasing populations, shrinking distances, and the rate of change of technology over the next 20 years.
2. Governments everywhere are increasingly a part of our every corporate action—often as a customer, but just as frequently as regulator, policeman, judge and jury.

Corporate Self-Renewal is the prime responsibility of Board of Directors

3. Large and growing international activities introduce a wide variety in legal, cultural, and national environments within which we must function. We must face economic philosophies with orientations ranging from those which are heavily socialistic to those characterized by relatively free private enterprise, plus all the divergence of views that operations within developed and developing countries imply.
4. With growth in size and complexity, the demands on our chief operating executives become increasingly intense. There can be no substitute for the full-time commitment of experienced, dedicated senior executives, but just because the demands are so intense, it is exceedingly difficult for such executives to spend the time necessary to study, to think quietly about, and to comprehend the impact of this rapidly changing internal and external environment. Yet it is imperative that we provide, at a very high level, just such thinking and deliberate comprehension of the corporation's total environment, both internal and external, and the changing problems and opportunities it presents.

THE BOARD OF DIRECTORS

Clearly, boards of directors have the responsibility to meet the challenges of this rapidly changing environment, but we at TI are also beginning to believe that by structuring our board properly, we might also represent a principal means to deal effectively with these external and internal environments and be much better prepared to fulfill the responsibility for assuring corporate self-renewal. Without interfering with the heavy and what must inevitably be the complete operating responsibilities which fall on our principal executives, we feel that our board must evolve mechanisms which will allow us to examine and influence, and in the final essence take responsibility for, corporate self-renewal by:

1. Assuring that the corporate structure, policies and practices are realistic, sufficiently elastic, and yet powerful enough to couple not just with the external national and international environment as it now exists but as it will be through future years and over the entire corporate span of interests.
2. Assuring that the corporation's products and services are truly innovative and really are contributing in a major way to constructive change in the world around it.
3. Assuring that an innovative, aggressive, properly educated and experienced staff of professional managers, scientists, engineers, and other specialists is available and being generated in sufficient depth and talent to meet the corporation's long-range goals.

There are, of course, many other board responsibilities besides these. I have chosen corporate renewal because I believe it is not only the most important but often the least expressed and understood. At TI we are still in the process of discussing how we can best accomplish the fulfilment of this responsibility. We, of course, intend to continue to examine our structure and our method of operation; but tentatively we have concluded that in addition to our full-time operating officers who serve as directors, it would also be desirable to have directors for whom this would be a principal occupation. This would ensure our having high-level, capable people who have the time to study, to think quietly about and to comprehend the impact of the rapidly changing internal and external environment and the relationship of both to our corporate self-renewal. These directors would have no operating responsibilities. Their duties would relate entirely to their function as directors and advisors to the board.

DIRECTORS FROM OUTSIDE THE COMPANY

Tentatively we concluded that it would be desirable initially to have one or two such directors whose principal experience has been developed as senior executives of Texas Instruments. In addition, we would like to have one or two whose principal experience will have been developed outside of the company. Typical backgrounds could be:

1. Service at a senior executive level in our government or in the industry.
2. Extensive research and development experience.
3. Extensive international experience, particularly at a senior executive level in government and industry.
4. A really top-notch, internationally qualified economist with experience equivalent, for example, to that attained on the President's Council of Economic Advisors.

Of course, a principal question is: "Can we really obtain from within and without the company directors of this quality willing to make a company directorship their principal occupation?" I believe we can if we structure our board and its operations to make clear the opportunity it represents to play a principal part in the development of an exciting industrial institution and the vital responsibility it possesses for contributions to corporate self-renewal.

My beginning quotation from John Gardner's book, *Self-Renewal*, highlighted his concern about whether or not an individual or an organization or a society might advance toward maturity without advancing toward rigidity and senility. Let me conclude with the remainder of that quotation:

> "Does this mean that there is no alternative to eventual stagnation? It does not. Every individual, organization or society must mature, but much depends on how this maturing takes place. A society whose maturing consists simply of acquiring more firmly established ways of doing things is headed for the graveyard—even if it learns to do these things with greater and greater skill. In the ever-renewing society what matures is a system or framework within which continuous innovation, renewal and rebirth can occur."

I have described in this paper our "system or framework" at Texas Instruments for corporate self-renewal and endeavoured to illustrate in a concrete and specific fashion our commitment to fulfill that vital responisbility. ■

Strategic Leadership through Corporate Planning at ICI

Alan I. H. Pink

Stimulated by the business problems of the early 1980s, the ICI Executive Directors changed their organizational role and now spend more time working as a closely knit team providing strategic leadership to the Group. The Corporate Planning Department supports the Executive Team in its strategic role. Over the last 6 years the Company has developed an interactive process which integrates corporate planning, business strategic planning, financial budgeting and strategic/financial control. Some planning techniques are used but they are secondary to business experience and judgement in helping the Corporate Planning Department work for the Executive Team on the one hand and with the business units on the other.

'The Executive Team are the Planners.' This is a statement made whenever a member of Planning Department discusses Corporate Planning at ICI. It is not a disclaimer, nor is it a sign of excessive modesty, but it is a statement of the fundamental philosophy which lies at the heart of both ICI's strategic planning process and the way it operates in practice.

The Chairman and the Executive Directors exert clear strategic leadership on the ICI Group. The role of Planning Department, with appropriate essential key inputs from Finance Department, is to support the Executive Team in its strategic role and to facilitate the strategic dialogue between the Executive Team and the units through whom corporate strategy must largely be implemented.

The role of the Executive Directors in strategic planning has not always been as it is today and we are, therefore, in a good position to see the advantages which flow from our current organization. Some background will help to put this in context.[1]

Alan Pink is General Manager, Planning, at Imperial Chemical Industries plc in London.

The Challenge

ICI is large and complex. It currently makes an annual profit of over £1bn from sales in excess of £10bn, manufactures products in 40 countries and sells to virtually all of the world's markets through its own sales offices in over 60 territories. It has a vast multiplicity of businesses ranging from pharmaceuticals to petrochemicals, all based on exploiting chemical, biological and related sciences and engineering. ICI is the most diverse and international of all the major world chemical companies.

The challenge is, on the one hand, to free business managers to develop individual businesses competitively and profitably whilst, on the other, directing the Group and managing the complex portfolio to achieve coherence and integration. This objective is captured succinctly by the statement 'the whole should be greater than the sum of the parts'. To this end the style of the direction and management of the Group has changed substantially over the last 6 years.

Changing Gear

In 1980 ICI declared losses in two quarters, and reluctantly cut its dividend for the first time since the 1930s. The exceptional drop in performance was due to a combination of factors—world recession following the oil shocks of the 1970s, particular weakness in the U.K. economy, high domestic inflation and an overvalued currency supported by oil, which was penal to a major exporter like ICI. The difficult situation in the external economic environment was exacerbated by the fact that ICI, in the late 1970s, had invested heavily for further growth, particularly in Plastics and Petrochemicals. This growth did not materialize and in the early 1980s capacity surpluses worldwide caused intense competitive pressure and a resultant squeeze on profit margins.

In the short term massive restructuring took place across the chemical industry in Europe, but the particular circumstances of the United Kingdom meant that ICI had to improve its cost base more rapidly than its competitors. Manpower in the United Kingdom was reduced by almost 30 per cent in 5 years and many older production units were closed. The intended capacity *expansions* of the late 1970s became effective modern low cost *replacement* plants. As a result, and helped by a range of portfolio exchanges, ICI was put into a strong competitive position and was poised to benefit from the improving economic conditions in the second half of the 1980s.

These moves were urgent and successful, albeit painful, reactions to a profits crisis. In addition a major reassessment of both the short-term performance objectives and the long-term strategy of the ICI Group was also clearly necessary. Part of the recovery plan called for a reappraisal of the role of the Executive Directors in planning for, directing and managing the Company. The financial budgeting and monitoring processes were also completely restructured and formed a key part of the overall new approach.

One major change was to delegate profit and operating responsibility for business units clearly and unambiguously to the level of management immediately below the Main Board. This left a smaller team of Executive Directors—reduced from 14 to now only eight—free to concentrate on Group financial performance and corporate direction as a whole, without having personal profit accountability for the individual parts of the Company worldwide. Executive Directors thus ceased to advocate for particular spheres of influence and started working as a more closely knit team to develop a shared vision for the ICI Group. They became better placed to determine where to take ICI as a whole and to decide objectively about the allocation of resources to the individual units in a way which best meets the corporate aims.

The problems faced by ICI in the early 1980s have already been defined broadly. They led to an urgent need to:

☆ Increase profit

☆ Improve profitability

☆ Achieve consistent improvement in performance.

This had to be done against the background of key issues faced by the chemical industry:

☆ Lower growth

☆ Overcapacity in commodity chemicals

☆ Greater competitive pressures

☆ More rapid change/more uncertainty

and particular issues faced by ICI:

☆ Overdependence on slow-growing U.K. economy

☆ Collapse of U.K. customer base

☆ For historical reasons, major involvement in sectors with most overcapacity

☆ Overvaluation of sterling

☆ Poor relative labour productivity.

The broad strategy was set, therefore, to achieve two major thrusts. These were to improve *competitiveness*, in terms both of costs and of the ability to add value, and to *change Group shape* in respect of both products and territorial spread.

In the case of products the aim was to move the balance away from the cyclicality and competitive vulnerability of commodity chemicals, particularly where these were exposed to foreign currency fluctuations, towards differentiated, high value-added, effect (speciality) chemicals. In the basic chemicals businesses in Europe the thrust was to achieve the maximum cost efficiencies of scale and concentration, whilst also adding value in the product chain in differentiated sectors of the market. The effect businesses to be emphasized included Pharmaceuticals, Agrochemicals, Seeds, Advanced Materials, Electronics, Polyurethanes, Films, Explosives, Colours and Speciality Chemicals. All of these were judged to have good growth prospects and potential for further development.

In the case of territories the emphasis was to increase business outside the slow-growing U.K. market towards the higher growth United States, Japan, and selected less developed countries, especially on the Pacific Rim.

ICI thus embarked upon a major and strategic problem-solving phase in which existing businesses had a key part to play alongside central initiatives directed at macro restructuring, generation of new businesses and achievement of targeted acquisitions. The last 5 years have seen the major problems largely solved and the need today is to build successfully on the solid base which has been established. Figures 1–3 illustrate in different ways the considerable changes achieved in the ICI Group between 1982 and 1986. The overall objective now is to move forward aggressively and to achieve sustained growth in earnings through time.

Against this objective the broad strategic thrusts on

	1982	1986
Return on Chemical Sales (%)	5	10.5
Return on Assets (%)	7	19
Earnings per Share (Pence 1986)	29	92

Figure 1. ICI performance

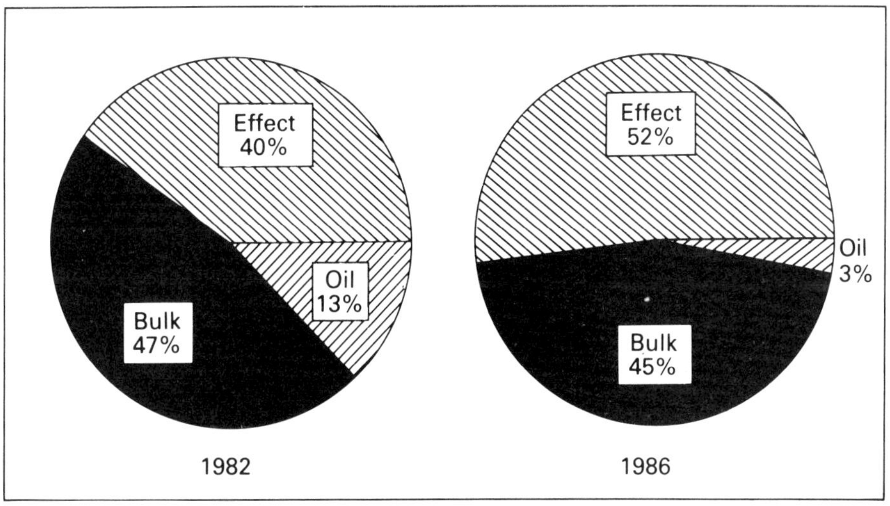

Figure 2. Product shape

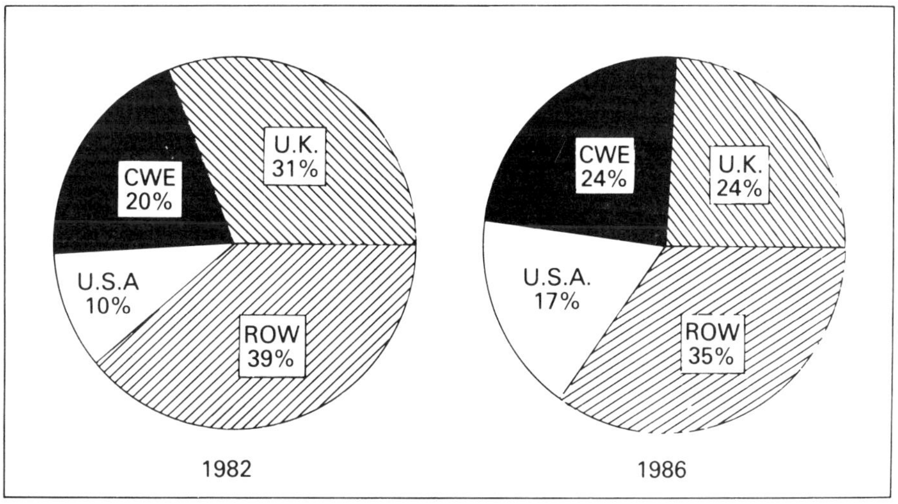

Figure 3. Chemical sales: territorial distribution

competitiveness and Group shape are still relevant. They are required now, less in the sense of urgent problem solving, but more to encourage a continuous evolution of appropriate competitive strategies for existing businesses and for developing new vehicles to bring ICI's core innovative skills to an ever-changing market. Blended together and applied to a mix of old and new, they are the means of sustaining the momentum of growth, renewal and more growth, through time. This strategic intent will be achieved only if the processes throughout the ICI Group enable and encourage good decision-taking by the level appropriate to the decision.

The Strategic Process

The strategic processes introduced in the early 1980s have been developed and refined to achieve a tightly integrated strategic planning and financial budgeting process which aims:

- ☆ to give the Executive Team the ability to steer the Group;
- ☆ to retain the necessary financial control at the ICI Centre;
- ☆ to delegate as much as possible responsibility and freedom of action to Chief Executives of operating units.

The need is to ensure that individual businesses and territories are following strategies which are consistent with Group strategy and that the implementation is broadly following the intended path on the required timescale. This means that at the heart of the process is the agreement by the Executive Team of a strategy for a unit, followed by subsequent monitoring of financial and strategic performance within the context of the agreed strategy.

At any time each unit has an agreed strategy to which it must work. There is no fixed pattern for a fundamental review of strategy, but a review will be called for if, from the perspective of the Executive Team, the strategy is clearly becoming untenable or if the Chief Executive Officer (CEO) of the unit believes he must offer different options.

* Strategy Paper and Background Review Documents Produced by Businesses in Consultation With Planning and Other Millbank Functions
* Papers Circulated by Business Director With Covering Letter Highlighting Key Issues. Single Brief Prepared by Corporate Functions
* Presentation by CEO to Executive Team
* Initial Feedback After Discussion by Executive Team; Minutes Issued by Secretary's Dept.
* Summary of Issues, Preferred Strategy and Milestones Prepared by Planning Dept. and Business
* Strategy Summary and Milestones Submitted For Main Board Approval

Figure 4. Business strategy review: the process in practice

The strategy review is carried out against a common economic background using central assumptions. It must provide an assessment of the range of strategic options available to the unit over a 10-year planning horizon (and for some business units a longer view is also appropriate), and should evaluate these against the background of ICI Group strategic aims.

When a preferred strategy is agreed it provides a framework in which the CEO can operate and it commits ICI Group resources in principle to the strategy. It also establishes definitive Milestones against which to measure progress of implementation of the strategy.

Figure 4 summarizes the process in practice. The Milestones cover a 10-year period, being more detailed and precise in the early years and less so later on. They are a mixture of quantitative and qualitative critical factors which provide reference points for the annual evaluation of budgets. They also act through time as key markers against which to test whether performance is meeting requirements or significantly and persistently falling short, indicating the need for strategy to be reappraised.

At any time the add-up of the business strategies indicates what the ICI Group as a whole will achieve if the businesses are successful in the execution of their strategies. The add-up may or may not match the aspirations that the Executive Team have for the ICI Group to achieve sustained growth of earnings and to be strongly competitive in its performance. In order to test this the Executive Team divorces itself from day-to-day activities and retreats, at least once a year, for 2 days to Hever Castle in Kent to reflect on both Group strategy and its implementation.

During these discussions corporate objectives are reviewed and the totality of business projections is tested for credibility, adjusted as appropriate, and the resulting overall forecast performance is compared against the corporate objectives. The total resources required to fund existing strategies are reviewed against available resources and the impact through time on Company financial ratios is assessed. In other words the strategy loop is closed and the Executive Team tests whether the totality is credible, acceptable and can be financed. It also identifies the need for additional initiatives which may be either offensive or defensive.

Also during these Hever discussions, the business portfolio is reviewed to judge its strength, to identify problems and to seek ways to eradicate weaknesses. The deployment of the Company's resources across the portfolio is assessed critically to ensure that the strong and profitable businesses are being adequately funded for maximum growth and that the poorer businesses are receiving minimum cash until their future is clear.

To help the process a simple broad, four-way categorization of businesses is used. The categories are Strong, Ongoing/Cash-generating, Problem and New. Figure 5 shows the characteristics and objectives for businesses in each sector. For the businesses in the ICI portfolio we have found this essentially qualitative approach to be more appropriate than such techniques as the Boston Consultancy Group Growth/Share matrix or the Shell Directional Policy matrix. The factors incorporated on the axes of those matrices, relating to industry

ONGOING/CASH	STRONG
Profitable Cash Generator But With No Major Growth Prospects — Run For Long-term Cash, Increasing Contribution by Improving Profits Through Limited Selective Investment Directed at Increasing Efficiency of Existing Operations in Preference to Expansion	Strong and Growing Profit Contributor Based on Good Competitive Position in Growing Good Quality Market — Stimulate Innovation and Invest to Sustain Profitable Growth and to Increase Total Size of this Sector
PROBLEM	**NEW**
Inadequate Profitability and Cash Generation — Turn Around, Divest or Close Down	New Business With the Potential of Being 'Strong' But Meanwhile Relatively High Cash Requirement With Relatively High Risk — Nurture; Then Select and Invest Sufficient Resources and Management Attention in Chosen Businesses to Develop 'Strong' Positions

Figure 5. Selectivity overview: characterization and objectives

sector prospects and our own competitive position within the industry, receive considerable attention. However, the process by which the Executive Team assesses the appropriate categorization for individual businesses, and then moves on from there to approve a specific strategy, embraces a wider range of relevant judgement factors including the Group corporate goals and objectives.

This approach is a particular example of a strongly fulfilled general determination that techniques should be kept in perspective as tools and should not become potential substitutes for applying business experience and judgement. Further in line with this general thesis the business categorization is not a mechanical fixed classification. It is a dynamic process with businesses moving between categories if this is justified by a strategy review.

A problem business, for example, which can develop a convincing and financially rewarding strategy to turn itself around, within a reasonable period, into a good cash business or perhaps eventually into a strong business, will get reasonable support through its time of crisis. There are some outstanding cases of successful turnarounds probably best exemplified by ICI's Polyurethanes business and its Fibres business. The corporate use of this selectivity quadrant is broad and units are encouraged to apply the same kind of categorization to their sub-portfolios. Many do and some elaborate the four categories into sub-groupings to define more accurately the strategic issues facing the businesses.

The categorization is simple, but the Executive Team finds it has provided it with a clearer overview of the portfolio and enabled it to arrive more quickly at decisions to encourage Chief Executives to divest poorly performing businesses with little recovery potential or, at the very least to limit resources until prospects improve. Similarly the Executive Team can ensure it is channelling sufficient resources into strong businesses and that enough 'patient' money is being devoted to the long-term development of new businesses without unduly straining current Group profitability.

The Executive Team believe they are now better placed to manage the diverse portfolio effectively, to direct resources towads making the maximum contribution to sustained growth of earnings and also to assess objectively management performance. The use of the categorization model down the organization is contributing to an upgrading of strategic thinking throughout the Group. It is helping the management to focus more consciously on the need to be selective in their use of resources and to apply strategically differentiated criteria in their business decisions. The quality of the strategic debate around the Group is sharper and is still improving against a heightened appreciation of the corporate direction.

Corporate Strategy *Does* Make the Difference

The iteration between the review of the whole Group strategy at Hever and the review of individual strategies with CEOs, coupled with the launching of central strategic initiatives aimed at improving the performance of the whole, provides the process for ensuring that, in spite of its diversity and complexity, the ICI Group moves forward coherently and proactively under positive strategic direction.

There are always critical decisions to be taken on the relative importance to be given to strategic and financial control of individual businesses. Some companies go unequivocally for one or the other. The ICI Executive seeks to balance the two so that in difficult times financial targets are met as closely as possible whilst key strategic initiatives are preserved. This is a very appropriate, but difficult, style of management which requires a considerable understanding by the Executive Team of the individual business issues and of the strategic parameters which are key to the future competitive success of the business. As will be seen later Planning Department has a role in highlighting key issues relevant to any debate with strategic implications. This does not set a restrictive agenda and additions are made by the Executive Team or by the responsible CEO, but it is expected to provide the core focus for the dialogue.

This role, together with the Department's formal and informal involvement in the total strategy process, will be seen to be at the heart of the contribution made by Corporate Planning at ICI towards the pursuit of corporate strategy. To quote Michael Porter 'Corporate Strategy is what makes the whole add up to more than the sum of its business unit parts',[2] and it is one of the factors which will ensure that ICI's future performance exceeds that of a diversified conglomerate.

The Budget Process

Each year the Executive Team, as a group, assisted primarily by Finance Department and also with input from Planning, reviews the budgets of all the main units for the next 3 years with each CEO in what is known colloquially as 'hell fortnight'. This is the key instrument of financial control and the agreed budget becomes a contract between the Executive Team and the Chief Executive of the unit.

At the budget review the Executive Team tests briefly whether the unit is proceeding along its agreed strategic path and whether the milestones are being passed. This provides an essential interlinking between the strategy process and the budget process (see Figure 6). The performance of a CEO against

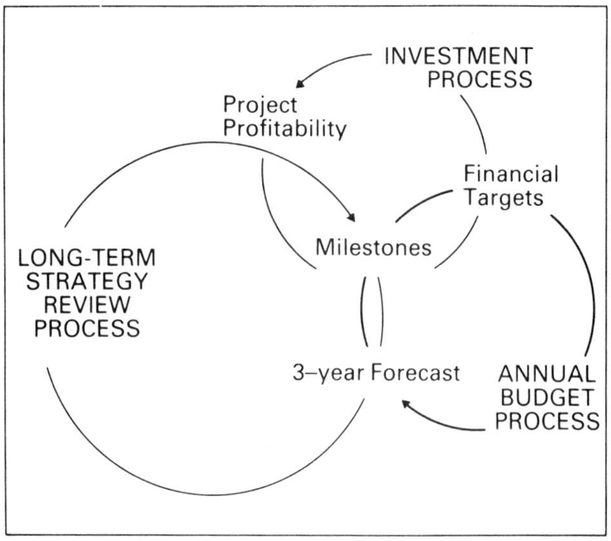

Figure 6. Interaction of strategy, budget and investment processes

his agreed profit and cash budgets is subsequently monitored quarterly to ensure business performance is on target. If it is not the CEO must take corrective action or persuade the Executive Team that dispensation is justified. It is under these circumstances that the debate will centre on whether to continue to incur costs on following longer term strategic goals.

Once a CEO has a budget agreed in the context of an established strategy the approval of capital investment subsequently falls naturally into the overall process, as illustrated in Figure 6.

Where the cost of a planned project or acquisition falls within the sanction authority delegated to a CEO, he can approve it provided he will still meet his profit and cash budgets. Where the cost exceeds his delegated authority, the CEO presents for consideration by the Executive Team a short paper outlining the case and the way the proposal fits the approved business strategy and the agreed budgets. Unless there are exceptional reasons for believing the business has moved off course there is no recycling of the strategic issues. The debate with the CEO, which is usually quite short, focuses on the market, technical and financial aspects of the proposal. The purpose is to establish whether the project is robust and of a quality which justifies the commitment of the requested capital. This is the final step in ensuring that financial resources are put to fully beneficial use consistent with the Group meeting its profitability targets.

The Result—Integrated and Interactive

Overall this adds up to a tightly knit process for corporate planning, business strategic planning, financial budgeting and strategic/financial control. As with all things it is capable of further improvement and refinement, but we believe that the broad pattern gives the necessary insights and stimulates the right debate between the Executive Team and those running individual businesses. The major interaction is between these, but Planning Department, along with Finance Department, have a key constructive and facilitating role to play and it is worth describing in some detail what this is.

Role of Corporate Planning Department

The key elements of the role of Corporate Planning Department can be summarized as follows:

☆ Provocation and catalysis of Executive Team strategic thinking, identifying Group strategic issues and possible new initiatives.

☆ Management and development of the strategic planning process.

☆ Acting as custodian of the Group strategy, proposing options on Group objectives and Milestones for achievement.

☆ Provision of strategic framework for discussion between Executive Team and business and territorial units.

☆ Provision of worldwide economic assumptions for planning and budgeting, and continuous assessment of the implications of economic trends on Group strategy.

☆ Assisting Units to put strategy proposals in corporate context.

☆ Assisting Executive Team in highlighting key issues for debate in Units' strategy or project proposals.

☆ Assisting Units in recording strategy summaries and developing appropriate Milestones.

☆ Assisting Executive Team in assessing Units' budgets for progress against strategic objectives and achievement of Milestones.

☆ Early identification of problems for the Group and its customers.

☆ Monitoring competitors and interpreting their strategies.

☆ Seeking out opportunities for the Group and ways to exploit them.

☆ Assessment of strategic relevance and value of potential acquisition targets.

☆ Making proposals for resolution of business-related organizational issues.

☆ Supporting the Executive Team in presenting and explaining Group strategy inside and outside the Group.

☆ Acting as a forceful advocate of strategic planning throughout the Group.

This role involves working for the Executive Team on one hand, with implications of a critique of the units' performance, whilst on the other hand working with the units themselves. This is a difficult dual role and can be carried out only by planners who are respected for their views and for the practical contribution they can make to thinking at both levels, whilst most importantly being, and being seen to be, honest. On many occasions a planner prematurely receives information, which used inappropriately would be unhelpful to the unit. The whole Department recognizes that they would not get a second opportunity to break this trust.

The Executive Team helps to guard the impartiality of Planning Department. The principle that briefs, which are written for the Executive Team about a unit's proposal, are also discussed with and received by the unit, helps to keep the process 'open'.

Three or four longer-term scenarios are considered by the Executive Team each year and they select the scenario to be used for planning purposes. The other scenarios are used to set the boundaries of upside and downside on the forecasts and to assist in judging whether the balance of probability lies above or below the planning assumptions. The scenarios are kept updated and are used as background for all strategy and budget projections.

A macro-economic model of the Group is maintained which gives the ability to test the effect of different economic growth rates and varying exchange rates on financial performance. The economic work is given a long-term dimension by a 'Futures' capability which projects social and technical trends. The purpose is to raise the Group's eyes above current horizons to try to spot trends and even discontinuities in markets and technology and to encourage use of this insight in identifying threats to existing business and also new opportunities of high potential.

Planning is a Department with a graduate strength of 20, divided into two mainstreams: a Planning Group and an Economics and External Studies Group. The former works largely internally on the corporate and business strategies and the latter is mostly involved with assessing the external environment. These skills must be integrated and information about the economic environment, the health of customer industries, competitor performance and major strategic thrusts of competitors is brought to bear on both ICI corporate strategy and the evaluation of individual business options. For many tasks, mixed discipline teams of people from across the Department are formed to provide the strongest possible blend of skills.

To assist integration within the Planning Department and also with other departments (principally Finance and the Acquisitions Team), a unified data base of internal and external data has been generated. Manipulation and clear display of these data is critical to their value in improving decision-taking. To this end a third group of Planning Department has been established to manage Information Technology (IT) in the ICI corporate headquarters.

The IT skills are developing very rapidly and a suite of models and displays is being created which will transform the capability to test interactively various options and events. Such a system needs to be tightly managed, but provides a powerful new tool in support of strategic thinking and dimensions to communication.

Planning in a Nutshell

The description if ICI's planning and budgeting processes and of the role of Corporate Planning has covered many of the key characteristics of the way the Company operates. It may be helpful to summarize these operational characteristics and add one or two more:

☆ An Executive Team with a strong strategic planning role

☆ A concise and precise statement of agreed strategies for Units, with achievement Milestones

☆ Short-term profit and cash budgets for Units set using the strategic Milestones to provide a linkage with their long-term strategies

☆ Close working between Corporate Planning Department and Finance Department

☆ A simple, flexible, action-oriented, portfolio management tool

☆ A quantitative vision of the Group 10 years ahead with assessment of availability and allocation of resources

☆ A process for setting corporate objectives and Milestones and for identifying potential shortcomings in the corporate achievement

☆ Strategic identification and justification for acquisitions

☆ Understanding of both customer industries and trends in society to provide early warning of changes or even discontinuities in ICI businesses

☆ Interpretation of competitor strategies

☆ Identification of territorial shifts and opportunities

☆ Ensuring changes in business shape are reflected by changes in employee skills and organizational structures

☆ Strategies for maintaining excellence in innovative skills central to competitive success in present and future business.

A corporate planning process with characteristics as diverse as these presents a challenging role to Planning Department to keep the various threads appropriately connected. The disparate issues must be sufficiently related to allow individual decisions, whilst at the same time they must be sufficiently separate to allow discrete decisions without over complicated debate on each and every subject. Planning Department, therefore, has a major role in ordering and allocating priority to issues and in helping to sort wood from trees.

Overall this adds up to a job which is difficult, challenging and hectic, but which is also stimulating and exciting for all concerned. A staff role, yes, but one which is involved, proactive and above all *additive*.

References

(1) Graham Turner, ICI becomes proactive, *Long Range Planning*, **17** (6), 12–16 (1984).

(2) Michael Porter, From competitive advantage to corporate strategy, *Harvard Business Review*, **65** (3), 43–59, May–June (1987).

Planning Global Strategies for 3M

Carol Kennedy

Minnesota Mining and Manufacturing, as it is formally listed in the *Fortune 500,* but better known to the business world as 3M, has long enjoyed the reputation of being one of the best managed and certainly most innovative American multinationals. It rated no fewer than 38 pages in the index of Tom Peters' and Robert H. Waterman's *In Search of Excellence,* more than any other example of 'America's best-run companies' studied by the two McKinsey consultants.

It has a record of product innovation second to none: what other company, after all, lives by the rule that a quarter of its annual sales must come from products invented or improved upon in the last 5 years? That has been a corporate goal since anyone can remember in this venerable business, founded in 1902, whose first commercially successful product, sandpaper, has grown into a list of nearly 50,000. They cut across virtually every industry from home entertainment to health care, construction to chemicals; products as diverse as kitchen scourers and video-cassettes, reflective road signs and surgical masks. More than 100 new products are introduced every year (see Figure 1).

3M's most famous product, 'Scotch' transparent adhesive tape, is literally a household name throughout homes and workplaces in the developed world; more recently, its ubiquitous yellow 'Post-it' notes have become a contemporary legend in product development.

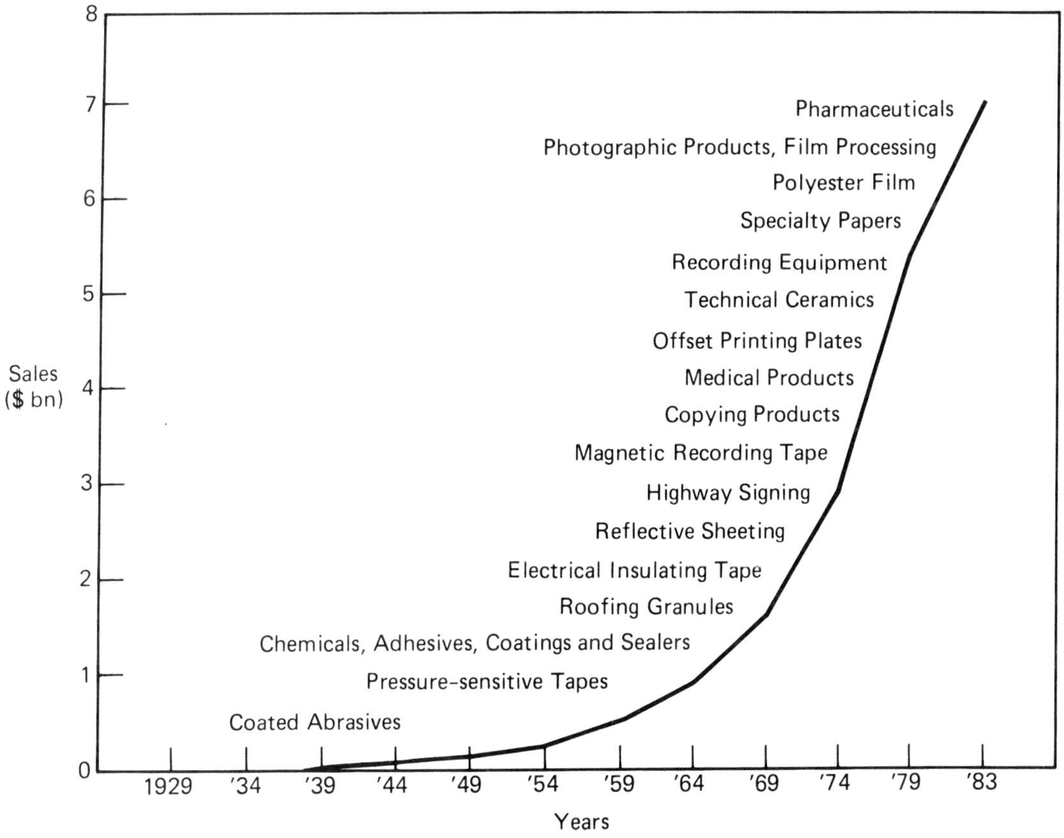

Figure 1. 3M historic growth

Carol Kennedy is a journalist and Deputy Editor of *Director*.

The company's well-known encouragement of its employees to pursue their own ideas by seeking development support anywhere within the organization has brought many product acorns to vast-spreading oaks. Tolerance of the small-scale, individual project, with the opportunity for its progenitor to manage it as it grows into a product, is still a characteristic of a company now generating \$8·6bn in global sales, 40 per cent outside the United States. As *Forbes* magazine once said: '3M marketing operates on a simple principle that no market, no end product is so small as to be scorned; that with the proper organization, a myriad of small products can be as profitable, if not more so, than a few big ones. More firmly than most, 3M management appreciates that the beach is composed of grains of sand, the ocean of drops of water.'

Those grains of sand were slow to make the beach. For the first quarter of its existence, 3M—the 'Mining' in the title is a relic of a corundum quarry that only ever produced one ton of saleable mineral—was virtually a one-product company. Its diversification out of sandpaper happened through the kind of interaction between sales force and laboratory for which 3M is now renowned. In 1923, its salesmen noticed that painters in automobile body shops were cursing the difficulty of keeping colours apart on the newly fashionable two-tone cars. A young lab technician named Richard Drew solved the problem in 2 years by producing a masking tape that could be stripped off without damage. Five years after Du Pont introduced Cellophane in 1930, Drew succeeded in putting adhesive on the back of it, and Scotch tape was born. Tape products now account for 17 per cent of all 3M sales.

Science and Salesmanship Formula

The story of 'Post-it' notes, the company's runaway success of the early 1980s, exemplifies both the unique cross-technical co-operation within 3M and the way that executives become product champions and salesmen. It was two senior managers who caused the market breakthrough for a product that had languished around the laboratories for 5 years because no one could think of a use for imperfectly adhesive glue. The chemist who discovered it, Spencer Silver, devised an application for bulletin boards, to which pieces of paper would self-stick, but a test marketing failed miserably. In a 'Eureka moment' which has already become part of innovation folklore, another lab technician, Arthur Fry, realized the product's true potential—attaching the adhesive to the paper rather than a bulletin board—when the slips of paper he used as markers in his church hymn-book kept falling out of the pages.

Conventional test marketing still failed, however, until the two executives took a hand. Enthusiasts themselves for the product, they realized its potential indispensability would only be appreciated if it got physically into the hands of potential customers. They gave away wads of the little notepads to secretaries, receptionists, bank clerks and businessmen, saying 'Here, try this', and watched people literally become addicted to the product.

That blend of science and salesmanship is the potent fuel on which 3M's vast and complex machinery is run in 100 different technologies and 49 countries. Chemical engineers dominate the senior management, including the current CEO, Allen F. Jacobson, but nearly all have worked as down-the-line salesmen. It is a formula that has worked consistently well: 3M is one of the most reliable profit performers in U.S. industry. In 1986, after one of its less successful years and admittedly helped by a weak dollar, it achieved a growth in earnings per share of 17·9 per cent, nearly twice its corporate goal; a return on capital employed of 23·5 per cent and a return on equity of 18 per cent. Stockholder dividends increased for the 28th year in succession. R & D spending rose from 4·6 per cent of sales to 6·5 per cent, well above average for U.S. companies, and Jacobson intends that it should fall no lower.

National Culture of an International Company

3M was almost half a century old before it moved its activities outside the United States; its international division was set up in 1951 and generated \$20m in its first year. In 1986 sales outside the United States totalled \$3·3bn—25 per cent of the total \$8·6bn in sales were in Europe. The overseas subsidiaries are run with a high degree of autonomy, financing their own expansion and operated overwhelmingly by non-U.S. citizens: out of 82,000 3M employees, 35,000 work outside the United States, but only about 100 of those are Americans. The 3M culture, however, freely crosses national boundaries: a French manager may easily be running a Korean operation, a Briton managing a subsidiary in Spain, or a Dane one in Germany.

At heart, though, it remains a very American company, rooted in Midwestern values down to the belief, enunciated by a chairman of the early 1970s, Harry Heltzer, and broadly shared by the current CEO, that small towns offer the best manufacturing locations because the work ethic is better there.

There is certainly no lack of work ethic at corporate headquarters in St. Paul, Minnesota (17,000 3Mers work in the Twin Cities of St. Paul and Minneapolis), where the CEO and his senior managers are invariably at their desks by 7.30 a.m. and breakfast meetings often start before that. The atmosphere fairly fizzes with intellectual energy and commitment, evoking the university campus to which visiting business writers often compare it; a comparison intensified by the physical size and self-containment of 3M's 400-acre complex, a 10-minute early-morning drive from downtown St. Paul.

Everywhere you look, people are bustling off to the meetings, often unscheduled and cutting across divisional or departmental boundaries, that characterize 3M's intense, informal style of internal debate and communication. (Meetings are not just occasions for brainstorming or generating paper, either: with the company's post-1980 acceleration of its quality drive, senior managers who get requests for decisions from the 1400 'quality action teams' are required to respond within 1 month, and do so, 95 per cent of the time.)

Communication was a prime reason for 3M's prominence in Peters' and Waterman's bible of excellence. Others included the way that product champions are encouraged to persist (successful ones being publicly recognized in a 'hall of fame' known as the Carlton Society after a former CEO); its 'nichemanship'; its closeness to the customer; its ability to turn ideas quickly 'into tin' and its high tolerance of failure. As a 3M executive once said, the company might occasionally stumble with a product, 'but you only stumble if you're in motion'.

Letting people make mistakes is as much a pillar of 3M culture as the '15 per cent' rule which expects R & D workers to spend 15 per cent of their time on their own projects, the company in turn underwriting 15 per cent of the costs of materials and development as 'capital to entrepreneurs'.

Introduction of Strategic Planning

Noticeably absent from Peters' and Waterman's criteria for excellence was any reference to strategic planning, which apparently did not rate highly in their assessment of what makes a well-run company. They believed, with some justice, that over-reliance on planning had distracted many companies from focusing closely on essentials like products and customer needs, and approvingly quoted *Business Week* as saying that neither Johnson and Johnson, TRW nor 3M, 'all regarded as forward thinking, has anyone on board called a corporate planner'.

That may have been true when '*Excellence*' was being written, but things are different now in St. Paul. 'This company was very late in adopting any kind of formalized, explicit style of strategic planning', admits Livio D. DeSimone, executive vice-president of 3M's industrial and consumer products sector, which generates one-third of the company's sales and half its profits. DeSimone was the first of three executive VPs on a rotating basis to head the corporate strategic planning committee when it was set up in 1981.

It was not until Lewis Lehr took over as chairman of the board and CEO in 1980 and embarked on a root-and-branch restructuring of the business that the previous loosely woven, intuitive consensus among senior managers on planning matters was channelled into a more disciplined system of thinking about where the company should be going and priorities for its multifarious businesses.

On the surface, there seemed no evident reason for change. The company was turning in good financial performances, a steady 20 per cent return on equity. Since its earliest days of selling sandpaper to industry, it had pursued a simple but effective strategy against competitors; quality products, priced fairly and sold aggressively, with a steady stream of innovation replenishing the market. But as technology and the business environment changed and product cycles shortened, such elemental strategies were not enough.

Outside pressures had changed too—inflation, volatile interest rates, regulatory changes, scarcity of key resources, declining demand in some major markets, competition had grown on a world-wide scale in such fields as film and magnetic memory technology, office products, pressure-sensitive tape and the graphic arts. There were more and sharper competitors both internationally and regionally in health care, transportation, electronics, construction, safety and communications. Though still performing strongly, 3M faced a decrease in what had been exponential growth since the war. It had also become so large that it was in danger of losing overall perspective.

'We had pushed decisions down to the product level of the company, and cross-functional teams were doing a pretty good job but they weren't steering the company', explains Michael A. Tita, director of planning services and development. The culture of the company, despite the long-term nature of many of its product developments, was essentially of the here and now.

'What really counted in this company was operational efficiency, operational results and predictability over a short term', says DeSimone, an affable, powerfully built man known to his colleagues as 'Desi'. (Nicknames are a part of the 3M 'family' culture; CEO Jacobson is known as 'Jake'.)

This pragmatic approach remains strong; there is a distinct air of 'it had better work' in management's attitude to strategic planning and constant questioning of planners' assumptions. 3M managers are wary about 'putting feet in concrete in the wrong place', as DeSimone says.

Lehr did not want 3M to lose its consensual style of determining goals, but he believed in the need for more structured planning. He felt the company was not fully exploiting its potential in consumer markets; something it has since done outstandingly in, for example, magnetic recording tape, initially manufactured for industrial use only. 3M is now a leading producer of domestic videotape cassettes and 3M U.K. is Europe's largest supplier. 'If you take everything that's sold in true consumer form, that's over $1bn—a big consumer company', observes DeSimone.

In pursuit of this goal, Lehr reshaped the company into four main business sectors: industrial and consumer (including such core products as industrial abrasives, adhesives, coatings, sealants and commercial office supplies); electronics and information technologies; graphic technologies and life sciences, which include safety and health-care products. Within these sectors are clusters of divisions: the industrial and consumer sector contains four groups of between three and five divisions each (see Figure 2).

By grouping operating units around related technologies Lehr acknowledged that a company like 3M could only continue to innovate on the scale it needed to if it shared and concentrated its technological resources. He also recognized the need to operate on a planned global strategic basis without losing the strong, autonomous, entrepreneurial flair of the divisions.

The division is the core business unit of 3M. There are 40-odd now compared with 25 a decade ago, and more are being added each year as projects develop to the size of viable businesses. Each division is responsible for its own planning and forecasting and, through its general manager, for product-planning on a world-wide scale. Cutting across the divisions since Lehr's restructuring are 20 strategic business centres or SBCs, essentially data-gathering and 'thought centres' as DeSimone puts it, which operate from a higher perspective than the operating units (see Figure 3).

Strategic Business Centres

Mike Tita has explained the thinking behind the SBCs in a paper to the New York Conference

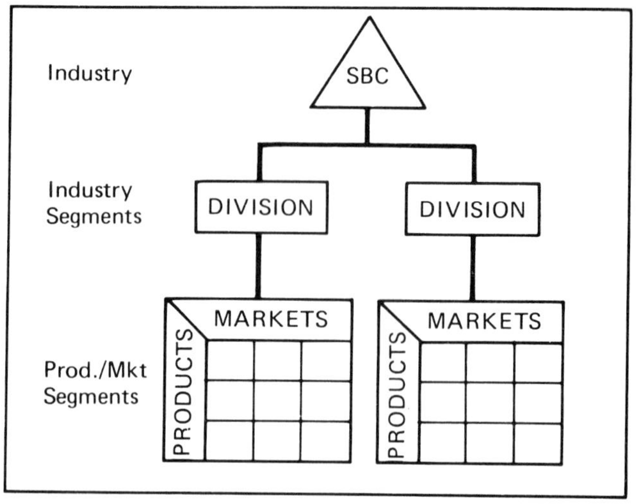

Figure 3. Planning centre (multi-division SBC)

Board. It was recognized that the first task confronting managers was to build a data base of information on markets and competitors. Only in this way could 3M's varied businesses set realistic goals and be assessed by tailormade performance measures. This posed a formidable problem for a company with about 200 organizational units world-wide—departments, projects and national subsidiaries—most of which had been accustomed to planning and operating on the basis of their own perceived requirements and opportunities.

Within the SBCs, set up in 1982, plans are worked out in true 3M 'bottom-up' style in conjunction with the key operating managers. They set out how each 3M business will manage its products and markets for best competitive advantage, consistent with the level of investment and risk that management is willing to support. Each plan defines the resources needed to achieve it and the performance measures that will be used.

As a first step, each industry in which the company operated is characterized by size and growth rate, external influences such as new technology and regulatory changes and, above all, by an analysis of key competitors; their market share and their perceived competitive strategies. 3M is then measured against them, whether as market leader or

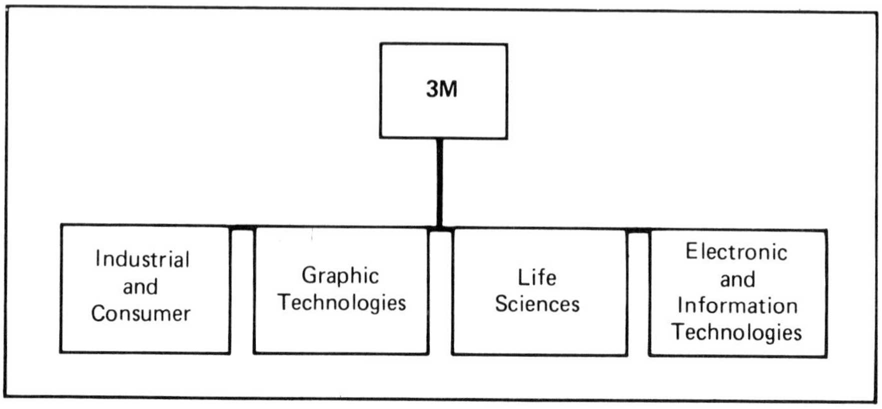

Figure 2. 3M response. 1981 reorganization into four sectors

occupying a niche which can be maintained or improved against competitors with broader product lines. Mike Tita's paper explained:

> The strategic condition of an SBC strongly influences appropriate strategies. For example, in embryonic industries 3M businesses emphasize market- or product-oriented strategies to improve their competitive position. As their industries mature, these businesses will very likely emphasize integration, efficiency, and rejuvenation through innovation. In the late stages of maturity, they'll move forward to consolidation and disinvestment.

(Among recent significant disinvestments has been the photocopying business: around 1970 probably half the company's earnings came from duplicating, copying, recording and office products.)

Performance measures are worked out on the basis of maturity of the industry, competitive position and strategy. Key financial measures include return on capital employed, operating income and cash flow, while non-financial yardsticks would include market share, product quality, distribution expansion and new product development. Finally the plan is assessed for its probability of success, in the context of developments within the industry and 3M's competitive position within it (see Figures 4 and 5).

Above the SBCs in the planning process, and forming the hinge of corporate strategy, comes the strategic planning committee, headed at vice-president level and composed of about 12 people from all four sectors, a representative cross-section of the company chosen, says DeSimone, for their 'aptitude for strategic thought'. Around March each division and its SBC will have prepared its detailed plan and financial summary for the year ahead. These, which cover the main international operating areas as well, are reviewed in late April at sector

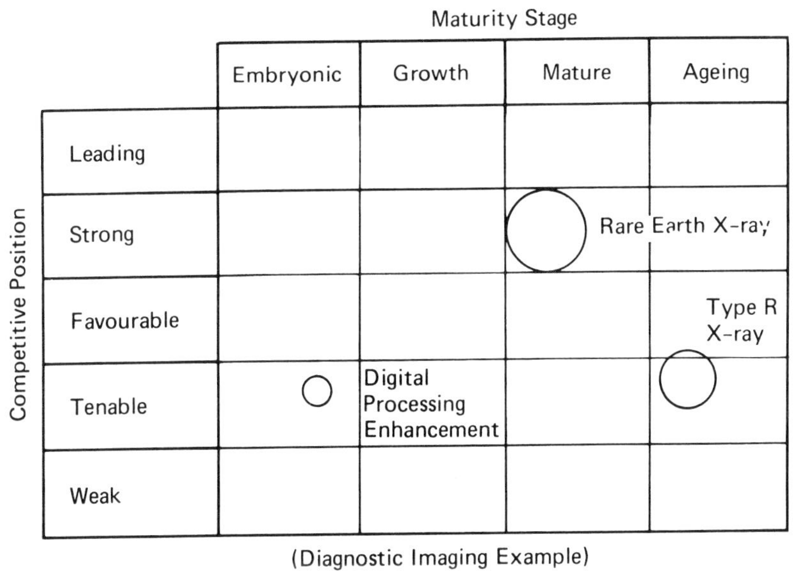

Figure 4. Product portfolio (illustrative)

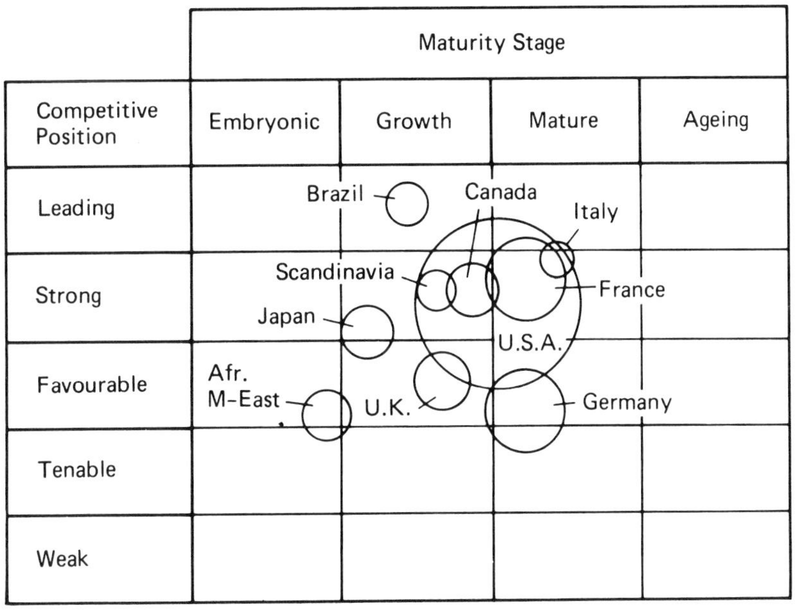

Figure 5. Strategic condition of 3M business by geographic market (illustrative)

level, when the strategic planning committee becomes involved, at least two of its members attending every meeting (see Figures 6 and 7).

In July a corporate review of plans is carried out over 3 days by the company's 34-strong management committee, of which all strategic planning committee members are a part. This is when investment priorities are voted on. Finally in December come the operating reviews, when world-wide and regional plans and forecasts are finalized together with those of the operating units themselves.

Around these key review points, the year falls broadly into two halves, global strategy (on a maximum time-scale of 5 years) being worked out in the first half and shorter-term action plans and budgets between June and December. Non-U.S. representatives come to St. Paul for planning sessions and at the end of the year senior members of 3M's management, including the CEO, are on the move themselves to most of the major operating countries. The plans are then discussed a final time (see Figure 8).

If it seems that the planning ground gets worked over repeatedly, that is by design. 'Iterative' is the word you hear most at 3M when discussing its planning process. The culture of consensus is still powerful, and there is as strong a belief in cross-fertilization of ideas and views at the planning level as there has always been at the technical level. What in fact has happened is that 3M's strategic planning system has transferred a culture into management which always existed scientifically.

Tita, who describes himself as a 'system engineer',

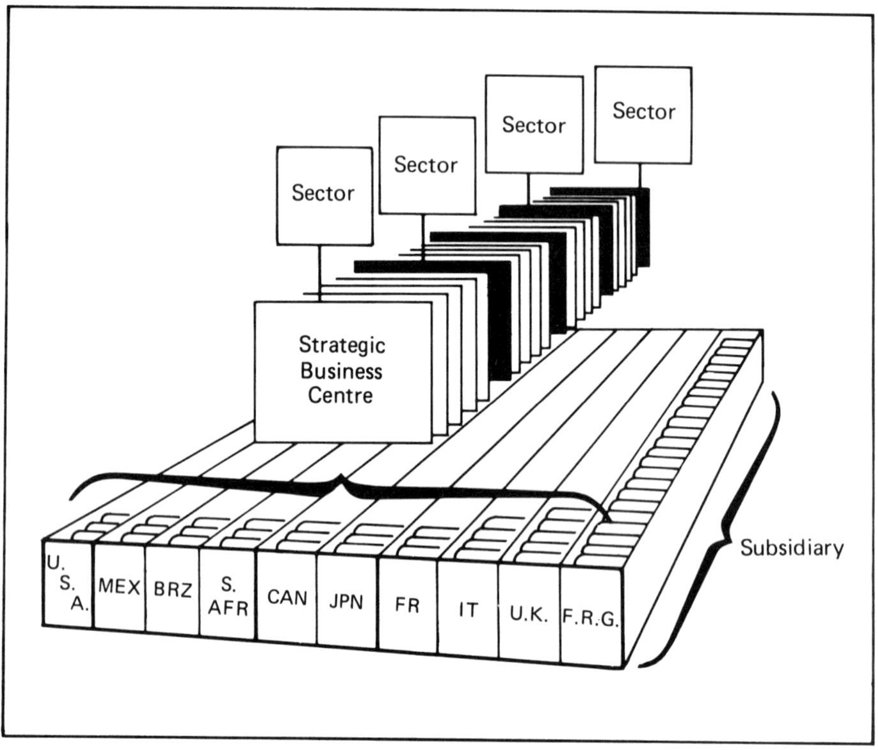

Figure 6. 3M global planning system

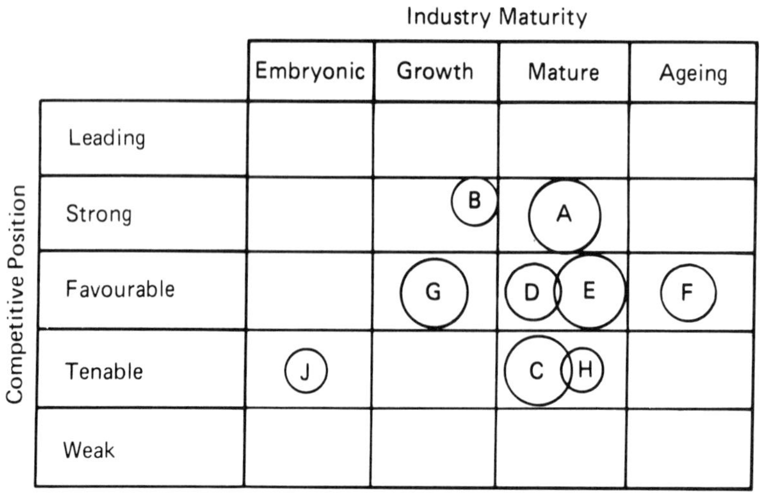

Figure 7. Corporate portfolio array (illustrative)

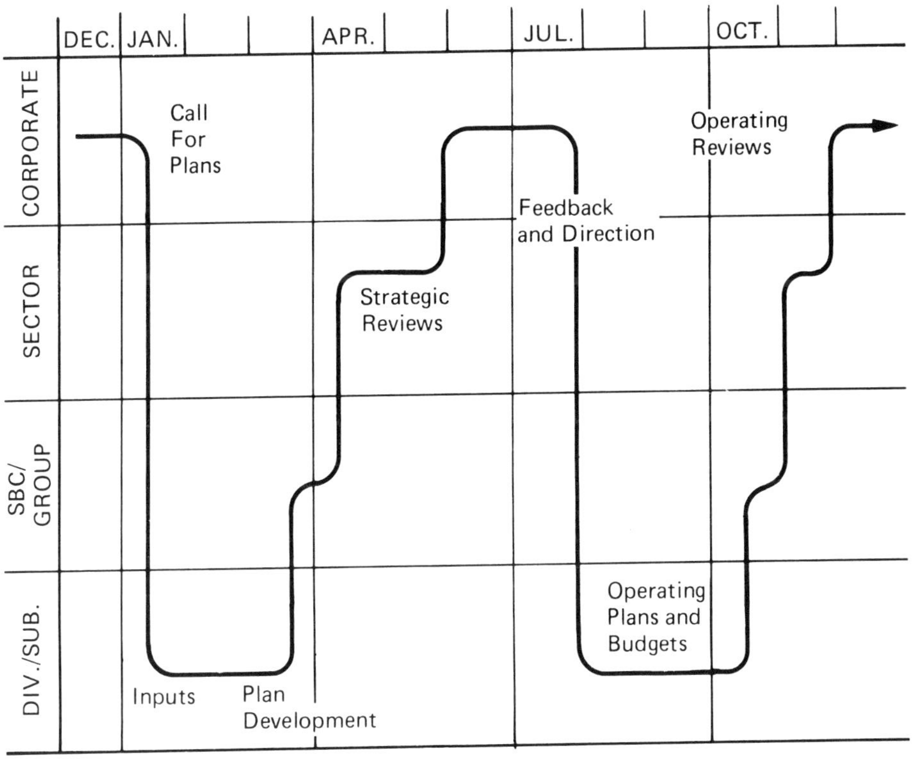

Figure 8. Planning cycle

constantly refining and fine-tuning the planning function, says the process has effectively 'created a business school' for management, with live cases.

> We have an iterative system which goes up and down and they talk to each other and we have input and feedback and perspective from every level. We have product functional and cross-functional people making product decisions, and we have corporate managers making decisions for prioritization of the businesses of the company and directional strategy. We've got each level making the decisions it ought to make.

The business of Tita's unit is to feed the planning mills with the grist they require in the shape of information. A core function is to furnish the SBCs and operating units with an analysis of 3M's 20 key corporate competitors throughout the world. It gathers these data from published sources and 3M's own global network, pulling it together and 'trying to get into the competitor's mind'. Lately, it has been 'prioritizing' the company's businesses and markets and concentrating on identifying key opportunities and new products.

Its current preoccupation is with the growth potential of 3M businesses outside the United States, focusing heavily on fast-growing areas of the world such as the Pacific basin. Twelve 3M companies operate in the Asia-Pacific region, the largest being a joint venture with Sumitomo of Japan. A technical servicing facility is being established in Singapore to capitalize on the growth of electronics manufacturing in the Far East. 3M is already selling electrical products in China and looking at a joint venture in India, one of the few major countries in which it does not yet operate.

The company has got out of a couple of African countries in recent years, but its preference is 'to get in for the long run', says Jacobson: 'We have what we call the FIDO principle—first in defeats others.'

Future Development

International markets are now the main target of 3M's growth strategy: the company's penetration of major overseas markets is about half that in the United States. DeSimone sees significant opportunity for his sector in overseas markets, which currently account for about 40 per cent of its volume. With improved market penetration, he believes, international business could eventually generate more than half.

New laboratories and technology centres in Europe and Japan are improving 3M's ability to tailor products more closely to local market needs, and the company has also concluded about 100 research agreements with 50 universities world-wide.

Perhaps the most fascinating of 3M's strategic planning activities, which take place before the pre-Christmas operating reviews, are the so-called 'Challenge 2002' brainstorming sessions (in 1988 they become 'Challenge 2003') in which the management committee and the strategic planning committee discuss trends and developments for the company's businesses over the next 15 years. The general manager of each business unit is required to 'paint the best picture' he can of his industry 15 years ahead—challenges, threats, likely product areas, market needs.

The outcome is a sort of 'unexpressed guide' for strategic planning. 'It's a very broad guide, a set of thoughts,' says DeSimone, but it undoubtedly has an influential role, standing in relation to the accountable areas of planning much as blue-sky research does to targeted work in the laboratories.

'One of the things we tried to do early on was to break away the accountability segment from the free-thought segment,' explains DeSimone. In these sessions, operating unit forecasts are looked at in a freewheeling, associative way. Products theoretically due for improvement or replacement after 5 years are examined for development potential over the next 4 or 5 years. New products are evaluated, acquisition horizons scanned. 'Then we look at what we don't want to forecast, because it is too conceptual or too early to make any commitment.'

There is a continuing need to assess new projects which might blossom into departments and ultimately divisions, without necessarily committing them to hard-and-fast forecasts. All this is 'a way of bridging pragmatic operating units and creativity in a non-accountable way', says DeSimone. To rate division status, a business does not have to generate \$500 m or \$1bn sales: it can work well enough at \$60m or \$70m providing it offers something new and exploitable. The average size is around \$200m in annual sales.

Some units are close to forming new divisions now: ceramics, currently a department, is not far from division status. Contractor products, a project servicing building contractors with such products as coated abrasives, tapes and adhesives, may develop into one in 2 or 3 years. Dental products became a division 2 or 3 years ago.

Some divisions split like amoebas; others are consolidated to attack a market more effectively, like automotive specialities a few years ago. Still others are formed that have no sales outside the company but whose value in production terms could be as much as \$400m. A recent one is speciality chemicals, which makes most of 3M's acrylic adhesives, all of its fluor chemicals and a whole series of speciality chemicals and polymers. A speciality film division exists to manufacture magnetic tape, X-ray and photographic film for the company; another was recently formed to centralize the manufacture of pressure-sensitive tape, 3M's largest business. Previously, seven different divisions had run their own manufacturing operations.

Mike Tita saw benefits to the planning system after its first year.

> We didn't make any major decisions but we had a sort of catharsis, got rid of all the junk, all the projects that had been hanging on and weren't being evaluated. After that first year the people in the laboratories and factories were saying, 'Now we know what we're doing.' The pay-off was in getting rid of things that were sucking us under. We got rid of about 300 projects in small departments.

But there has also been a major change in terms of 3M's outward focus on competitors, which Tita says has fostered a 'pro-active rather than reactive stance'.

Another change will become evident this year (1988) when, long shy of corporate advertising, 3M emerges as a sponsor of the Olympic summer and winter games, which will entitle it to use the immediately recognizable Olympic rings on 12 of its products.

In the upper levels of 3M management there is a hint of scepticism over the value of the planning system for identifying new business opportunities. 'Our system is an exceptionally good one for the analysis and direction of existing businesses. I don't know if it's as good for generating new ones,' muses DeSimone. Allen Jacobson believes it has given the company some useful directions for avoiding future problems. He calls it 'pretty good corporate life insurance', but says that in 3M and most other companies he has talked to, it's been 'pretty low' on identifying opportunities.

> It's a good process for identifying critical mass in a business, and some that might not make it. But opportunities come from other places, and I guess I am very concerned about identifying opportunities, needs and potential future needs in the market-place. Those are the things that are going to make us grow and get us profits.

When Jacobson, 40 years with 3M (he started as a product engineer in the tape laboratory), took over the top seat in March 1986, there had been some fallback in the company's four main corporate goals: annual earnings per share growth of 10 per cent or better; return on capital employed of 27 per cent or better; return on stockholders' equity of between 20 and 25 per cent, and the famous 25 per cent new products rule. He is said to be a 'one sheet of paper man' where planning data is concerned, unlike DeSimone who 'soaks up information like a vacuum', and he saw his priority clearly: to stop tinkering and start implementing.

In his 14th-floor office with its distant panorama of the Twin Cities, he says drily:

> When you get a new chief executive and strategic planning together, people expect dramatic change. I'm not the least bit interested in drama, I'm interested in seeing our business progress. Our company is multi-product, multi-technology, multi-national and multi-market. We probably sell to a greater variety of commercial, industrial and consumer markets than anybody else.
>
> Now with that variety, that diversity, you can't make all the

important decisions on the 13th or 14th floor of this building. You have to have a system that depends on your people, or on the people closest to the job, the technology and the customer.

He concedes, however, that there is now

a lot more St. Paul involvement in seeing that business plans are consistent with overall strategy, and that we are exploiting all of the opportunities in an area rather than cherry-picking.

For 3M, the world is clearly full of cherry orchards.

PART FIVE

Improving Performance by Changing Corporate Culture

The Quest for Quality at Philips

Kees van Ham and Roger Williams

All over the western world during the last few years companies have been introducing total quality programmes. Their objective is to regain or maintain market leadership. Top management understands the importance of company-wide quality for strategic positioning and actively leads the companies in these excellence movements. All aim at improving performance through top management leadership, total involvement of all members of the organization, rebuilding organizational and management practices and systematic, deep, long-term change strategies. At Philips such a movement started company-wide 3 years ago. This article describes the background to the programme, gives some of the results achieved so far and looks ahead to possible future developments.

The Need for Total Quality

In order to understand the major changes currently taking place in organizations in their quest for quality, it is necessary to look at how the western business environment has changed since World War II. Over the last few decades markets have become far more difficult to satisfy. Perhaps this is most clear in the consumer goods area. In this field the situation in the late 1940s was one of shortages. Customers had been starved of goods during the period of hostilities and thus could be relatively easily satisfied. The result was that the determinants of commercial success became price and availability in the market place, and the production function formed the pushing power. There was virtually no international competition and sales forces were often merely order-takers.

However, industrial capacity built up rapidly and national tariff barriers were slowly dismantled. As a result the first signs of market saturation appeared. Consumers started to become more critical as the shelves began to fill up. At the same time changes in distribution patterns led to the number of buying points in many markets being drastically reduced with the consequent swinging of influence towards the retailer. At about the same time, consumer organizations began to use the mass media effectively in order to inform the public about competing products quality, reliability and price performance.

Manufacturers, in this new climate, had to become more concerned with customer desires. More attention had to be paid to marketing and to information about product characteristics, instructions for use and service facilities. The production function was no longer the driving force and organizations became much more market driven.

The continuing battle for low prices led to the movement of business to cheap labour areas and insistence on economies of scale. Throughout the 1960s and 1970s this trend towards increasing customer power continued steadily. Not only price but also product quality and reliability became essential. Those companies which could not meet these demands were shaken out of the business. Markets became global, facilitated by lower tariff barriers and cheaper transport and this, in turn, was followed by a globalization of product development and manufacturing. In the fight for competitive advantage, providing maximum choice for the customer became a favoured weapon. The situation now is that new products are appearing more and more frequently and product life cycles are shrinking rapidly.

In addition, the options available to customers, have developed dramatically. For example the number of different types of television sets produced by Philips trebled in under 10 years (Figure 1).

Kees van Ham is Senior Director of Corporate Organization and Efficiency at Philips International, Eindhoven and Roger Williams is based at Erasmus University, Rotterdam.

BRUCE KYLE PRIZE: 1986

This article has been awarded the Bruce Kyle Prize for 1986 as an innovative paper based on experience which is of practical value to planners and senior managers.

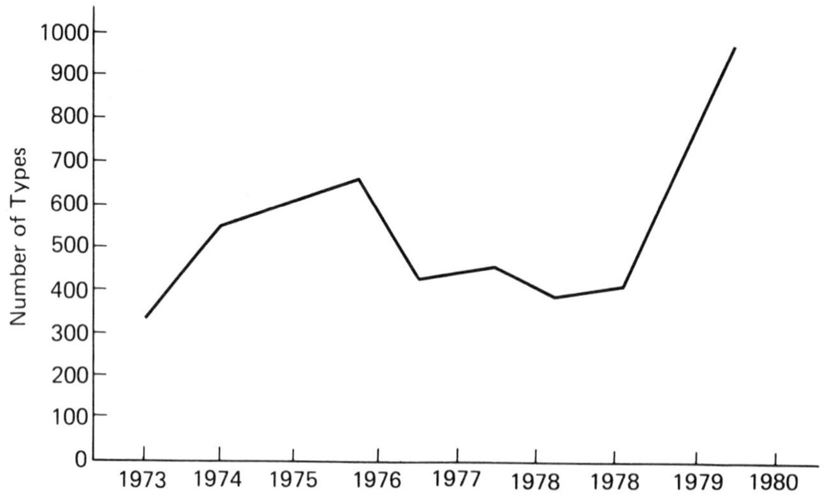

Figure 1. Television sets: increase in product range

Markets now demand top performance not just in terms of price and quality but also in terms of innovation and variety in product range. New product development times have had to be drastically reduced and manufacturing flexibility increased. Initially the introduction of new technology in development, production and marketing was often seen as the possible cure for all these woes by manufacturers, but soon it became clear that this, of itself, was not enough. Such major changes in the business environment necessitated important adjustments not only in technology but also in management styles, organizational structures and social systems.

New Corporate Capabilities
Although we have taken as our example the changes in the business environment of consumer goods, similar increases in customer demands have been occurring in a wide variety of markets both in the industrial and service areas. The systems and ways of working which were successful in the 'production push' period, when customers were hungry for goods, are no longer fit to cope with for ever upward spiralling demands for product variety, reliability and quality.

Many long-established and previously highly successful practices had to be changed (Table 1).

Table 1. The evolution of effective approaches to quality improvement

Was effective	Current
☆ Partial improvement approach per business function	☆ Interrelated improvement approach per business process
☆ Quality improvement efforts concentrate on production	☆ Quality improvements efforts throughout all areas of the business
☆ Quality: responsibility of specialist function	☆ Quality: responsibility of line management
☆ Improvement mainly through experts	☆ Improvement through involving all employees
☆ Inspection to correct mistakes made	☆ Prevention designed into product, service and process
☆ Complex control systems	☆ Stimulation of self regulation
☆ Standardized repetitive tasks	☆ Experiments with enlarged individual responsibility
☆ Suppliers chosen on basis of narrow range of criteria	☆ Suppliers chosen on basis of wide range of criteria
☆ Contract based relationship with many suppliers	☆ Co-makership agreements with selected suppliers

Management has realized that it has to take a clear lead in directing the organization in the quest for quality of performance. It is the people in the organization that make the vital difference. And to move into new patterns of working, management has to express and practice the new values which it believes will lead to the development of new capabilities.

Changing company cultures unfortunately cannot be learned only from books. There are no standard techniques for overall application. The procedure manuals have still to be written. The process has to start at the top and work its way slowly and thoroughly right down through the organization. This process takes time, dedication and persistence.

Company-Wide Quality Improvement at Philips

Philips is a large, diverse and complex company. It operates within many different national environments with a great variety of product/market combinations and thus a great diversity of customer circumstances (Table 2).

During the late 1970s and early 1980s awareness was growing that new initiatives would have to be taken

A case: the birth of a new business group

In the early 1980s one of Philips' Business Groups was facing major problems. Many of their products were outdated and market share was declining. There was talk of removing some of the business to other units and as a result, morale amongst the employees was poor.

In 1982 a major change process was started. Structural measures were taken to shape the Business Group into a more self-contained organization encompassing ownership of all necessary functions. Markets were thoroughly investigated, the necessary financial investments were made and development of new products started. Despite this new approach there remained a high degree of scepticism amongst many of the employees. The whole culture of the organization had to be seen to change, and to help this process, employees were kept fully informed every fortnight on production, sales, market movements and competitive developments. Then management formed groups from the next two hierarchical levels to assist them in developing business plans. Next, at a meeting attended by everyone, all were asked to say what their major problems were with working in the Group. From this list the 'top ten most important' problems were identified. And during the next 6 months priority was given to ensuring their solution. By this means trust in management and staff was revived. At the same time as these changes were being implemented, a structured total improvement plan was developed. This plan addressed basic issues like quality, reliability and flexibility, and was discussed with all employees. Their suggestions were then incorporated and put into action. As a result a wide variety of operational improvements covering work stations, routing, lay-out, procedures and organization of the work flow were achieved.

Within 2 years product quality has increased such that customer complaints have become almost non-existent. And today, each and every complaint is addressed with top priority throughout the organization. Production throughput time and thus 'response to market' time has been reduced from 6 weeks to a few days, and the production area is now capable of producing any sales order within a few weeks.

As a result, efficiency has been improved and customers have regained confidence in the products. Prices have been reduced, market share has risen and the Group has become profitable once more. The original goals of the change programme were to improve quality, reliability and flexibility. The result was increased efficiency and thus the opportunity both to lower prices and yet to increase profits, and hence to ensure continuity, which is the ultimate objective of any improvement activity.

Table 2. Some facts about Philips (1985)

Sales: U.S. Dollars	24 billion	
Fields of activity:	(as a percentage of total turnover)	
	Lighting	12·4%
	Consumer electronics	26·3%
	Domestic appliances	10·3%
	Professional products and systems	27·8%
	Components	18·1%
	Miscellaneous	5·1%
Employees: 345,000		
National organizations in approximately 60 countries		
420 factories throughout the world		

in order to keep the company up amongst the world leaders. From the late 1970s onwards more and more information became available from internal change projects which were enabling differing parts of the organization to adjust successfully to the new business environment. In addition, information about approaches taken in other organizations and careful competitive analysis clarified the picture still further (Table 3).

Table 3. Characteristics of the new road to success

- ☆ The drive for absolute customer satisfaction
- ☆ The need for management to take full responsibility in leading the quality improvement movement
- ☆ The need for the integration of functional capabilities in a total approach with clearly set priorities
- ☆ The need for involvement of all employees, functions and suppliers

In 1983 these internal and external signals were brought together by the Board of Management, and resulted in a policy statement issued by the President in October 1983. He stated that: 'The quality of products and services is of the utmost importance for the continuity of our company' and continued: 'The Board of Management has decided to give vigorous direction to a Company-wide approach to quality improvement'. He went on to outline the major elements of the new quality policy. This statement was sent to all senior executives of the company who were shortly afterwards invited to attend seminars where the message was further elaborated and discussed. During the seminars the Board of Management asked all senior executives to communicate the message to their own organizations and to personally start a change process along the lines indicated.

The Approach

In such a complex company careful consideration had to be given to the question of how far the new approach should be centrally prescribed in a standard format or how much freedom should be allowed for local initiative and adaptation. It was decided that all units should start from the corporate policy statement issued in October 1983 and from the basic principles discussed during the seminars (see Table 4).

Existing management reporting systems would be used to monitor progress and to give new impulses where needed. However, within these boundary conditions, local management was free to develop its own approach, using local resources as far as possible. The whole company thus entered an era of intensive 'learning by experimentation'. To foster local initiatives a central resource team was set up to

Table 4. Company-Wide Quality Improvement principles

(1) Customer satisfaction
A perfect interface must be achieved between company performance and customer needs in all aspects that customers consider to be important.

(2) Leadership
Quality improvement is primarily a task and responsibility of management as a whole.

(3) Total involvement
There must be total involvement of all employees at all levels and in all functions. Equally important is the complete involvement of all suppliers of goods and services.

(4) Integrated approach
Integration must be achieved between functions and between levels. Traditional organizational barriers must be removed.

(5) Systematic approach
A systematic approach must start with a clearly defined business strategy which is then translated into an improvement policy, objectives and priorities. These must be followed by detailed planning, implementation and monitoring of progress.

(6) Defect prevention
Defects must be prevented from occurring. Performance must be the result of built-in capabilities.

(7) Continuous improvement
The approach should not have the character of a campaign or a project. Excellence can only be achieved by continuously investing in improvement, step-by-step, year after year.

(8) Maximum quality
Long-term objectives must be set which reflect the will to strive for excellence. The path towards excellence must be marked by challenging but achievable and acceptable targets.

(9) Education and training
Widespread attention will be given to education and training. A new work culture can only be realized if all people are more than ever prepared to make their contribution.

provide support through consultancy and information dissemination and to help encourage the growth of networks of managers and specialists. The creation of such networks, it was hoped, would intensify and accelerate the exchange of local experience and knowledge.

Five Main Activities
In all approaches five main activities involved in bringing about change have been utilized (Figure 2).

It is possible to start the process with any of the five activities, depending on the specific circumstances and wishes of the units concerned, and thence to proceed in any order, but eventually all five activities have to be worked through; because only then will all facets of the change process have been covered. Only then will the changes be really embedded in the organization.

All these five activities must be worked through within the organization level after level, in a vertically linked process. Corporate improvement policy must be split down into policies for specific product divisions and national organizations, and these must be further translated into improvement policies for particular business groups and then finally for each individual operational unit. Activities at any one level must dovetail into the levels both above and below.

Results

Once a year a major evaluation is carried out for the Board of Management of the progress which has been achieved. Two and a half years after the official start, results are promising. Significant performance improvements have already been achieved, some of which, of course, are the results of initiatives taken well before October 1983. Improvements have been achieved in many different performance areas including throughput times, service respond times, system reliability, accounting reporting dates, stock levels, product call-rate, accuracy of files and documents and reachability (see Table 5).

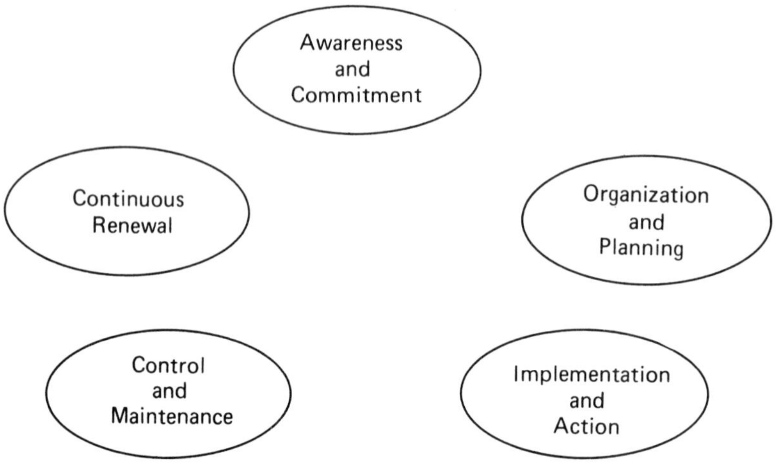

Figure 2. The five main activities involved in bringing about change

Table 5. Some examples of results

Typical measures	Typical improvements 1983	1984	1985
Development throughput time	18 months	18 months	15 months
Outgoing defect level	3%	2%	0·2%
Number of approved suppliers	0	0	10
Change-over time in production	1 hour	1 hour	5 min
Stock level (as % of turnover)	15 days	9 days	6 days
Fall off rate	25%	20%	9%
% Errors in invoicing	6%	4·3%	2·3%

*In a credit control area the percentage of overdues as % of total debt decreased from 23% in 1981 via 16% in 1983 to 13% in 1985.

*The Q-factor indicating the absence of defects in the operational process of a computer centre increased in 1 year from 92% to the targetted value of 98%.

*Implementation of a CWQI-programme in a Commercial Department decreased sales costs within 2 years by nearly 30%.

Essentials for a Learning Process

This is only the start of a long-term learning programme. There are three essentials for a successful organizational learning process. The learning must be seen to be legitimate, possible to achieve and worth achieving. All three are built into the programme. The issue of legitimacy has been achieved by choosing, from the beginning, a top-down strategy and making it quite clear that management at all levels regarded Company-Wide Quality Improvement as a top priority matter. Secondly, through holding up examples of successful programmes in comparative organizations, both within and without Philips, it is emphasized how it is possible for any unit, in any situation, to start improving their quality performance. To this end many different forms of communication are used ranging from laservision to a common logo and newsletters, from video tapes to internal discussion forums or informal get-togethers.

It is hardly necessary, in a well-run organization, to point out that quality improvement is worth achieving. However, in addition to this natural desire to succeed, through the introduction of a Philips Quality Award system, management teams are given something extra at which to aim. Competition to show excellence, compared to ones peers, is highly motivating. Such quality awards not only provide a little extra spice to normal day-to-day working, but they also make clear the standards towards which to aim and give clear unambiguous feedback to all involved of their progress (see Figure 3).

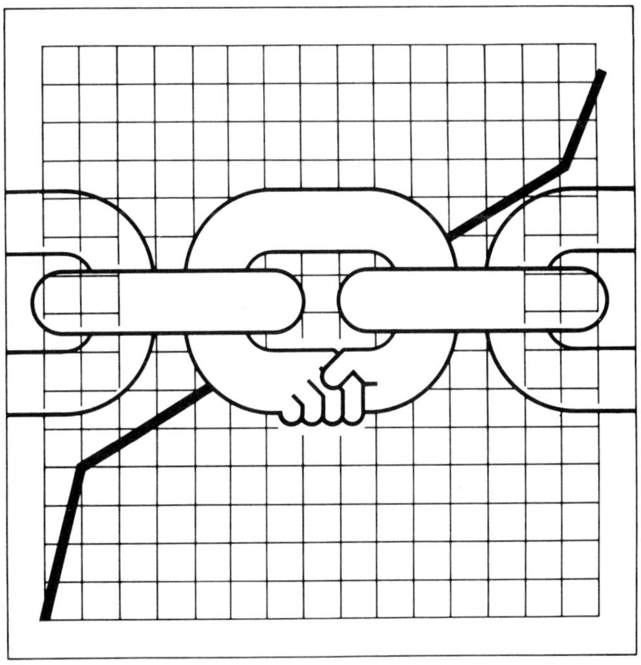

Figure 3. The Company-Wide Quality Improvement logo

Evaluation and Conclusion

In the past years awareness of the need for quality improvement and knowledge on how to manage improvement programmes has been communicated through over 250 awareness and commitment seminars to well over 15,000 managers. By now structured programmes are running in more than 150 organizational units, together employing more than 60,000 people. These units not only include production facilities but also sales groups, supporting functions and administrative departments. In evaluating what has been learnt to date the following conclusions can be drawn:

☆ The top-down cascade model has proven to be successful in spreading awareness and commitment. It is not a once-and-for all-input by top management. Rather it requires their continued attention at regular intervals in order to maintain momentum, especially if there are to be clear and lasting changes in company values.

☆ Management ownership of the programme is a basic condition for success. Best results are achieved in those places where managers lead improvement programmes from personal conviction. One of the worst things which may happen is a manager delegating responsibility for the programme to a specialist.

☆ Involvement of all organization members is crucial if improvement is ever to become a routine part of every day life, but this is not easy to achieve. It must come from personal example and commitment. For example, if involvement is forced upon supervisory management, it may well become a mere window-dressing exercise and thus fail and be difficult to repair.

☆ There must be consistency between what management says and what management does. People will not believe in the importance of new values unless their application is demonstrated by the hierarchy.

☆ Small-scale improvement is relatively easy to achieve. Merely focusing management's attention on this area will achieve a few percentages points improvement. On the other hand breakthroughs in performance can only be realized by breakthroughs in traditional habits. These take time, dedication and persistence and can lead to frustration. Some of our organizations are disappointed that, even after 2 years, breakthroughs are not yet in sight. This necessitates continuous encouragement by management. Perseverence can also be helped by the knowledge that other, eventually successful, breakthroughs have also often taken so long.

☆ Market performance evidence seems to be the only argument which convinces managers to spend time and energy on a total quality programme. If this evidence is lacking or if it is not hard enough, organizations may go through the motions, but will not take the difficult decisions needed for breakthrough.

☆ There is indeed no standard way, no recipe which guarantees success. Many quality improvement packages are available for the market. Philips has by now experience with most of them. The conclusion is that such programmes can help in starting up the change process, but units then have to be able to 'personalize' the package in some way and to develop their own skills and resources, if they are to maintain the momentum.

Company-Wide Quality Improvement is a programme of strategic significance. It helps management to build up the capabilities needed to obtain an improved position in the market place.

Bibliography

For more detailed comment, on the general issue of developments in manufacturing industry see:

P. T. Bolwijn and T. Kumpe, Towards the factory of the future, *The McKinsey Quarterly,* Spring, pp. 40–49 (1986).

P. T. Bolwijn *et al., Flexible Manufacturing: Integrating Technological and Social Innovation,* Elsevier, Amsterdam (1986).

For more detail concerning the general Philips approach see:

C. J. van Ham, Company-Wide Quality Improvement. New ways to involvement and co-operation, *Proceedings of the 8th Annual Industrial Engineering Managers Seminar,* Institution of Industrial Engineers, Washington D.C. (1986).

For information on other companies' approaches see:

Y. K. Shetty and V. M. Buehler, *Productivity and Quality Through People,* Quorum, Westport (1985).

Planning for a Rapidly Changing Environment in SAS

Olle Stiwenius, Senior Consultant, SAS Management Consultants, Sweden

The author describes how Scandinavian Airlines achieved a turnaround from unprofitability and loss of market share. The creation and development of a corporate culture revitalized personnel and initiated a new management role, business-oriented rather than administrative. Punctuality became a specific goal and won for SAS the reputation of being Europe's most punctual airline. The change process is likely to continue into the future and the new internal management systems will change to meet these needs.

The dramatic turnaround of SAS probably owes more to changes in people and organization than to anything else. There is no doubt that the changes in profitability are exciting. However, once we have carefully studied the annual reports they are merely historic facts. The major transformation was from a production-oriented airline to a market-oriented service company. The management of SAS realized they had to become customer-oriented—simply to start working as a service company. One of our directors pointed out that 'the battle for the air will have to be fought on the ground'. The change has also emphasized the role of the manager in corporate renewal and the adoption of an explicit business philosophy in order to gain commitment and involvement.

Something had Happened Out There

For a long time SAS had lived in a steadily growing market very much protected by the international air line agreements. The business was managed to profitability by generally economizing and reciprocally dividing the markets.

As the market grew 'automatically' we were simply taking orders. Profitability was reached by keeping down costs and protecting our investments in aeroplanes and other assets. And we did very good business, focusing on technical improvements and selling our aircraft—very successfully (Figure 1).

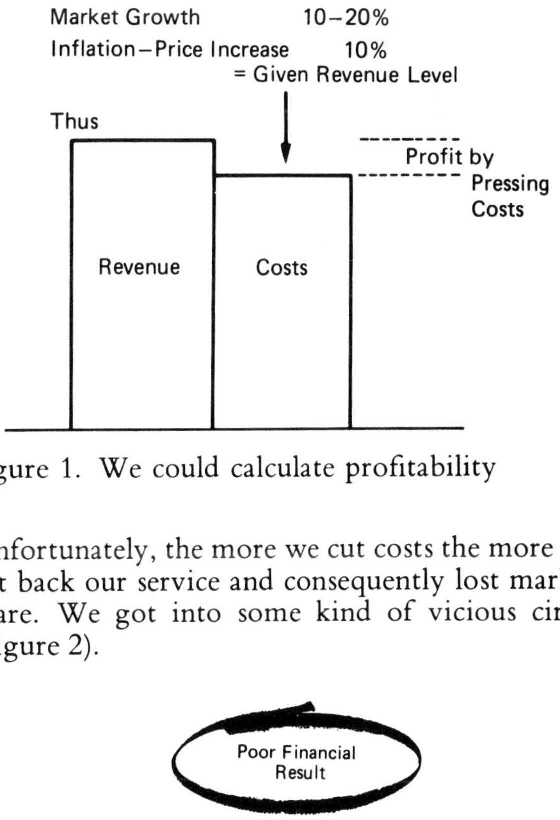

Figure 1. We could calculate profitability

Unfortunately, the more we cut costs the more we cut back our service and consequently lost market share. We got into some kind of vicious circle (Figure 2).

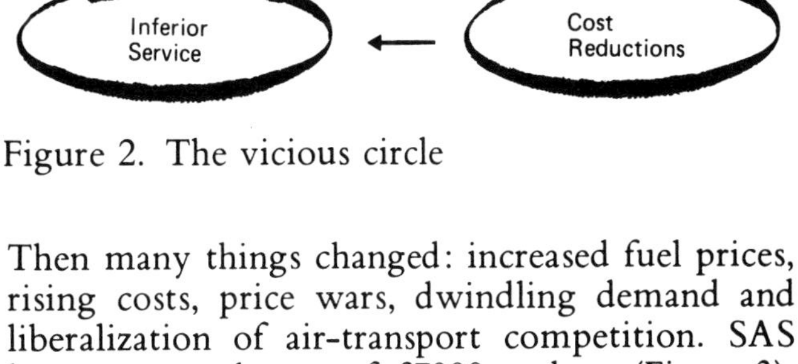

Figure 2. The vicious circle

Then many things changed: increased fuel prices, rising costs, price wars, dwindling demand and liberalization of air-transport competition. SAS lost money at the rate of £7000 per hour (Figure 3).

The author is Senior Consultant, SAS Management Consultants, Sweden.

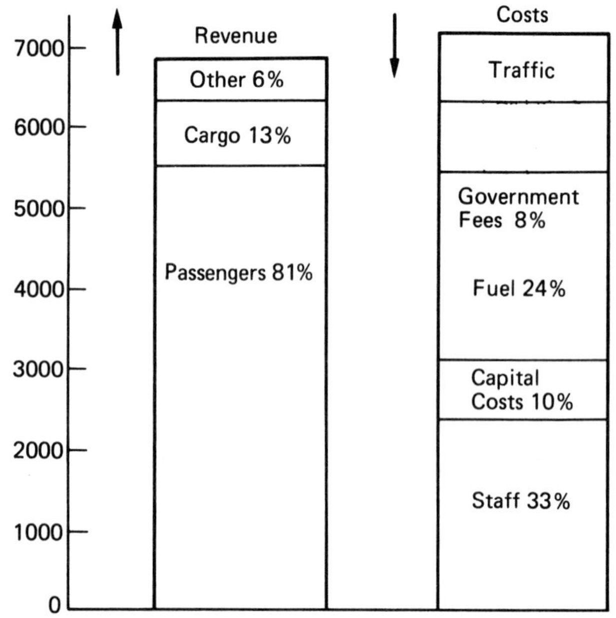

Figure 3. Revenues and costs 1980/1981

It became apparent that a competitive market called for an entirely new corporate philosophy, and our deteriorating service was having disastrous consequences.

Now, an airline like business can adapt to any level of market-share, but cannot live on with a falling trend. So we had to make a quick pull-up and to work together on becoming the world's best service airline. To master the accelerating deficits, caused by the vicious circle, we had to act and act fast (Figure 4).

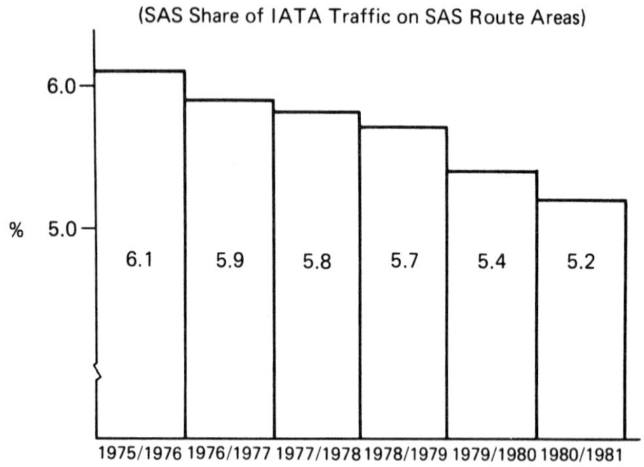

Figure 4. SAS market share

Influence on Organizational Culture

The aim was to adapt to the market preferences. This meant that we had to become attractive to our passengers by meeting their demands.

As our President pointed out

> We can have as many beautiful aircraft as we like and still not survive if we don't have passengers who would rather fly SAS than our competitors.
>
> Because the only ones who are willing to pay our cost next year are the satisfied customers of today

This also meant that we had to look upon our costs as a potential basis for income and to generate income by market-orientation.

Obviously the staff closest to the market tend to notice market-changes first, but our organization was not arranged to pick up the signals fast enough. Thus we might have been a bit late in adapting to the new environment.

The major reason for our former slowness was unquestionably that we had put too many restrictions on the behaviour of our front line employees, who account for roughly 50 per cent of our personnel. Living by the detailed rules and regulations did not allow our 'front soldiers' to give the service our customers demanded.

Who is in the best situation to adapt to the market's needs? Who has the most frequent contacts? Who is able to initiate better service and who knows the market's need the best? The Front Line of course!

With our 'Front line personnel' we already had all the knowledge we always tried to buy in market surveys. So we 'classified' all other human resources as 'support troops' or 'support functions', who are supposed to look upon the 'Front line' as their primary customer.

These basic circumstances called for a reorganization in order to achieve the greatest possible market contact and the greatest possible delegation of responsibility and authority to the 'Front line'.

In fact, no instructions or regulations whatsoever, could possibly 'direct' our annual 40–100 million individual passenger contacts to create customer satisfaction. It called for an entirely new view on 'the customer in focus' (Figure 5).

Towards a New Corporate Philosophy

The SAS turnaround had to be directed towards the reality that the only thing that counts in a service company is a satisfied customer.

Our company's philosophy and its organizational structure were based on the same prevailing ideas as industrial society. It was created to satisfying growing market needs by effective use of production resources, i.e. primarily managing investing capital—to keep installations profitable.

Many corporate reorganizations during the 1970s tried to bring about profitability by planning from their own production resources out to the market (Why don't they buy our super-product?). All

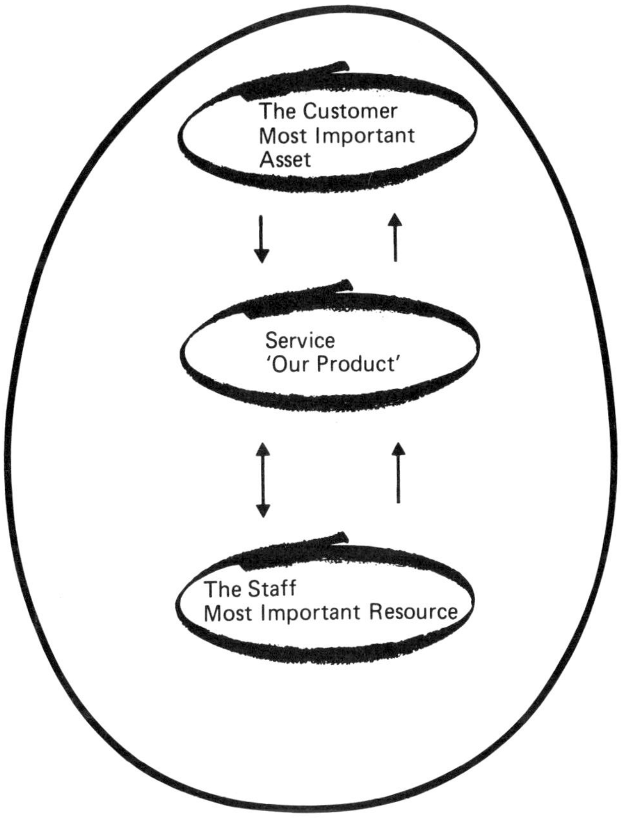

Figure 5. SAS concept

business education aimed at handling cost-cutting programmes, and the salesman's job was just to sell what the company produced.

SAS also fell into that trap. Specialist functions and specialists were created for every conceivable task—functional organizations were supposed to look after the assets, but rather they tended to preserve the investments already made. And manuals were produced abundantly with the aim of making us produce even more effeciently. The bitter truth however was that we were putting more and more restrictions on our employees' methods of working (Figure 6).

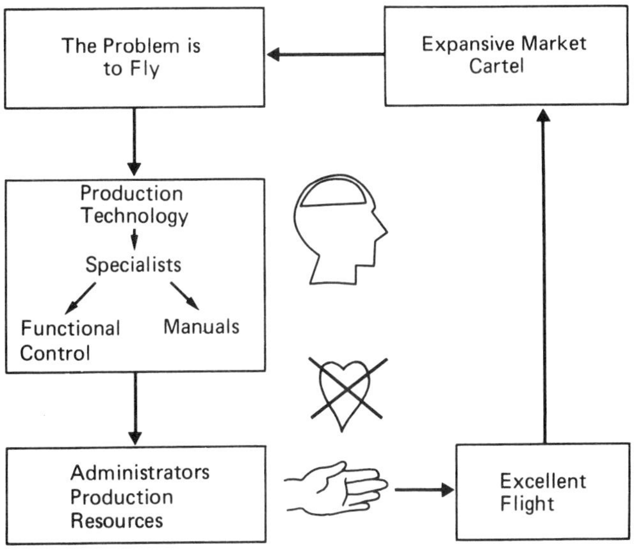

Figure 6. Old SAS

This belief in one 'right' course of action worked very well for a long time. But looking around in the world of uncertain income SAS management realized we had to start with the market, not with our resources. Product development and planning called for reversing our strategic approach.

As the growth in sales slowed down we started to look upon market development as our major challenge (Figure 7).

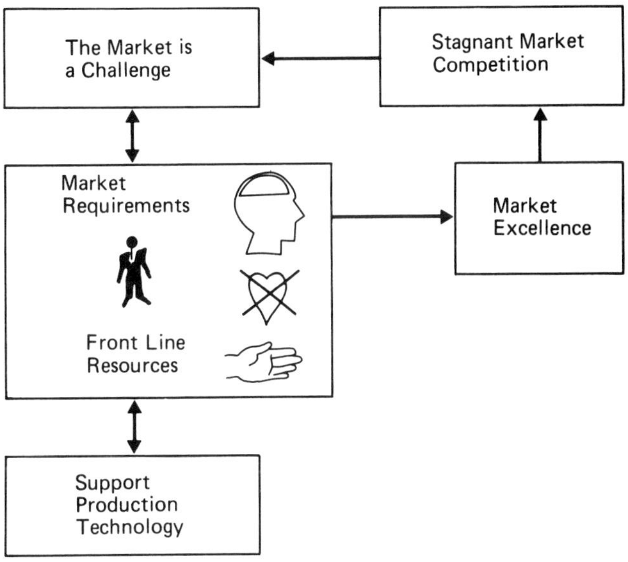

Figure 7. New SAS

Our strategic decision thus became firstly, an offensive directed towards market-segments we singled out. And secondly, we marshalled our resources to the needs of those markets, i.e. strengthening the 'Front Line'. Our corporate philosophy was reformulated thus:

> In a stagnating market, where competitive forces are set free, a company can achieve profitability only by adjusting and aggressively investing to meet customer needs better than the competition.

SAS Enters 'The Virtuous Circle'

One of the basic facts in business is that a deficit will arise if costs are higher than revenues. So to reverse the situation, you either have to reduce the costs or increase your income.

SAS decided to do both at the same time.

Our strategy meant that we had to bring our resources into line with their revenue-making potential. In other words simply cutting costs across the board would not be the solution to meet customer needs. Our President gave an expressive illustration of this, pointing out that:

> you have to set a car moving before you apply the brakes. Otherwise no other change may occur but the obvious risk that you may step through the floor and damage the car.

In practice we worked hard on helping our staff to understand what they should expect. The entire change process was supported by clear and simple information (brochures, videotapes, debates, in-house magazines, etc.) on our course of action. The introductory information on our new strategies was published in a brochure called 'Let's get in there and fight'.

This communication produced an increase in motivation, like all understanding does, and this was further reinforced by 'service-training'. Our third basis for the virtuous circle was an extensive management training programme to increase the organization's ability to act according to our new philosophy.

In short we created consciousness, knowledge and desire to change to the new approach.

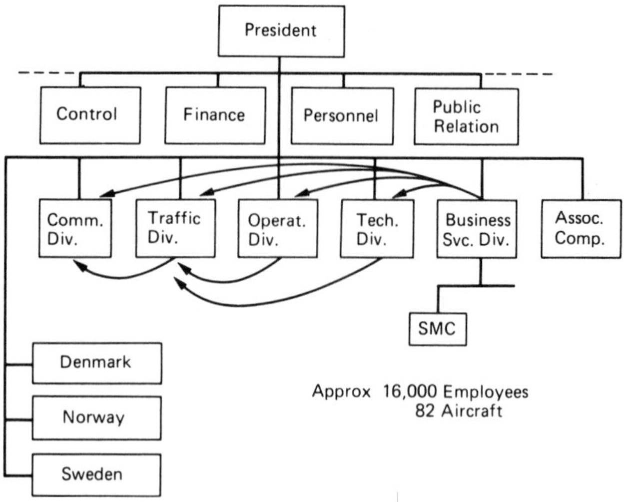

Figure 8. SAS organizations

Organizational Structure and Service Management

We had to adjust our organization to the fact that income is created by offering the customers those products they are prepared to pay for (basics in a market-orientated organization as opposed to a technology- and production-orientated one). Clearly, market segmentation is nothing new. On the contrary, it seems so evident that many industries have overlooked it in their struggle for production efficiency.

In the case of SAS we created the 'businessman's airline', in which we offered the business traveller a product to suit their needs.

Now, what about the costs? Certainly we focused on those as well, but we decentralized the initiative to managers closer to the market than our head-office. And this is where the service concept is so important.

Costs are largely incurred in the 'delivery system' of a company's structure, i.e. primarily in the human resources. We realized we had to improve our performance in these areas, to the concept of service, where you engage yourself in solving the customer's problems.

So we moved staff from the back office to more needed functions closer to the customer/passenger, to provide peripheral services (booking, checking, waiting, comfort, attentiveness, etc.) in the front line 'delivery-system' and we trained them for the new tasks.

We are now organized in relatively small, result-oriented and independent functions. We have discarded the old military organization where hierarchies tend to disrupt the communication patterns, thus delaying vital decisions close to the customer/passenger (Figure 8).

Strengthened Market-Organization

The new SAS organization is adjusted to market-demand and based on wide spread delegation. It could be viewed as a wheel, where the customer/passenger constitutes the hub.

This kind of structure encourages the customer-orientation and flexibility. It opens up possibilities for competent personnel to develop quickly and take responsibility for results without direct supervision. The organization form also emphasizes communication, co-operation and co-ordination. And it is supported by a very ambitious programme of personnel and management development.

The Significance of SAS 'Cultural Patterns'

A corporate culture is the pattern of habits, goals, concepts, ideas and behaviour that are found within a company. It is strongly influenced by the formulas which management develops to the benefit of the company. In a successful enterprise the culture reflects the market situation. It develops differently in a situation of growth than in a stagnating market.

Thus, the corporate culture should harmonize with the commercial environment. When this changes, the culture has to change as well, if the company is to survive.

This change took place and is still taking place in SAS. In fact our organizational market-orientation meant a new Corporate Culture. We believe that in order to maintain SAS as an excellent service company we have to have the same basic values shared among all our staff. We are convinced that a satisfied customer continues to fly SAS rather than simply to fly, and is therefore the result of a market investment. Our values also suppose that customers want to be treated as individuals, they want personal service, to feel at home and to be taken care of by SAS.

We have described this culture by concluding that 'SAS lives with its customers' and 'a satisfied customer is our only real asset'. We also try to treat our own staff as individuals. We have created a culture where our customer is in the centre and creates opportunities for individual initiative and commitment that invests in market segments and 'backs winners'.

Open Attitudes

A major transformation calls for radical structural and cultural changes. And changing an obsolete success formula, deeply embedded in the minds of key company personnel, also calls for strong action. Probably, before meaningful changes can be carried through, it is imperative to demonstrate dramatically that the former, well-proven formulas are no longer valid.

The SAS way of doing this has been to provide generous and open information to create new attitudes towards the customer and to colleagues. For example the consequences of market orientation had to be clearly formulated and communicated. The new SAS philosophy states that 'change is a condition for survival and thus provides security'. So we focused very much on our view that the only way to survive is through a continuous process of change in people and organization.

We also made it our responsibility to give information fast, and to back it up with concrete initiatives. As we openly declared that 'our staff is our foremost resource' we made it our policy that 'everyone is responsible for making sure that we have satisfied customers' and 'seek the information you need so that you can assume your responsibility'.

When Something Goes Wrong . . .

There are always reasons when things go wrong. But we made it acceptable to risk mistakes. One of our most important messages from Management was that 'Mistakes can be corrected, but lost time can never be regained'. So we had to allow our staff to make decisions so that the customer's needs were satisfied immediately. The normal procedure would be *not* to refer the matter to a superior, who primarily has a supporting function and the responsibility to develop the quality of staff.

In the 'New SAS' the philosophy is rather to allow oneself a few misses now and then by testing new ideas instead of spending excessive time to be absolutely certain that the decision will be a complete success.

When things go wrong, information must immediately be given, internally and externally, explaining what has gone wrong.

The reasons why the problem occurred and the current position must be clearly formulated. The opposite, to emphasize uncertainty by total silence, will only result in confusion, scepticism and irritation. This is the core of SAS's new, open attitude.

New Supervision and Leadership

To focus so much on the employee requires supervision and leadership to support those who provide the customer-service. It also requires that product planning and the product itself are arranged so that the contact between personnel and passengers is positive.

All the components work upon each other, thus enabling every employee to provide a service to the individual customer/passenger, which creates positive feelings—the 'Moment of Truth' for SAS.

New Goals and Strategies

To support the individual in his decisions, our philosophy includes providing goals and strategies that are so easy to understand that all staff can help according to their abilities. The framework, set by management, has to allow our departments to change operations on the basis of market demand instead of keeping to detailed internal requirements. Thus, during the change process we have lived roughly with only one goal:

> to create such a profit by 1990 that we can favourably finance the need for new aircraft by then.

And we regard all costs as potential resources for the market. Even our own support functions have defined their 'internal markets', because services produced internally have 'buyers', who can define their need, volume, quality, etc. just like other purchasers (Figure 9).

Our main strategy is to develop 'The business traveller's airline', and as many resources as possible were directed towards this task. We also produced complementary strategies like marginal-, concentration-trading- and transformation-strategies. Of these none was allowed to influence our 'Main strategy'. Thus everybody was focused on serving our business travellers in all situations.

The Change

The most important feature of our transition was maybe the strategy of speed. The organizational restructuring was carried through in approximately 5 months. It was probably our 'crisis-awareness'

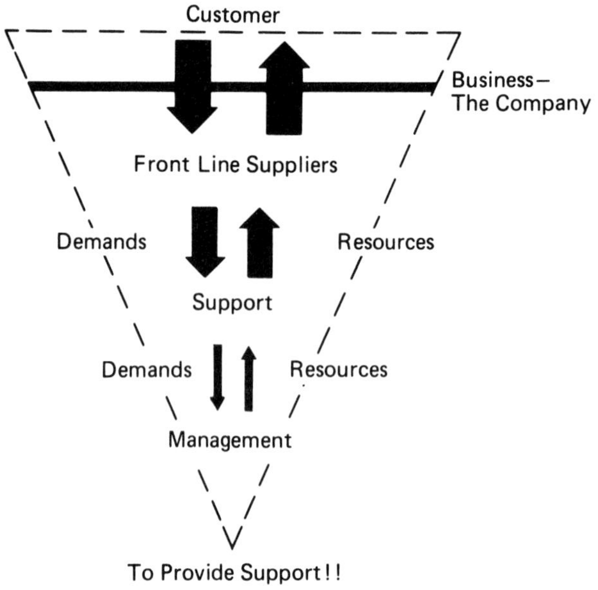

Figure 9. What is the purpose of the 'organization'?

that triggered the start. Everyone came to understand that our heavy deficits called for something to be done. Thus all of the staff wanted to change things (Figure 10).

Also, the direction of change was carefully communicated. At an early stage we gathered around the slogan: 'Let's get in there and fight', which clearly pointed out our strategy. It was formulated in a booklet sent to each employee's home which outlined SAS's goals, philosophy and course of development.

Popularly it was referred to as 'Carlzon's Little Red Book' and it was very helpful for working out decentralized strategies and change-programmes, which were achieved within 2 months.

One of the most interesting messages our President presented was 'to become 1 per cent better in a hundred details rather than 100 per cent better in one detail'. The change was heavily supported with an extensive information-plan, internally, to help the staff to understand what was happening and to encourage them to participate in changing their way of working.

Creation of Credibility

To build up a belief in communication a detailed programme of activities was worked out and carried through.

To realize our business strategies we invested $20m in 150 projects to become more customer-orientated, like e.g. 'business-traveller's airline, Euroclass and First business class'. This orientation towards market potential involved most of our staff in work to create 'a new SAS' instead of becoming too problem-oriented.

Simultaneously we carried through a comprehensive Management Development programme for approximately 2000 'key-persons' among upper and middle management. And in addition we offered all our 10,000 front line staff a 2-day course in 'Personal Service through personal development'. There is no doubt that this programme brought about a remarkable change in attitudes among our employees.

Emphasis on Training

The reason for the SAS success is that we were able, through training and combined information efforts, to create a new, creative and market-sensitive 'climate'. Our organization with very

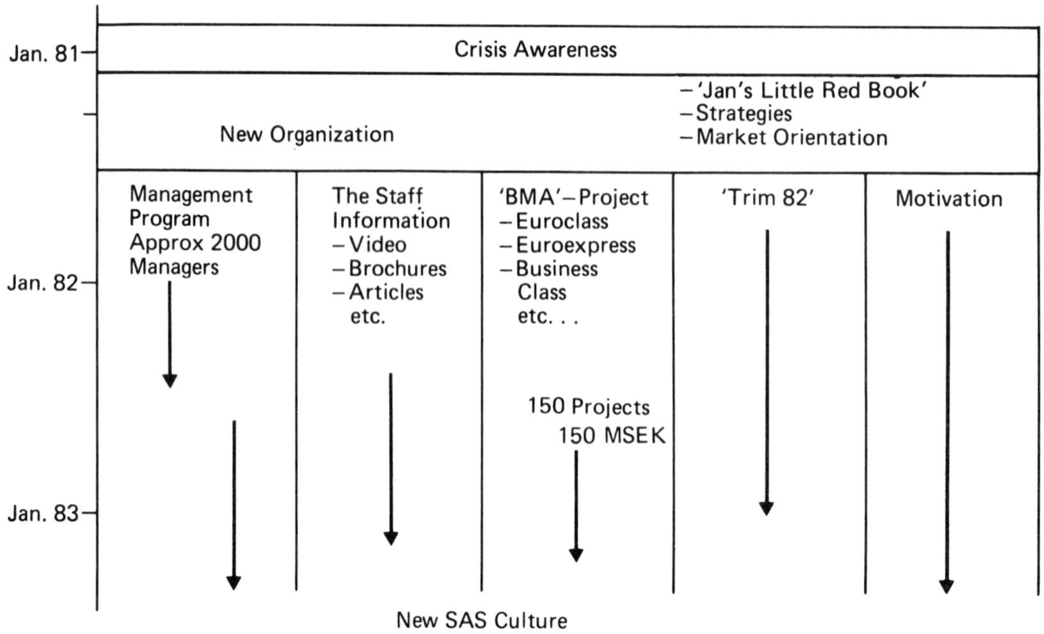

Figure 10. Plan of activities for the SAS change

open channels for communication has become more venturesure through this intensive programme of spreading our philosophy.

The basic programme has now been completed by bringing more middle managers, supervisors and foremen into training. As everything is aimed at changing our 'corporate culture' the subjects have included strategy finance and service management.

Market-Value Analysis

A vital element in the change-process was to relate resources to needs. This was carried through in the form of a decentralized value/activity–analysis, performed by each new division.

By holding a serious discussion between internal service functions (support-functions) and the receivers of this support (mainly front line personnel) we were able to define our 'over-capacity', i.e. services nobody was prepared to pay for. As a consequence these resources were transferred to other activities, where a shortage of resources could be found. This strengthened the front line organization by offering better service to our 'key-staff', meeting our customers in numerous 'moments of truth'.

New Management Role

This also means that a completely new management role has been recognized in SAS, that is the task of maintaining the continued development of our 'Corporate Culture', where will-power, energy and ability to push through a new policy might be decisive for success or failure (Figure 11).

From	To
Production Orientation	Marketing Orientation
Cost Responsibility	Result Responsibility
Centralization	Decentralization
Administrators	Businessmen
Instruction	Information
Force	Freedom
Reaction	Action
Problem	Possibility

Figure 11

It requires a business-oriented and participative leadership to imbue a team-spirit and to revitalize personnel attitudes. Thus management must be supportive and inspirational, setting goals and guidelines and delegating operational responsibility in a strong and clear manner.

In addition there is a strong emphasis on being result-orientated, where it is the result which is assessed and judged rather than the course of action that led up to the result.

In this result-orientated organization, department heads are expected to be businessmen rather than administrators, to cause action instead of reaction and to give information rather than instructions.

In other words the new leadership in SAS means that a manager's primary responsibility is to develop the quality of his or her staff.

The Future

We are pretty sure that our markets will undergo substantial changes in the future and that these changes will occur very swiftly. We also recognize that it is frequently difficult for existing management to review an earlier market-situation and radically question, re-orientate or reject former activities. Therefore we will probably be faced with the continuous re-organization of our business in order to formulate new demands, new goals, a new management philosophy and new strategies to achieve these goals.

We must also be prepared to draw up new internal management systems to change our company's culture and revise the modes of thinking among 'key personnel'.

Such changes are already taking place. We are now organizing for a 'Total Travel and Service concept' in order to adapt to new market requirements, and the change process goes on, or rather a new one is already emerging.

So, now that we have been successful in making a quick pull-up, we are building for the 1990s.

Leadership
No doubt the turnaround of SAS has been greatly inspired by the new type of leadership that Jan Carlzon represents. Some key characteristics could be noted:

- ☆ SAS staff at an early stage were made aware of the clear vision of the future that our President held, i.e. ideas about probable changes in the market-situation.
- ☆ He believes in the individual's ability to take on greater responsibilities given the opportunities.

This is of course a supportive management philosophy, executed by Mr. Carlzon and many others which clearly challenges people to be more adventurous and entrepreneurial.

- ☆ He has communicated very skilfully during the entire change. In a very simple and understandable manner our weak and strong points have been described. And through visual communication our staff has been encouraged to handle the business in an unorthodox way.
- ☆ Knowledge is also vital to carry through major changes. As Mr. Carlzon had experience of managing a successful domestic airline—and other travel businesses—he could act very confidently and this gave other people confidence in carrying out his decisions.

Changing the Corporate Image

The actual change in SAS service was quickly noticed by our passengers and aroused much interest from the media. Also our image as 'the businessman's airline' was projected in a number of brochures and advertisments, distributed to our customers and to our own staff. The distribution was based on the idea that 'you should not inform your customers better than your own employees'.

The presentation of the company's image is so vital in a change process that SAS management decided to change the firm's 'brand image'. We changed our logotype, colours, uniforms and made a complete redesign of our aircraft and office interiors. Not only did this signal an important change in the eyes of customers and employees, it was also intended to prolong the economic life-time of our assets.

We chose 'punctuality' for special attention as a central part of our image. For an airline employee 'punctuality' is the one thing everyone can easily do something about. Our President put up a TV monitor in his office so at any time of the day or night he could check our punctuality. And he had this particular priority projected to customers and employees. Thus we could all see how important 'punctuality' was to the new SAS.

The Role of Project Teams

SAS management believes in the effectiveness of project teams in solving specific problems and consciously uses them in the change process. The best example is probably the goal 'to become the most punctual air line in Europe'. A project team was asked what it would cost SAS to reach that goal. After a short time a comprehensive report was presented. Management, however, was primarily interested in the cost—estimated to some million Swedish kronor. They decided that 'punctuality' was worth that amount, and they gave the project an immediate 'go-ahead'.

In less than 3 months SAS was the most punctual airline in Europe, and our President summarized his conclusion in these words:

> We became Europe's most punctual airline. It didn't cost millions. It cost a fraction of the estimate, and we don't know how the money was spent.

If the project team had been given detailed instructions on how to make the airline more punctual, it would probably have spent the millions to find out they could not carry out the task.

It is this freedom of action which now guides all our project teams at SAS.

The NFC Buy-Out—A New Form of Industrial Enterprise

Sir Peter Thompson, Chairman, National Freight Consortium plc

When the Conservative Government's plans for floating the National Freight Company, Britain's biggest road freight business, on the Stock Exchange were delayed by economic factors, senior management in the business put together a scheme to buy NFC. In what became Britain's largest employee buy-out, with over 10,000 employees and pensioners putting up £6·187m of the purchase price, a new form of industrial enterprise was created. In this article Sir Peter Thompson, leader of the buy-out team and now Chairman of the National Freight Consortium plc, describes the background to the buy-out, the complex financial, legal and communications activities involved, and the way in which employee-involvement has become an integral part of the operation of what has proved to be a commercially successful business providing exceptional returns on investment.

When the employees of National Freight were offered the opportunity to acquire the ownership of their business, in February 1982, by buying shares, we had a vision for the future of the company. As I wrote in the Prospectus at that time, we believed, as we do today, that

> by creating a company controlled and owned mainly by employees, we were launching a new kind of industrial enterprise. We believed that this would help to get rid of the conflicts between management and workers traditional to British industry—the 'us and them' attitude. In its place would be a new attitude of co-operation which should lead to improved efficiency, better prospects for employment and better profitability.

In working hard to put flesh on that vision, we also knew that commercial success was essential—not only to retain the confidence of our investors, most of whom worked in the business, but also to invest in the long-term future of the enterprise and, of course, to reward shareholders for their investment.

Our results for 1983–1984, our third year of operation, demonstrate how successful we have been in building a strong, profitable and expanding business (Table 1). This success has been fuelled by record levels of investment in NFC, but the hidden 'plus factor' has undoubtedly been employee ownership and, here again, we have worked hard to bring as many employees as possible into a share in the ownership—our most recent campaign, in March this year, resulting in a further 3000 members of our staff buying shares.

Employee ownership and professional management have proved a very powerful combination, and there is no question in my mind that a company owned by a large part of its workforce has proved immensely attractive to customers, not only as a concept but also for the expectation of better service from a highly motivated staff. While we are still seeing more buyers than sellers at each of the quarterly share-dealing days in our internal trading system, we are now having to look at the possibility of flotation on the Stock Exchange some time after February 1987—and, most particularly, at whether we can offer an attractive investment opportunity without losing the important advantages which we believe are inherent in our particular form of ownership and control. There is no guarantee that we will float, but I believe we have to offer the present shareholders a choice on which to vote at a future AGM.

Just what have we achieved, and how did we come to buy the business in the first place? Although the answers may not provide a blueprint for others, I think they have a great deal of significance for many parts of British industry—not least in the staff commitment which a real share in the ownership creates.

The Buy-Out

When we bought NFC in 1982, 10,300 employees and pensioners bought shares. Today we have around 16,500 such shareholders—almost all the

Sir Peter Thompson is Chairman of the National Freight Consortium, The Merton Centre, 45 St. Peters Street, Bedford MK40 2UB.

Table 1. How NFC turnover and trading profit have moved in the 3 years since the buy-out

Three-Year Comparisons of NFC Turnover and Trading Profit*

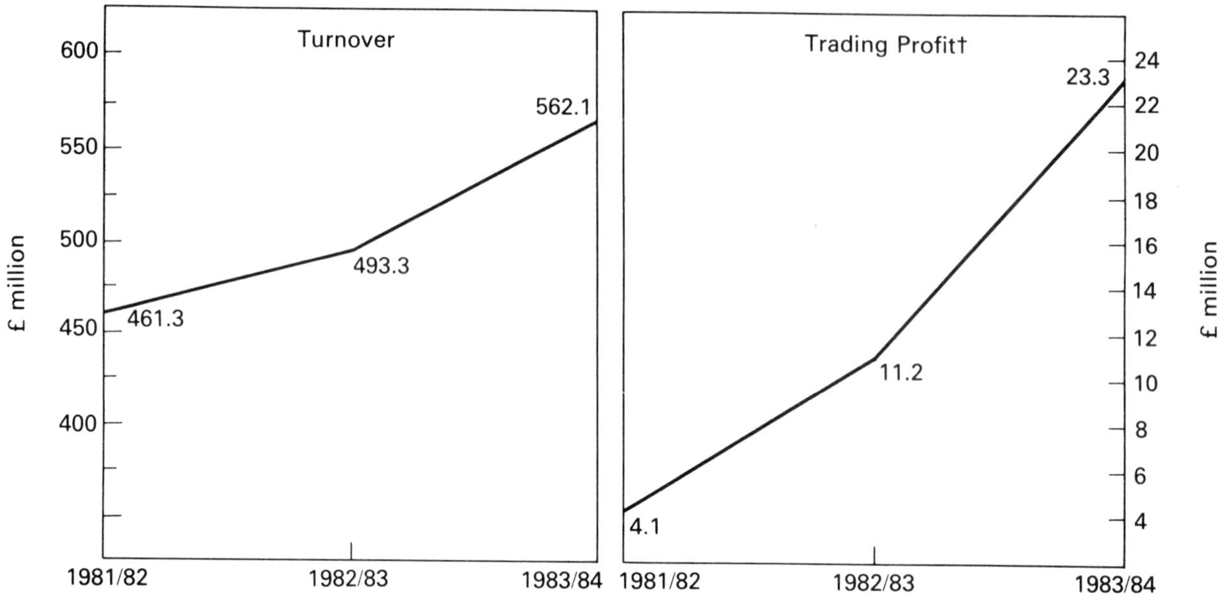

*1981/82 and 82/83 for 52 weeks 1983/84 for 53 weeks.
†Trading profit after deducting redundancy payments. In 1983/84 costs of £1.3m relating to properties held for disposal were charged against profits on disposal of land and buildings. In earlier years such costs were charged in arriving at trading profits.

increase having come from more employees buying into the business. NFC employees, pensioners and their immediate families hold 83 per cent of the equity—the remaining 17 per cent being held by the syndicate of banks which lent us money for the buy-out. Those who bought shares at that first opportunity in 1982 have seen their holdings increase more than 12-fold in value, so even those who bought the minimum of 100 £1 shares have seen that investment grow to £1240. Meanwhile, dividends have increased strongly year on year.

This increase in capital value (established quarterly by chartered accountants Ernst and Whinney, in the absence of a Market quotation) has been well ahead of the FT all-share index and is shown in an accompanying table; so is the growth in dividends. As indicated earlier, the improvement in financial results, which have strongly affected the reward for investors, has come increasingly from a considerable investment programme. For example, in 1983–1984 we committed over £100m to the business—far more than ever before. Much of this was to provide the property, vehicles and equipment to meet customer demand for dedicated distribution and other contract-backed activities. We plan to exceed this level of investment in the current year and have set ourselves a target of over £500m over the next 5 years to support the very strong growth—mainly at home but also overseas—which we are intent on achieving, not least as a basis for improved job opportunities, which we see as particularly important in an employee-owned business.

Dividends paid on NFC shares to date

Date		Dividends paid (net) p	Amount of dividend per original £1 holding p
July 1982	Interim	4·5	4·5
Oct. 1982	Interim	4·5	4·5
March 1983	Final	3·0	3·0
March 1983	Interim	5·0	5·0
May 1983	Interim	5·0	5·0
Aug. 1983	Interim	2·5*	5·0
Nov. 1983	Interim	2·5*	5·0
March 1984	Final	2·0*	4·0
March 1984	Interim	3·0*	6·0
May 1984	Interim	1·5†	6·0
Aug. 1984	Interim	1·5†	6·0
Nov. 1984	Interim	2·8†	11·2
March 1985	Final	0·52‡	10·4
March 1985	Interim	0·56‡	11·2

*Dividend per share after scrip issue.
†Dividend per 50p share.
‡Dividend per 10p share.

Last year for the first time we also covered all our outgoing from trading profit alone, having accepted from the time of the takeover that we would need to rely partly on property sales in the first couple of years. This situation has now changed, as the accompanying financial results table demonstrates (see Table 2): not only have total profits increased very sharply but the quality of those profits has improved, with much the biggest

Table 2. A comparison of the financial results of NFC over the past 2 years (1982–1983 and 1983–1984) shows how a very strong increase in profitability has been accompanied by an improvement in the quality of profit—i.e. more from trading activities and much less from property disposals

How the Consortium Performed

Profit and Loss Account for the year to 6 October 1984	**1983–1984 53 weeks £m**	1982–1983 52 weeks £m	% change
Turnover (sales of services or goods to customers)	**562·1**	493·3	+14
Less: Costs incurred (wages and salaries, hire of vehicles, fuel, licences, maintenance, depreciation, etc.)	**536·5**	477·0	+12
Trading profit	**25·6**	16·3	+57
Less: Redundancy	**(2·3)**	(5·1)	−55
Trading profit after redundancy	**23·3**	11·2	+108
Add: Profits on property disposals	**4·7**	11·6	−59
Operating profit	**28·0**	22·8	+23
Less:			
Interest on medium-term loan and overdrafts	**(11·1)**	(11·0)	
Overseas taxation	**(0·3)**	—	
Extraordinary items	**(1·3)**	(2·5)	
Minorities' share of profits	**(0·5)**	(0.1)	
Dividends, paid and proposed (including cost of Advance Corporation Tax paid by the Consortium)	**(4·3)**	(2·6)	+65
Profit retained in the business	**10·5**	6·6	+59

contribution coming from our trading activities—despite heavy losses in one section of our business.

With the growth in revenue and profit we have not only been able to begin to invest in operations abroad as well as in the U.K., but have had the confidence to create a challenging long-term strategy for the business, to which I would like to return in greater detail at the end of this article. First, let me remind you about our origins.

Where We Came From

As Britain's largest transport, storage, distribution and travel business, NFC was shaped by a long line of political decisions. The post-war Labour Government nationalized commercial long-distance road haulage, in 1953–1956 a Conservative Government partially denationalized it, and Mrs. Barbara Castle's 1968 Transport Act formed the remaining State road transport businesses into the National Freight Corporation, with the addition of the road haulage activities of British Rail, which became National Carriers.

The new Corporation operated from 1969 for 10 years, initially with large revenue grants, then with chequered financial results—some small profits in one or two of the early years, heavy losses in 1975 and, after some structural and management changes in the following year, a slow growth to reasonable profitability at trading level.

When the Conservative Party came to power in 1979 the intention was to float us on the Stock Exchange and with this in mind the Corporation, whose assets were held mainly through 40 subsidiary limited companies, was replaced by the newly created National Freight Company Limited, its equity share capital owned entirely by the government. Plans for the flotation were upset by the economic recession and its effect on our profitability, and then crucially by British Rail shutting its collected and delivered parcels service for which our National Carriers provided vehicles and drivers—an almost immediate loss of over £20m in annual revenue.

The government was therefore advised by its merchant bankers that a successful flotation could not be considered for some 2 years—which left it in a difficult position in view of the election manifesto. We sensed that they would seek some other way to sell the business and we feared, in particular, that it might be sold piecemeal or offered to a single purchaser who could well be more interested in stripping out the substantial property assets than in continuing to run a low-margin transport business.

There were still some 25,000 employees in the business (extensive redundancy made necessary by the bad trading conditions of 1980–1981 had reduced the workforce from over 30,000) and we were concerned about their future as well as the possible effects on the business of the arrival of an asset stripper. It was at this point that a group of us—senior managers—began to consider whether we might mount a bid to acquire the company. Preliminary discussions with merchant banks made it clear that unless the management was prepared to accept a position where the bid was, in practice, an institutional one with the management simply providing a small percentage on top, two things would have to happen: first, the scope would have to be widened to include the entire workforce—to obtain not only sufficient finance for success but also to obtain commitment to the change of ownership; and, secondly, institutions would need to be persuaded to lend the majority of the purchase price without acquiring a majority of the equity capital.

The resolution of these two problems was to occupy the small group of senior managers concerned for over 9 months but the principles which were established very early on, and which were subsequently published unchanged in the Prospectus, were:

- The business must be controlled by employee-investors.
- All employees, not just management, must have an equal right to invest.
- Investors should receive dividends in proportion to their investment.
- The business must be professionally managed with a board of directors responsible to the shareholders.

These were the main principles which distinguished our concept from a management buy-out on the one hand and a co-operative on the other. We had quickly come to see the possibility of creating a new type of industrial enterprise.

The ownership of shares in a business does not usually imply that the shareholder has any direct involvement in the running of the business—though there have been many creditable attempts over the years to involve employees more, especially through the issue of shares as an annual bonus or as part of a company saving scheme.

I see ownership in terms of the positive ownership of a piece of the company which varies in value as the health of the company fluctuates. For me it is important, indeed crucial, to see ownership of part of the business operating as a direct factor in the control of the business.

Government, Bank and Management Reactions

In NFC we had long-established staff consultation procedures at all levels of the business, and equally well-established (and rare in the public sector), we had devolved decision-making. The management of its activities was through subsidiary operating companies, and profit centres at almost all of the hundreds of branches, and this had important implications for the success of our particular kind of privatization. We had the first practical evidence of this when we brought together our top 130 managers in 1981 to put before them, in great confidence, our proposals to buy the business from the government. A little while previously we had opened confidential discussions with Barclays Merchant Bank, who proved keen to help us, and in May, after some stringent financial and management exercises, we had put an outline of our plans to Transport Secretary Norman Fowler. He was delighted with what we suggested and gave the senior management group conditional approval to see whether we could sell the idea to the employees and make it work. At the same time he put his own legal and financial advisers to work on evaluating our proposals.

We had, of course, had to keep the NFC's Board informed of our proposals as they developed and, while the Board throughout maintained the correct stance of a body which had a legal obligation to safeguard the public interest in a State undertaking, it formally recognized our plans as perhaps the best for the future of the business and carefully 'held the ring' on behalf of the shareholder—the government.

At the highly confidential meeting of our 130 most senior managers from headquarters and operating subsidiaries throughout the NFC, the reception—after the initial startled silence—was enthusiastic. Each participant was asked to fill in, anonymously, a questionnaire which simply asked three questions:

(1) Will you be prepared to support the concept financially yourself?

(2) How much, approximately, do you think you will be investing?

(3) Are you prepared to endorse the concept and encourage your own people to take part?

Over 95 per cent said 'yes' to questions (1) and (3) and the answers to question (2) indicated that we should be able to raise the minimum equity which we had provisionally set at £5m. The amount from this group alone was likely to be well over £1m.

Armed with this reaction we were able to go back to the Secretary of State and make a firm offer, subject to the settlement of price and other conditions. So far as the government was concerned, they were sympathetic from the start about what we wanted to do, and we now had the banks behind us as well, subject to an enormous amount of detailed work in preparing the loan agreements and other complicated documents, and—not least—in arranging security for the medium-term loan which would provide the bulk of the purchase price. To give an example of the amount of paperwork and discussion involved, Barclays' original acceptance letter ran to nine closely-typed pages and was based on a scheme which it was hoped would avoid falling foul of Section 54 of the 1948 Companies Act, which came to haunt us over the coming months.

Put simply, Section 54 stopped people buying a company on the security of its own assets. It was designed to prevent fraud, but not designed to deal with the unique situation of employees trying to buy their company from the government with the government's blessing. It was that Section 54 which prevented NFC giving Barclays security on bank loans backed by its properties, and which sent us down tortuous alternative avenues—from which we were eventually rescued by the last minute appearance of the Seventh Cavalry in the shape of the Companies Act 1981. This measure was before the House as a Bill when our buy-out arrangements were nearing completion and it was brought into effect, not entirely coincidentally, in December 1981 just in time for Sections 42–44 to provide a route whereby loans from the banks could be secured against the NFC's properties—though in a rather complicated way in our case.

Back in May–June 1981, however, we had yet to discover the reactions of the rest of our management and all our other employees, the trade unions, the press and the public at large to our proposed buy-out. Since the Secretary of State, Norman Fowler, had set 18 June as the day on which he proposed to tell the House of our proposals to buy NFC, we had to ensure that our employees would be informed simultaneously, and we also had to tell the trade unions and the news media.

At very short notice we arranged for the printing of 25,000 copies of an information sheet for every employee, explaining the proposed buy-out in simple terms, and had these distributed in sealed bundles to all our branch managers with instructions that they were not to be opened until the afternoon of 18 June, but then every employee was to receive one before close of business. Also at short notice, arrangements were made for senior NFC managers to brief the General Secretaries of the main unions having membership in NFC, and for a press conference in the City of London. Although this had to be set at the normally unpopular time—for the press—of mid-afternoon, we had an excellent turn-out, reflecting the good relations which we had built up with sections of the press over the years through a very open attitude towards the media, and also the lunch meetings with senior financial journalists in 1980 in preparation for the intended flotation. This relationship almost certainly played a part in the next day's press reports which, almost without exception, were enthusiastic; and most of the press remained supportive throughout the whole of the buy-out period—and still do today.

The reaction of the trade unions was understandably less enthusiastic: three of the four main unions with members in NFC took the view that while they opposed denationalization as a matter of policy, our scheme was probably the best way forward in the circumstances. The fourth, and much the biggest, declared its opposition and campaigned against the buy-out.

This was a situation we had to live with but meanwhile we had some rapid communicating to do. We had set ourselves a very tight programme for the buy-out and, while the complex financial and legal issues were being tackled behind the scenes, we had to discover whether we could interest 24,000 employees and their families and 18,000 pensioners in putting up some money to help us buy the business between us. We started with six large regional meetings at which the leading members of our 'cabal' and myself put our proposals to the rest of our 2500 managers—with very much the same enthusiastic response which the senior managers had given.

A Major Communications Exercise

We now had the task of educating, informing and persuading a large and geographically widespread audience that our novel proposition was in their best interests, against the background of the bankers saying, in effect: 'If you can raise at least four and a quarter million pounds between you we will lend you the rest to pay the £53·5m purchase price and the attendant costs.'

Video was the main medium chosen for the mass communications exercise, which was not such an obvious choice in 1981 as it might seem today. The main practical considerations were that the equipment was fairly portable and simple to operate. More significantly, the philosophical choice of video was based on the need to communicate the enthusiasm and commitment of myself and my colleagues in far more locations than we could possibly visit; the fact that visual images were needed to put over a novel and complex message; and the simple fact that the television screen is such a familiar source of information.

There were multiple messages to get across: the basic facts about the buy-out proposals, the enthusiasm of the management team, the probable timetable, the nature of shareholding and its rights and obligations, and the variety and scope of NFC's business—since hitherto employees' main interest and knowledge would have centered on their own branch or company. Fortunately the resulting videotape did its job, and so did a second one dealing largely with questions and concerns raised by employees. It was shown just after the prospectus had been issued, and so also dealt with share application.

Backing up the video thrust were printed progress reports, a booklet *Buying Your Own Company*, freephone advice sessions involving senior managers and, of course, the prospectus itself. The latter was obviously a vital piece of communication and, in City terms, ours was a very odd animal indeed. We were determined that, even if all the usual legal and financial information had to be packed in, it would be accompanied by readable, illustrated material in plain English. The fact that over 40 proofs were needed says something for the conservatism of the banking and legal professions and much for our obstinacy. In the end, I think we got it about right and it won considerable acclaim in the financial press for its clarity (Figures 1 and 2).

Waiting for Success

The application lists for buying NFC shares (there were 6,187,500 Ordinary £1 shares on offer at par,

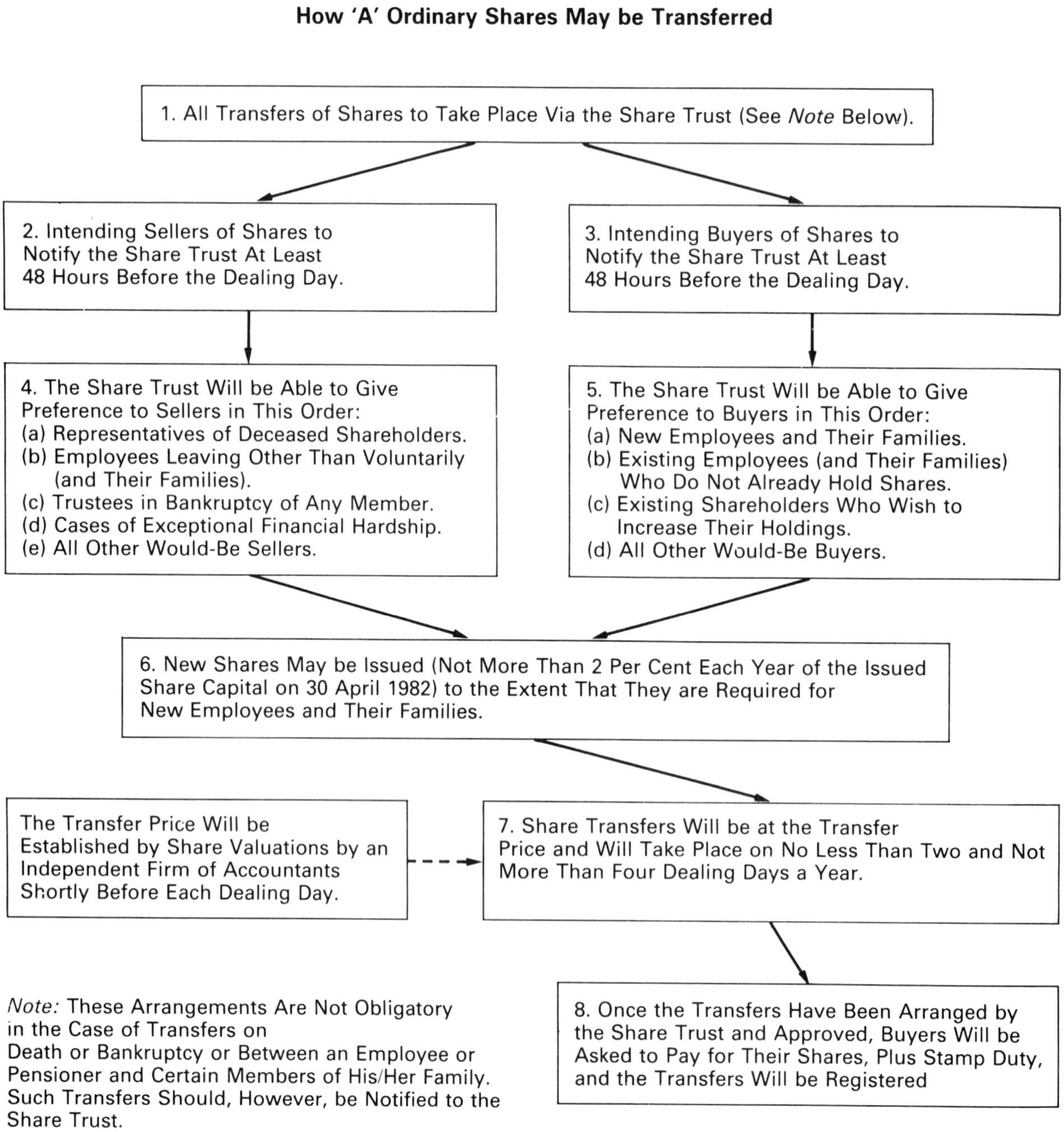

Figure 1. An example of how diagrams were used in the 1982 Prospectus to put over complicated concepts—in this case, how the share scheme would work. The Prospectus diagrams were hand-drawn and printed in colour.

How the Purchase Will be Financed

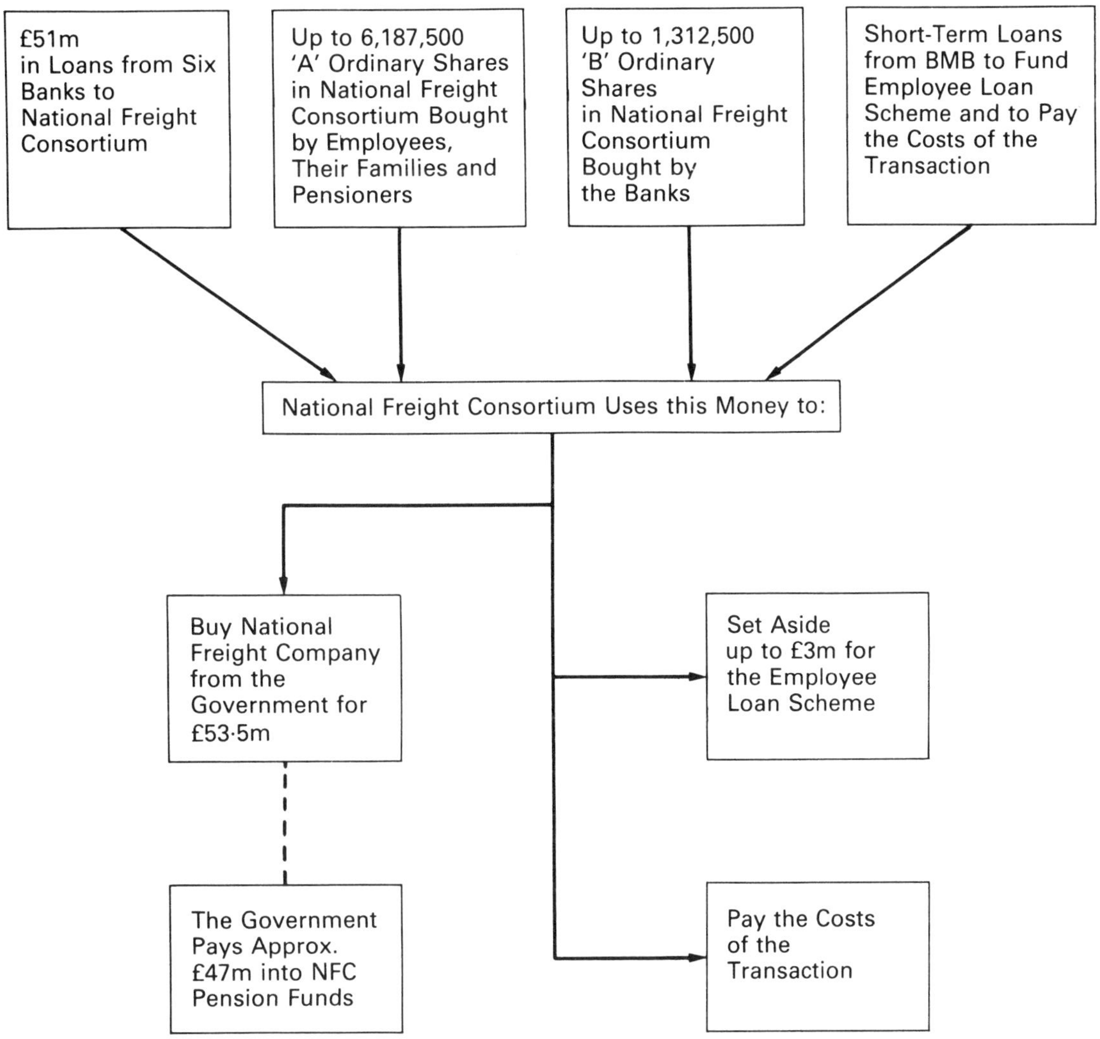

Figure 2. Another diagram from the 1982 Prospectus

payable in full on application) opened on 25 January 1982 and closed on 16 February. Interest-free loans of up to £200 for share purchase were made available to employees, and a target of £4·125m had been set as the minimum total subscription necessary for success.

At first the response was terrifyingly slow, but it soon became clear that we had a great success on our hands. Applications for over seven million shares were received and, though it went very much against the grain, the applications had to be scaled down and over £800,000 returned.

When people ask me about the relevance of NFC's buy-out success for other businesses I always stress the background from which we came as well as the unusual circumstances which gave us a window of opportunity. One of the most important was the fact that NFC never represented more than about 8 per cent of the market it was in, and this vulnerability to competition—unusual in the public sector—meant that managers were keenly aware of the relationship between productivity and profit. They were also aware of the relationship between effort and reward; some years ago we instituted performance target setting for the top hundred or so managers in the business, and this process has been extended to managers at all levels and, more recently, to clerical staff. As much as 12·5 per cent of a manager's salary can be dependent upon achieving agreed quality objectives during the year, while once-off bonus payments related to the achievement of cashflow and profit targets can be as much as 30 per cent of salary, depending on the extent to which targets are exceeded. Bonusing is in most cases on a work-unit basis so that many people share in achieving financial targets and benefit thereby. Such a background, I believe, made the acceptance of the risks and corresponding potential of shareholding itself more likely.

Involving the Shareholders

Having bought the business we resolved to involve our new 'owners' in a way that would set NFC apart from other large public companies. Shareholders—most of them employees—have been given opportunities to give management their views. We hold quarterly shareholder meetings chaired by directors in eight regions of the U.K.; we have used MORI to survey all our shareholders' views about business development, dividend policy, shareholder communication, donation and sponsorship policy, shareholder representation and a host of other issues; we send them a quarterly newsletter about company progress and a range of shareholder matters; we deliberately structure our AGM agenda to promote discussion and the involvement of shareholders in policy decisions; and last year we had a postal ballot of all shareholders to elect a 'shareholder director' to represent their views at Board level. Inevitably many of the questions raised in such forums are more about operating matters than about the wider direction of the business, but that is no bad thing. These people are close to the commercial roots and it can be daunting as Chairman to address an AGM knowing that the shareholders (and we typically have nearly 2000 at such a meeting) are closely involved and extremely well informed about what actually goes on at the workface. At our 1985 AGM we saw industrial democracy very much in action, with voices and votes used very effectively to decide significant issues—and not always in the way the Board intended. I see that as a strength of our policy.

While the shareholders have been quick to use their opportunities to comment—and to vote—they have also proved ready to be guided by the Board and professional management on issues where business experience and judgment are vital. For example, in accepting a modification of our original debt-reduction strategy (involving top priority for paying off our main loan) when we were presented with unprecedented business opportunities requiring investment in new resources.

Broadening the Ownership

One of the subjects on which we have communicated and consulted with shareholders has been the widening of the share ownership among employees, which the Board sees as important. We have had AGM approval for two wider share ownership campaigns—in 1983 and 1985—with new prospectuses, and these have brought over 6000 more employee-investors. We have continued to offer an interest-free loan for share purchase by new employees. Our policy is also to keep the 'entry price' low, so as the share value has risen we have split the shares three times to reduce the unit price. Few employee-shareholders have sold out (only 4 per cent last year) and, as Table 3 shows, buyers have been strongly outnumbering sellers in our internal quarterly trading. While this continues we can take the long view about whether or not to float NFC on the Stock Exchange—which in 1982

Table 3. On the internal share market, buyers have continued to exceed sellers. This table shows the requests for shares at Dealing Days 3–10, covering 1983 and 1984

Requests for shares at Dealing Days

Dealing Day	Offered	Required	Offered as a % of required
1983— 3	49,548	374,473	13
4	169,184	348,486	48
5	135,815	208,320	65
6	266,042	317,987	84
1984— 7	169,098	524,193	32
8	109,326	421,648	26
9	148,300	300,433	49
10	170,335	327,768	52

NB. Share split after Dealing Day No. 6 discounted.

we undertook not to do for at least 5 years, and then only with the approval of shareholders in General Meeting. However, if the strong buying trend was reversed, this would obviously argue cogently in favour of broadening the market beyond NFC itself.

Whatever decision is eventually taken by shareholders, the need to retain the driving power of employee control is obviously going to be a crucial issue. We do not want to destroy the valuable thing we have created and become like any other transport company owned by the City—exchanging one set of faceless shareholders for another. I would also suggest that NFC in its unique new form has earned its exclusion from the political arena.

Meanwhile we have set our strategy for the next 5–10 years after long and deep management discussion and a widespread consultation among shareholders. It is summed up in our new business mission:

> NFC will become a broad based International, Transport, Distribution, Travel and Property Group with a high reputation for service in all its activities. It will retain its commitment to employee control and will use this commitment to expand into associated product areas where service levels are critical. It will have a participative style associated with first class results-orientated employment packages. It will seek increased employment opportunities and real growth of dividends and share values for its shareholders.

It is a strategy for growth, for high service levels and improved job opportunities, and particularly for a better balanced business. While investing more in U.K. activities than was ever the case when it was State-owned, NFC intends to put about a quarter of its investment into overseas activities, mainly in the U.S.A. where the returns from transport and distribution activities are about twice those in Britain. In the past NFC has been almost totally dependent on the U.K. for its income and the intention is to spread the risks and the returns internationally, so that we are no longer so dependent on the comparatively poor-performing home economy. And, while investing heavily in our U.K. transport and distribution activities and their modern-technology support, we are committed to developing our property interests and expanding our travel business—which is already one of the biggest agencies in Britain.

It is, I think, a measure of the understanding and support of our shareholders that they have accepted this broad view of our future direction. It is also a measure of how employee-shareholders are involved in a business whose ownership they are very conscious of sharing.